VANDOVER AND THE BRUTE

VANDOVER AND THE BRUTE

BY
FRANK NORRIS

INTRODUCTION BY
Warren French

UNIVERSITY OF NEBRASKA PRESS
LINCOLN AND LONDON

Introduction Copyright © 1978 by the University of Nebraska Press

First Bison Book edition: 1978

Most recent printing indicated by the first digit below:

1   2   3   4   5   6   7   8   9   10

Library of Congress Cataloging in Publication Data

Norris, Frank, 1870–1902.
   Vandover and the brute.

   Reprint of the 1942 ed. published by Doubleday, Garden City, N.Y.
   I. Title.
[PZ3.N792Van   1978]   [PS2472]   813'.4   78–8537
ISBN 0–8032–3300–0
ISBN 0–8032–8350–4 pbk.

Reprinted by arrangement with Doubleday & Company, Inc.
Manufactured in the United States of America

CONTENTS

INTRODUCTION

Vandover and the Brute was probably the first novel that Frank Norris completed, but it was the last to be published, twelve years after his death in 1902. In a foreword to the original edition, the author's brother, Charles Norris, a prolific novelist himself, offered an explanation for this curious state of affairs.

American publishers were not ready in the 1890s for a history of personal degeneration as depressing as Vandover's; consequently, the manuscript was packed away in a San Francisco warehouse. When this building was destroyed by the fire following the San Francisco earthquake of 1906, the manuscript was assumed to have been lost. Several years later, however, it turned up in an improperly labeled trunk that had been moved to safety just before the warehouse caught fire. Although Norris's signature was missing, an alert reader recognized his style; and the supposedly lost novel was recovered and posthumously published.

Thus ran Charles Norris's account. Recently, however, the best history yet of the novel's reclamation, James D. Hart's *A Novelist in the Making*, has explained that as late as 1899, when publishers found the story "hardly available," Norris probably abandoned work on it, but left it in his wife's hands. There it remained until it was published at last in 1914, when genteel standards of decorum were collapsing. Hart also thinks that Norris completed the novel in 1895, earlier than any other, and that he did not substantially revise it thereafter, although he borrowed material from it for *Blix* (1899), a lighter-hearted tale of San Francisco life, and even for his last novel, *The Pit* (1903). Hart argues persuasively that *McTeague* and *Blix* may, in fact, have originated as subplots for *Vandover*.

Most valuable of all Hart's contributions to clearing up the history of the novel is his reprinting of a group of student themes which Norris submitted to Lewis E. Gates's English 22 class at Harvard between November 16, 1894, and April 30, 1895. Of the forty-four themes that have been located, Hart points out that twenty-seven are related to *Vandover*. Eleven have some relationship to *McTeague* and seven to *Blix*. Hart also questions Charles Norris's recollections seventeen years later in a letter to Franklin Walker, Frank Norris's biographer, that the brother added some five thousand words to the text (nearly 5 percent of its length) before its publication in 1914. Hart speculates plausibly that any additions were not nearly so extensive as Charles Norris recalled. Certainly the novel was never finally revised for publication. Hart points out duplications of passages within the novel itself and duplicate passages in other novels. The lack of transitions between chapters also makes the novel read like a collection of preliminary sketches.

The place of *Vandover and the Brute* in Frank Norris's career seems now clearly established. It is a first novel, quite a remarkable one, largely if not entirely the work of Norris's year as a special student at Harvard, and a mine that he was to draw upon for later works when his loss of hope for its own early publication led him to abandon polishing it into final form. It is thus indispensable to an understanding of the development of a prolific young man's remarkable legacy—six published novels and a large number of shorter stories and critical essays in the seven years of his lamentably brief career. If it were important only in relationship to Norris's career, James D. Hart's edition would admirably satisfy scholarly needs. *Vandover and the Brute* is, however, an extraordinary work in its own right; and the present edition is undertaken in an effort to establish this still undeservedly neglected novel in its proper place in the evolution of American fiction.

For a long time, Stephen Crane's *Maggie: A Girl of the Streets* (1893) and Norris's *McTeague* (1899), in many ways a companion piece to *Vandover*, have posed a problem to historians of American literature. These two works that shocked contemporary readers and genteel authors and reviewers when they were published are distinctly more cynical and pessimistic about man's progress than even the subsequent works of their authors.

The genteel tradition still dominated Anglo-American letters at the end of the nineteenth century, and William Dean Howells had pronounced its credo in *Criticism and Fiction* (1891), "The manners of the novel have been improving with those of its readers. . . . Generally people now call a spade an agricultural implement." This improvement in manners was made to seem an illusion by Crane's and Norris's early efforts. Puzzled as to how to deal with such an unprecedented portrayal of American urban society, historical critics have sought to label the works "naturalistic" and to see them as landmarks in the emergence of a new literary frankness and freedom in the twentieth century. The early deaths of Crane and Norris have been mourned as setbacks to the consistent evolution of a naturalistic movement in American letters.

Now, however, as we reach the unmistakable end of that long period in the early and mid-twentieth century that has been labeled "modernist," we can see Crane's and Norris's work in a larger perspective that brings the whole theory of American naturalism into question. Edwin F. Cady has argued in *The Light of Common Day: Realism in American Fiction* (1971) that "there are really no nauralists in American literature." Critics like Thomas A. Gullason have also argued persuasively that as early as *The Red Badge of Courage* (1895), Crane had begun to move beyond a naturalistic approach and to develop an ironic style that presages modernism, while his last novels are commonplace romances. Tendencies are harder to detect in Norris's brief career, but his final completed work, *The Pit*, and his projected trilogy about the Battle of Gettysburg suggest a growing conservatism and reconciliation with the genteel tradition.

Neither author in his early fiction seems to have opened the vein that he would have developed into the new century, as Theodore Dreiser did in *Sister Carrie*. (It should be added here, however, that although Dreiser continued to publish into the 1940s, he never really developed any new concept for a novel after 1914.) Thus we can see that *Maggie*, *McTeague*, and *Vandover* did not lead anywhere in particular, even in their own authors' careers. They were not the kind of harbingers of a new art that James Joyce was producing during the same period in Ireland, but rather the outraged reactions of two remarkable, brash young men to a tradition turned rotten.

Recent activities have also made us aware that these three novels were not such isolated phenomena in their own time as they have long appeared to be. After years of neglect, Harold Frederic's *The Damnation of Theron Ware* (1896), with its chilling portrayal of a naive, genteel clergyman "awakened" into a cynical politician, has attracted many interpreters; even more important has been the revival of interest, largely through the growing feminist movement, in another novel that horrified turn-of-the-century critics: Kate Chopin's *The Awakening* (1899), the story of a married woman's rejection of her family for illicit romance and suicide. New interest has stirred in the novels of H. B. Fuller; and the even more startling, long suppressed fiction of George Cabot Lodge has been published. Charlotte Perkins Gilman's extraordinary short story "The Yellow Wallpaper" (1892) has also been discovered as a precursor of these works which strike a discordant note in our literature. It is quite likely that still more fiction in this vein may await notice among those works spurned by the arbiters of genteel taste.

What our awareness at last of this body of work illuminates is the existence during the dying years of the nineteenth century of an American "decadent" literature, comparable to that of the *Yellow Book* period in England, yet quite different from the elegant drawing-room decadence of Oscar Wilde and Aubrey Beards-

ley which even Frank Norris deplored. While "decadence," like every literary label, has been so variously
and casually used that it has become virtually meaningless, it can have a specific meaning helpful in isolating
the common qualities of the small but arresting body of
work produced by Crane, Norris, Chopin, Frederic,
Fuller, Lodge, and others during a few years at the end
of the nineteenth century; it can be helpful as well in
assessing the significance of these works in the development of American literature and our national culture
generally.

Strictly speaking, "decadence" is a biological state
that living matter enters after it has passed its maturity
or "ripeness" and has begun to rot or deteriorate.
Applied metaphorically to artistic constructs like paintings or novels, the term can distinguish those works
that concentrate on the representation of "decadent"
states in the matter portrayed. Writers in the genteel
tradition, like Howells and Henry James, concentrated
on the approbatory portrayal of exemplary responsible,
mature persons like the significantly named Adam and
Maggie Verver in *The Golden Bowl*. Decadents, like
Charlotte and the Prince in the same novel, were
subjects for correction. The manners of the novel, to
extend Howells's observation, not only improved with
those of its readers, but should work to effect further
improvements in those readers.

But as in all things a surface glow begins in time not
to externalize an interior harmony but to provide a
veneer over interior disintegration, so manners become
affectations that place upon delicate individuals an
undue strain leading to their collapse. One is struck

especially by the similarities between the behavior of Norris's Vandover and Edna Pontellier in Kate Chopin's *The Awakening*. Despite Norris's frequent theatrical pronouncements about the triumph of the bestial side in man's nature in *Vandover*, which Donald Pizer and James Hart attribute to the influence of Professor Joseph LeConte's teachings at the University of California, Vandover's main problem—as Joseph R. McElrath, Jr., has recently pointed out in one of the rare analyses to focus perceptively on *Vandover and the Brute*—is that he lacks the energy to meet the demands placed on the individual by a society that measures worth in terms of one's adherence to meaningless but exhausting conventions. (Characters in other early Norris novels like *Moran of the Lady Letty, McTeague*, and *Blix* are threatened by similar demands.)

Similarly, Kate Chopin's Edna is not a deliberately wicked or perverse individual, but one who is bored and fatigued by rituals of a society with what McElrath calls an "archaic life-vision." Both Vandover and Edna succumb to the blandishments of forbidden activities from the lack of the drive (so often present in characters of novelists otherwise so unlike as Henry James and Horatio Alger, Jr.) to dedicate themselves to the achievement of the lofty goals that their societies presumably prize. Near the end of Norris's novel, even Vandover's self-indulgences no longer amuse him very much: "Everything was an *ennui*, and [he] began to long for some new pleasure, some violent, untried excitement." Using remarkably similar language, Kate Chopin describes Edna at the dinner party that crowns her drive for emancipation as feeling "the old ennui overtaking her; the hopelessness which so often assaulted her" and "overpowering her at once with a sense of the unattainable."

The distinction of *Vandover and the Brute* lies thus in its contribution to the brief but intense outburst of a preoccupation with decadence in late nineteenth-century American literature. It is the dynamic response of a sensitive young artist to his distressed perceptions of a decline in the romantic idealism that had fostered his nation's growth (a sentiment that he expounded also in many of his critical essays). While critics have often read *Vandover* as the moralistic record of the deterioration of an individual who succumbs to the beast within him, we need to weigh the arguments of Joseph McElrath. The novel may most satisfactorily be read as a protest against an inert and constricting society that, like a vampire, destroys individuals in order to give its already dead form a semblance of life.

If the customary response has tried to place Norris too much in the nineteenth-century tradition of "self-reliance," McElrath may make him too prescient a prophet of twentieth-century alienation; but his argument is valuable in forcing us to consider whether an adequate interpretation of this novel lies somewhere between the two theories. (McElrath's arguments also help make sense in context of episodes like the maritime disaster described in chapter 9.) Perhaps only now that the modernist sensibility which has shaped our vision for more than seventy years has reached its own decadence—as presented in such novels as John Barth's *Lost in the Funhouse*, Thomas Pynchon's *Gravity's Rainbow*, and Kurt Vonnegut, Jr.'s *Breakfast of Champions*—can we perceive the similar relationship of the last novels of the previous genteel era to its tradition.

If Vonnegut and others depict the final complete withdrawal of the alienated individual into his own head to the utter exclusion of an outside world, a state at which any further development of the particular vision becomes impossible, so the complete separation of external manners from internal feelings marked the end of a tradition that posited its concept of progress upon the emblematic revelation of internal states through external behavior. *Vandover and the Brute* is important to readers in the late twentieth century for its unusually powerful dramatization of the terminal point at which an earlier generation had arrived. At that point its most gifted fictional interpreters saw the necessity of embarking upon the new path which has led us to the terminal point that we have recently reached. Their work enables us to see as well what most people at the time could not.

Paradoxically, the very abruptness of the transitions in *Vandover and the Brute* (which suggest the jump-cuts of recent film) gives the novel an air of modernity that Norris is hardly likely to have deliberately contrived. From his viewpoint the work remained a sketch. Art students today, however, tend to value, for example, preliminary sketches of Romantic landscape artist John Constable over finished works because of the spontaneous vision the first impressions preserve. In a similar way, Norris's unrevised fiction provides us with both a unique symbol and a record of the fragmentation of sensibilities in the decadent scene that he preserves. We can enter more fully into the feelings of an age with significant parallels to our own through this then rejected work than through the elegantly finished works that the age itself prized.

WARREN FRENCH

*Indiana University–Purdue University
  at Indianapolis*

CHRONOLOGY

1870   March 5, Benjamin Franklin Norris, Jr., born in Chicago.

1884   Norris family moves to California and settles in 1885 into Henry Scott mansion at 1822 Sacramento Street, San Francisco. Frank attends preparatory school at Belmont, California.

1887   Norris family goes to Paris and Frank enrolls in the Bouguereau Studio to study painting.

1890   Frank enters the University of California at Berkeley.

1891   Mrs. Norris subsidizes publication of Frank's first book, *Yvernelle*, a ballad poem.

1894–
1895   Frank studies creative writing under Lewis Gates at Harvard and works on *Vandover and Brute* and *McTeague*.

1898   Frank goes to New York to work for *McClure's Magazine*; his first published novel, *Moran of the Lady Letty*, appears in November.

1899   *McTeague* and *Blix* published; Frank becomes a reader for Doubleday, Page and Company and advocates publication of Theodore Dreiser's *Sister Carrie*.

1900   Frank marries Jeannette Black on January 12;
        A Man's Woman published.
1901   *The Octopus* published.
1902   Jeannette Norris, Jr., Frank's only child, born
        February 9; Frank Norris dies of peritonitis on
        October 25.
1903   *The Pit* published posthumously after serializa-
        tion in the *Saturday Evening Post; A Deal in
        Wheat and Other Stories* and *The Responsibili-
        ties of a Novelist* published.
1914   *Vandover and the Brute* edited by Charles Nor-
        ris and published.

FOR FURTHER READING

Cooperman, Stanley, "Frank Norris and the Werewolf of Guilt," *Modern Language Quarterly* 20 (1959): 252–58, argues that in *Vandover and the Brute* and *McTeague*, Norris's "naturalistic" commitment to scientific determinism is simply superimposed upon a basically Calvinist philosophy that instinct is evil.

French, Warren, *Frank Norris* (New York: Twayne, 1962), pp. 52–61, argues that the novel is not so much a tract against self-indulgence as, like *McTeague*, the portrayal of an individual "unable to cope with the practical problems of living in an urban society and to accept the responsibilities of mature man in a civilized state."

Hart, James D., editor, *A Novelist in the Making: A Collection of Student Themes, and the Novels* Blix *and* Vandover and the Brute (Cambridge, Mass.; Harvard University Press, 1970), issued during the year of the centenary of Norris's birth, is the standard source book for study of the novel. It includes not only the text, but a collection of themes that Norris wrote at Harvard containing material later used in *Vandover and the Brute*, along with a long introduction setting the record straight about the history of the manuscript and summing up significant criticism of the novel.

McElrath, Joseph R., Jr., "Frank Norris's *Vandover and the Brute*: Narrative Techniques and the Socio-Critical Viewpoint," *Studies in American Fiction* 4 (1976): 27–43, reads the novel not as a moralistic attack upon Vandover, but rather as an attack on "nineteenth-century morality and the archaic life-vision of a world of fixed certainties which informed it."

Pizer, Donald, *The Novels of Frank Norris* (Bloomington: Indiana University Press, 1966), pp. 31–52, is the final form of the arguments of the outstanding Norris scholar that *Vandover* and *McTeague* are examples of "evolutionary ethical dualism" and that in *Vandover*, "Norris was most powerful and suggestive when he abjured both explicit analysis and massive symbol for pictorial representation."

Walker, Franklin, *Frank Norris: A Biography* (Garden City, N.Y.: Doubleday, Doran, 1932), an affectionate account by the principal promoter of the San Francisco Bay area's literary heritage, remains the standard biography, drawn in large measure from personal interviews with Norris's family and friends.

VANDOVER AND THE BRUTE

VANDOVER AND
THE BRUTE

CHAPTER ONE

It was always a matter of wonder to Vandover that he was able to recall so little of his past life. With the exception of the most recent events he could remember nothing connectedly. What he at first imagined to be the story of his life, on closer inspection turned out to be but a few disconnected incidents that his memory had preserved with the greatest capriciousness, absolutely independent of their importance. One of these incidents might be a great sorrow, a tragedy, a death in his family; and another, recalled with the same vividness, the same accuracy of detail, might be a matter of the least moment.

A certain one of these wilful fillips of memory would always bring before him a particular scene during the migration of his family from Boston to their new home in San Francisco, at a time when Vandover was about eight years old.

It was in the depot of one of the larger towns in western New York. The day had been hot and after the long ride on the crowded day coach the cool shadow under the curved roof of the immense iron vaulted depot seemed very pleasant. The porter, the brakeman and Vandover's father very carefully lifted his mother from the car. She was lying back on pillows in a long steamer chair. The

3

three men let the chair slowly down, the brakeman went away, but the porter remained, taking off his cap and wiping his forehead with the back of his left hand, which in turn he wiped against the pink palm of his right. The other train, the train to which they were to change, had not yet arrived. It was rather still; at the far end of the depot a locomotive, sitting back on its motionless drivers like some huge sphinx crouching along the rails, was steaming quietly, drawing long breaths. The repair gang in greasy caps and spotted blue overalls were inspecting the train, pottering about the trucks, opening and closing the journal-boxes, striking clear notes on the wheels with long-handled hammers.

Vandover stood close to his father, his thin legs wide apart, holding in both his hands the satchel he had been permitted to carry. He looked about him continually, rolling his big eyes vaguely, watching now the repair-gang, now a huge white cat dozing on an empty baggage truck.

Several passengers were walking up and down the platform, staring curiously at the invalid lying back in the steamer chair.

The journey was too much for her. She was very weak and very pale, her eyelids were heavy, the skin of her forehead looked blue and tightly drawn, and tiny beads of perspiration gathered around the corners of her mouth. Vandover's father put his hand and arm along the back of the chair and his sick wife rested against him, leaning her head on his waistcoat over the pocket where he kept his cigars and pocket-comb. They were all silent.

By and by she drew a long sigh, her face became the face of an imbecile, stupid, without expression, her eyes half-closed, her mouth half-open. Her head rolled forward as though she were nodding in her sleep, while a long drip of saliva trailed from her lower lip. Vandover's father bent over her quickly, crying out sharply, "Hallie! — what is it?" All at once the train for which they were waiting charged into the depot, filling the place with a hideous clangor and with the smell of steam and of hot oil.

This scene of her death was the only thing that Vandover could remember of his mother.

As he looked back over his life he could recall nothing after this for nearly five years. Even after that lapse of time the only scene he could picture with any degree of clearness was one of the greatest triviality in which he saw himself, a rank thirteen-year-old boy, sitting on a bit of carpet in the back yard of the San Francisco house playing with his guinea-pigs.

In order to get at his life during his teens, Vandover would have been obliged to collect these scattered memory pictures as best he could, rearrange them in some more orderly sequence, piece out what he could imperfectly recall and fill in the many gaps by mere guesswork and conjecture.

It was the summer of 1880 that they had come to San Francisco. Once settled there, Vandover's father began to build small residence houses and cheap flats which he rented at various prices, the cheapest at ten dollars, the more expensive at thirty-five and forty. He had closed out his business in the East, coming out to California on account of his wife's ill health. He had made his money in Boston and had intended to retire.

But he soon found that he could not do this. At this time he was an old man, nearly sixty. He had given his entire life to his business to the exclusion of everything else, and now when his fortune had been made and when he could afford to enjoy it, discovered that he had lost the capacity for enjoying anything but the business itself. Nothing else could interest him. He was not what would be called in America a rich man, but he had made money enough to travel, to allow himself any reasonable relaxation, to cultivate a taste for art, music, literature or the drama, to indulge in any harmless fad, such as collecting etchings, china or bric-à-brac, or even to permit himself the luxury of horses. In the place of all these he found himself, at nearly sixty years of age, forced again into the sordid round of business as the only escape from the mortal *ennui* and weariness of the spirit that preyed upon him during every leisure hour of the day.

Early and late he went about the city, personally superintending the building of his little houses and cheap flats, sitting on saw-horses and piles of lumber, watching the carpenters at work. In the evening he came home to a late supper, completely fagged, bringing with him the smell of mortar and of pine shavings.

On the first of each month when his agents turned over the rents to him he was in great spirits. He would bring home the little canvas sack of coin with him before banking it, and call his son's attention to the amount, never failing to stick a twenty-dollar gold-piece in each eye, monocle fashion, exclaiming, "Good for the masses," a meaningless jest that had been one of the family's household words for years.

His plan of building was peculiar. His credit was good, and having chosen his lot he would find out from the banks how much they would loan him upon it in case he should become the owner. If this amount suited him, he would buy the lot, making one large payment outright and giving his note for the balance. The lot once his, the banks loaned him the desired amount. With this money and with money of his own he would make the final payment on the lot and would begin the building itself, paying his labour on the nail, but getting his material, lumber, brick and fittings on time. When the building was half-way up he would negotiate a second loan from the banks in order to complete it and in order to meet the notes he had given to his contractors for material.

He believed this to be a shrewd business operation, since the rents as they returned to him were equal to the interest on a far larger sum than that which he had originally invested. He said little about the double mortgage on each piece of property "improved" after this fashion and which often represented a full two-thirds of its entire value. The interest on each loan was far more than covered by the rents; he chose his neighbourhoods with great discrimination; real estate was flourishing in the rapidly growing city, and the new houses, although built so cheaply that they were mere shells of lath and plaster, were nevertheless made gay and brave with varnish and cheap mill-work. They rented well at first, scarcely a one was ever vacant. People spoke of the Old Gentleman as one of the most successful realty owners in the city. So pleased did he become with the success of his new venture that in course of time all his money was reinvested after this fashion.

At the time of his father's greatest prosperity Vandover himself began to draw toward his fifteenth year, entering upon that period of change when the first raw elements of character began to assert themselves and when, if ever, there was a crying need for the influence of his mother. Any feminine influence would have been well for him at this time: that of an older sister, even that of a hired governess. The housekeeper looked after him a little, mended his clothes, saw that he took his bath Saturday nights, and that he did not dig tunnels under the garden walks. But her influence was entirely negative and prohibitory and the two were constantly at war. Vandover grew in a haphazard way and after school hours ran about the streets almost at will.

At fifteen he put on long trousers, and the fall of the same year entered the High School. He had grown too fast and at this time was tall and very lean; his limbs were straight, angular, out of all proportion, with huge articulations at the elbows and knees. His neck was long and thin and his head large, his face was sallow and covered with pimples, his ears were big, red and stuck out stiff from either side of his head. His hair he wore "pompadour."

Within a month after his entry of the High School he had a nickname. The boys called him "Skinny-seldom-fed," to his infinite humiliation.

Little by little the crude virility of the young man began to develop in him. It was a distressing, uncanny period. Had Vandover been a girl he would at this time have been subject to all sorts of abnormal vagaries, such as eating his slate pencil, nibbling bits of chalk, wishing he were dead, and drifting into states of unreasoned melancholy. As it was, his voice began to change, a little golden down appeared on his cheeks and upon the nape of his neck, while his first summer vacation was altogether spoiled by a long spell of mumps.

His appetite was enormous. He ate heavy meat three times a day, but took little or no exercise. The pimples on his face became worse and worse. He grew peevish and nervous. He hated girls, and when in their society was a very bull-calf for bashfulness and awkward self-consciousness. At times the strangest and most morbid fancies took possession of him, chief of which was that every one was looking at him while he was walking in the street.

Vandover was a good little boy. Every night he said his prayers, going down upon his huge knees at the side of his bed. To the Lord's Prayer he added various petitions of his own. He prayed that he might be a good boy and live a long time and go to Heaven when he died and see his mother; that the next Saturday might be sunny all day long, and that the end of the world might not come while he was alive.

It was during Vandover's first year at the High School that his eyes were opened and that he acquired the knowledge of good and evil. Till very late he kept his innocence, the crude raw innocence of the boy, like that of a young animal, at once charming and absurd. But by and by he became very curious, stirred with a blind unreasoned instinct. In the Bible which he read Sunday afternoons, because his father gave him a quarter for doing so, he came across a great many things that filled him with vague and strange ideas; and one Sunday at church, when the minister was intoning the Litany, he remarked for the first time the words, "all women in the perils of child-birth."

He puzzled over this for a long time, smelling out a mystery beneath the words, feeling the presence of something hidden, with the instinct of a young brute. He could get no satisfaction from his father and by and by began to be ashamed to ask him; why, he did not know. Although he could not help hearing the abominable talk of the High School boys, he at first refused to believe that part of it which he could understand. For all that he was ashamed of his innocence and ignorance and affected to appreciate their stories nevertheless.

At length one day he heard the terse and brutal truth. In an instant he believed it, some lower, animal intuition in him reiterating and confirming the fact. But even then he hated to think that people were so low, so vile. One day, however, he was looking through the volumes of the old Encyclopædia Britannica in his father's library, hoping that he might find a dollar bill which the Old Gentleman told him had been at one time misplaced between the leaves of some one of the great tomes. All at once he came upon the long article "Obstetrics," profusely illustrated with old-fashioned plates and steel engravings. He read it from beginning to end.

It was the end of all his childish ideals, the destruction of all his first illusions. The whole of his rude little standard of morality was lowered immediately. Even

his mother, whom he had always believed to be some kind
of an angel, fell at once in his estimation. She could
never be the same to him after this, never so sweet, so
good and so pure as he had hitherto imagined her.

It was very cruel, the whole thing was a grief to him, a
blow, a great shock; he hated to think of it. Then little
by little the first taint crept in, the innate vice stirred in
him, the brute began to make itself felt, and a multitude
of perverse and vicious ideas commenced to buzz about
him like a swarm of nasty flies.

A certain word, the blunt Anglo-Saxon name for a lost
woman, that he heard on one occasion among the boys at
school, opened to him a vista of incredible wickedness,
but now after the first moment of revolt the thing began
to seem less horrible. There was even a certain attraction about it. Vandover soon became filled with an overwhelming curiosity, the eager evil curiosity of the school-
boy, the perverse craving for the knowledge of vice. He
listened with all his ears to everything that was said and
went about through the great city with eyes open only to
its foulness. He even looked up in the dictionary the
meanings of the new words, finding in the cold, scientific
definitions some strange sort of satisfaction.

There was no feminine influence about Vandover at
this critical time to help him see the world in the right
light and to gauge things correctly, and he might have
been totally corrupted while in his earliest teens had it not
been for another side of his character that began to develop
about the same time.

This was his artistic side. He seemed to be a born
artist. At first he only showed bent for all general art.

He drew well, he made curious little modellings in clayey mud; he had a capital ear for music and managed in some unknown way of his own to pick out certain tunes on the piano.   At one time he gave evidence of a genuine talent for the stage.   For days he would pretend to be some dreadful sort of character, he did not know whom, talking to himself, stamping and shaking his fists; then he would dress himself in an old smoking-cap, a red table-cloth and one of his father's discarded Templar swords, and pose before the long mirrors ranting and scowling.   At another time he would devote his attention to literature, making up endless stories with which he terrified himself, telling them to himself in a low voice for hours after he had got into bed.   Sometimes he would write out these stories and read them to his father after supper, standing up between the folding doors of the library, acting out the whole narrative with furious gestures.   Once he even wrote a little poem which seriously disturbed the Old Gentleman, filling him with formless ideas and vague hopes for the future.

In a suitable environment Vandover might easily have become an author, actor or musician, since it was evident that he possessed the fundamental *afflatus* that underlies all branches of art.   As it was, the merest chance decided his career.

In the same library where he had found the famous encyclopædia article was "A Home Book of Art," one of those showily bound gift books one sees lying about conspicuously on parlour centre tables.   It was an English publication calculated to meet popular and general demand.   There were a great many full-page pictures of

lonely women, called "Reveries" or "Idylls," ideal
"Heads" of gipsy girls, of coquettes, and heads of little
girls crowned with cherries and illustrative of such titles
as "Spring," "Youth," "Innocence." Besides these
were sentimental pictures, as, for instance, one entitled
"It Might Have Been," a sad-eyed girl, with long hair,
musing over a miniature portrait, and another especially
impressive which represented a handsomely dressed
woman flung upon a *Louis Quinze* sofa, weeping, her hands
clasped over her head. She was alone; it was twilight;
on the floor was a heap of opened letters. The picture was
called "Memories."

Vandover thought this last a wonderful work of art and
made a hideous copy of it with very soft pencils. He was
so pleased with it that he copied another one of the pictures and then another. By and by he had copied almost
all of them. His father gave him a dollar and Vandover
began to add to his usual evening petition the prayer that
he might become a great artist. Thus it was that his
career was decided upon.

He was allowed to have a drawing teacher. This was
an elderly German, an immense old fellow, who wore a
wig and breathed loudly through his nose. His voice was
like a trumpet and he walked with a great striding gait
like a colonel of cavalry. Besides drawing he taught
ornamental writing and engrossing. With a dozen curved
and flowing strokes of an ordinary writing pen he could
draw upon a calling card a conventionalized outline-pic-
ture of some kind of dove or bird of paradise, all curves
and curlicues, flying very gracefully and carrying in
its beak a half-open scroll upon which could be inscribed

such sentiments as "From a Friend" or "With Fond Regards," or even one's own name.

His system of drawing was of his own invention. Over the picture to be copied he would paste a great sheet of paper, ruling off the same into spaces of about an inch square. He would cut out one of these squares and Vandover would copy the portion of the picture thus disclosed. When he had copied the whole picture in this fashion the teacher would go over it himself, retouching it here and there, labouring to obviate the checker-board effect which the process invariably produced.

At other times Vandover copied into his sketch-book, with hard crayons, those lithographed studies on buff paper which are published by the firm in Berlin. He began with ladders, wheel-barrows and water barrels, working up in course of time to rustic buildings set in a bit of landscape; stone bridges and rural mills, overhung by some sort of linden tree, with ends of broken fences in a corner of the foreground to complete the composition. From these he went on to bunches of grapes, vases of fruit and at length to more "Ideal heads." The climax was reached with a life-sized Head, crowned with honeysuckles and entitled "*Flora.*" He was three weeks upon it. It was an achievement, a veritable *chef-d'œuvre.* Vandover gave it to his father upon Christmas morning, having signed his name to it with a great ornamental flourish. The Old Gentleman was astounded, the housekeeper was called in and exclaimed over it, raising her hands to Heaven. Vandover's father gave him a five-dollar gold-piece, fresh from the mint, had the picture framed in gilt and hung it up in his smoking-room over the clock.

Never for a moment did the Old Gentleman oppose Vandover's wish to become an artist and it was he himself who first spoke about Paris to the young man. Vandover was delighted; the Latin Quarter became his dream. Between the two it was arranged that he should go over as soon as he had finished his course at the High School. The Old Gentleman was to take him across, returning only when he was well established in some suitable studio.

At length Vandover graduated, and within three weeks of that event was on his way to Europe with his father. He never got farther than Boston.

At the last moment the Old Gentleman wavered. Vandover was still very young and would be entirely alone in Paris, ignorant of the language, exposed to every temptation. Besides this, his education would stop where it was. Somehow he could not make it seem right to him to cut the young man adrift in this fashion. On the other hand, the Old Gentleman had a great many old-time friends and business acquaintances in Boston who could be trusted with a nominal supervision of his son for four years. He had no college education himself, but in some vague way he felt convinced that Vandover would be a better artist for a four years' course at Harvard.

Vandover took his father's decision hardly. He had never thought of being a college-man and nothing in that life appealed to him. He urged upon his father the loss of time that the course would entail, but his father met this objection by offering to pay for any artistic tuition that would not interfere with the regular college work.

Little by little the idea of college life became more attractive to Vandover; at the worst, it was only postponing the Paris trip, not abandoning it. Besides this, two of his chums from the High School were expecting to enter Harvard that fall, and he could look forward to a very pleasant four years spent in their company.

Out at Cambridge the term was just closing. The Old Gentleman's friends procured him tickets to several of the more important functions. From the gallery of Memorial Hall Vandover and his father saw some of the great dinners; they went up to New London for the boat-race; they gained admittance to the historic Yard on Class-day, and saw the strange football rush for flowers around the "Tree." They heard the seniors sing "Fair Harvard" for the last time, and later saw them receive their diplomas at Sander's Theatre.

The great ceremonies of the place, the picturesqueness of the elm-shaded Yard, the old red dormitories covered with ivy, the associations and traditions of the buildings, the venerable pump, Longfellow's room, the lecture hall where the minute-men had barracked, all of these things, in the end, appealed strongly to Vandover's imagination. Instead of passing the summer months in an ocean voyage and a continental journey, he at last became content to settle down to work under a tutor, "boning up" for the examinations. His father returned to San Francisco in July.

Vandover matriculated the September of the same year; on the first of October he signed the college rolls and became a Harvard freshman. At that time he was eighteen years old.

CHAPTER TWO

THERE was little of the stubborn or unyielding about Vandover, his personality was not strong, his nature pliable and he rearranged himself to suit his new environment at Harvard very rapidly. Before the end of the first semester he had become to all outward appearances a typical Harvardian. He wore corduroy vests and a gray felt hat, the brim turned down over his eyes. He smoked a pipe and bought himself a brindled bull-terrier. He cut his lectures as often as he dared, "ragged" signs and barber-poles, and was in continual evidence about Foster's and among Leavitt and Pierce's billiard-tables. When the great football games came off he worked himself into a frenzy of excitement over them and even tried to make several of his class teams, though without success.

He chummed with Charlie Geary and with young Dolliver Haight, the two San Francisco boys. The three were continually together. They took the same courses, dined at the same table in Memorial Hall and would have shared the same room if it had been possible. Vandover and Charlie Geary were fortunate enough to get a room in Matthew's on the lower floor looking out upon the Yard; young Haight was obliged to put up with an outside room in a boarding house.

Vandover had grown up with these fellows and during all his life was thrown in their company. Haight was a well-bred young boy of good family, very quiet; almost every morning he went to Chapel. He was always polite, even to his two friends. He invariably tried to be pleasant and agreeable and had a way of making people like him. Otherwise, his character was not strongly marked.

Geary was quite different. He never could forget himself. He was incessantly talking about what he had done or was going to do. In the morning he would inform Vandover of how many hours he had slept and of the dreams he had dreamed. In the evening he would tell him everything he had done that day; the things he had said, how many lectures he had cut, what brilliant recitations he had made, and even what food he had eaten at Memorial. He was pushing, self-confident, very shrewd and clever, devoured with an inordinate ambition and particularly pleased when he could get the better of anybody, even of Vandover or of young Haight. He delighted to assume the management of things. Vandover, he made his protégé, taking over the charge of such business as the two had in common. It was he who had found the room in Matthew's, getting it away from all other applicants, securing it at the eleventh hour. He put Vandover's name on the waiting list at Memorial, saw that he filled out his blanks at the proper time, helped him balance his accounts, guided him in the choice of his courses and in the making out of his study-card.

"Look here, Charlie," Vandover would exclaim, throwing down the Announcement of Courses, "I can't make this thing out. It's all in a tangle. See here, I've got to fill up my hours some way or other; *you* straighten this thing out for me. Find me some nice little course, two hours a week, say, that comes late in the morning, a good hour after breakfast; something easy, all lectures, no outside reading, nice instructor and all that." And Geary would glance over the complicated schedule, cleverly untangling it at once and would find two or three such courses as Vandover desired.

Vandover's yielding disposition led him to submit to Geary's dictatorship and he thus early began to contract easy, irresponsible habits, becoming indolent, shirking his duty whenever he could, sure that Geary would think for the two and pull him out of any difficulty into which he might drift.

Otherwise the three freshmen were very much alike. They were hardly more than boys and full of boyish spirits and activity. They began to see "college life." Vandover was already smoking; pretty soon he began to drink. He affected beer, whisky he loathed, and such wine as was not too expensive was either too sweet or too sour. It became a custom for the three to go into town two or three nights in the week and have beer and Welsh rabbits at Billy Park's. On these occasions, however, young Haight drank only beer, he never touched wine or spirits.

It was in Billy Park's the evening after the football game between the Yale and Harvard freshmen that Vandover was drunk for the first time. He was not so drunk but that he knew he was, and the knowledge of the fact so terrified him that it kept him from getting very bad. The first sensation soon wore off, and by the time that Geary took charge of him and brought him back to Cambridge he was disposed to treat the affair less seriously. Nevertheless when he got to his room he looked at himself in the mirror a long time, saying to himself over and over again, "I'm drunk — just regularly drunk. Good Heavens! what *would* the governor say to *this?*"

In the morning he was surprised to find that he felt so little ashamed. Geary and young Haight treated the matter as a huge joke and told him of certain funny things he had said and done and which he had entirely forgotten. It was impossible for him to take the matter seriously even if he had wished to, and within a few weeks he was drunk again. He found that he was not an exception; Geary was often drunk with him, fully a third of all the Harvard men he knew were intoxicated at different times. It was out of the question for Vandover to consider them as drunkards. Certainly, neither he nor any of the others drank because they liked the beer; after the fifth or sixth glass it was all they could do to force down another. Such being the case, Vandover often asked himself why he got drunk at all. This question he was never able to answer.

It was the same with gambling. At first the idea of playing cards for money shocked him beyond all expression. But soon he found that a great many of the fellows, fellows like young Haight, beyond question steady, sensible and even worthy of emulation in other ways, "went in for that sort of thing." Every now and then Vandover's "crowd" got together in his room in Matthew's, and played Van John "for keeps," as they said, until far into the night. Vandover joined them. The stakes were small, he lost as often as he won, but the habit of the cards never grew upon him. It was like the beer, he "went in for it" because the others did, without knowing why. Geary, however, drew his line at gambling; he never talked against it or tried to influence Vandover, but he never could be induced to play "for keeps" himself.

One very warm Sunday afternoon in the first days of April, when the last snows were melting, Vandover and Geary were in their room, sitting at opposite ends of their window-seat, Geary translating his Monday's "Horace" by the help of a Bohn's translation, Vandover making a pen and ink drawing for the next *Lampoon*. A couple of young women passed down the walk, going across the Yard toward the Square. They were cheaply and showily dressed. One of them wore a mannish shirtwaist, with a high collar and scarf. The other had taken off her gloves and was swinging a bright red cape in one of her bare hands. As the couple passed they stared calmly at the two young fellows in the window; Vandover lowered his eyes over his work, blushing, he could not tell why. Geary stared back at them, following them with his eyes until they had gone by.

All at once he began laughing and pounding on the window.

"Oh, for goodness sake, quit!" exclaimed Vandover in great alarm, twisting off the window-seat and shrinking back out of sight into the room. "Quit, Charlie; you don't want to insult a girl that way." Geary looked at him over his shoulder in some surprise, and was about to answer when he turned to the window again and exclaimed, grinning and waving his hand:

"Oh, just come here, Skinny; get on to this, will you?

Ah, come here and look, you old chump! Do you think they're nice girls? Just take a *look* at them." Vandover peered timidly around Geary's head and saw that the two girls were looking back and laughing, and that the one with the red cape was waving it at them.

At supper that night they saw the girls in the gallery of Memorial. They pointed them out to young Haight, and Geary at length managed to attract their attention. After supper the three freshmen, together with two of their sophomore acquaintances, strolled slowly over toward the Yard, lighting their pipes and cigarettes. All at once, as they turned into the lower gate, they came full upon the same pair of girls. They were walking fast, talking and laughing very loudly.

"Track!" called out one of the sophomores, and the group of young fellows parted to let them pass. The sophomore exclaimed in a tone of regret, "Don't be in such a hurry, girls." Vandover became scarlet and turned his face away, but the girls looked back and laughed good-naturedly. "Come on," said the sophomore. The group closed around the girls and brought them to a standstill; they were not in the least embarrassed at this, but laughed more than ever. Neither of them was pretty, but there was a certain attraction about them that pleased Vandover immensely. He was very excited.

Then there was a very embarrassing pause. No one knew what to say. Geary alone regained his assurance at length, and began a lively interchange of chaff with one of them. The others could only stand about and smile.

"*Well*," cried the other girl after a while, "I ain't going

to stand here in the snow all *night*.   Let's take a walk;
come along.   I choose *you*."   Before Vandover knew it
she had taken his arm.   The sophomore managed in some
way to pair off with the other girl; Haight had already
left the group; the two couples started off, while Geary
and the other sophomore who were left out followed
awkwardly in the rear for a little way and then disappeared.

Vandover was so excited that he could scarcely speak.
This was a new experience.   At first it attracted him, but
the hopeless vulgarity of the girl at his side, her tawdry
clothes, her sordid, petty talk, her slang, her miserable
profanity, soon began to revolt him.   He felt that he
could not keep his self-respect while such a girl hung upon
his arm.

"Say," said the girl at length, "didn't I see you in town
the other afternoon on Washington Street?"

"Maybe you did," answered Vandover, trying to be
polite.   "I'm down there pretty often."

"Well, I guess yes," she answered.   "You Harvard
sports make a regular promenade out o' Washington
Street Saturday afternoons.   I suppose I've seen you
down there pretty often, but didn't notice.   Do you stand
or walk?"

Vandover's gorge rose with disgust.   He stopped
abruptly and pulled away from the girl.   Not only did
she disgust him, but he felt sorry for her; he felt ashamed
and pitiful for a woman who had fallen so low.   Still he
tried to be polite to her; he did not know how to be rude
with any kind of woman.

"You'll have to excuse me," he said, taking off his hat.

"I don't believe I can take a walk with you to-night. I — you see — I've got a good deal of work to do; I think I'll have to leave you." Then he bowed to her with his hat in his hand, hurrying away before she could answer him a word.

He found Geary alone in their room, cribbing "Horace" again.

"Ah, you bet," Geary said. "I shook those chippies. I sized them up right away. I was clever enough for that. They were no good. I thought you would get enough of it."

"Oh, I don't know," said Vandover after a while, as he settled to his drawing. "She was pretty common, but anyhow I don't want to help bring down a poor girl like that any lower than she is already." This saying struck Vandover as being very good and noble, and he found occasion to repeat it to young Haight the next day.

But within three days of this, at the time when Vandover would have fancied himself farthest from such a thing, he underwent a curious reaction. On a certain evening, moved by an unreasoned instinct, he sought out the girl who had just filled him with such deep pity and such violent disgust, and that night did not come back to the room in Matthew's. The thing was done almost before he knew it. He could not tell why he had acted as he did, and he certainly would not have believed himself capable of it.

He passed the next few days in a veritable agony of repentance, overwhelmed by a sense of shame and dishonour that were almost feminine in their bitterness and intensity. He felt himself lost, unworthy, and as if he could never again look a pure woman in the eyes unless with an abominable hypocrisy. He was ashamed even before Geary and young Haight, and went so far as to send a long letter to his father acknowledging and deploring what he had done, asking for his forgiveness and reiterating his resolve to shun such a thing forever after.

What had been bashfulness in the boy developed in the young man to a profound respect and an instinctive regard for women. This stood him in good stead throughout all his four years of Harvard life. In general, he kept himself pretty straight. There were plenty of fast girls and lost women about Cambridge, but Vandover found that he could not associate with them to any degree of satisfaction. He never knew how to take them, never could rid himself of the idea that they were to be treated as ladies. They, on their part, did not like him; he was too diffident, too courteous, too "slow." They preferred the rough self-assertion and easy confidence of Geary, who never took "no" as an answer and who could chaff with them on their own ground.

Vandover did poor work at Harvard and only graduated, as Geary said, "by a squeak." Besides his regular studies he took time to pass three afternoons a week in the studio of a Boston artist, where he studied anatomy and composition and drew figures from the nude. In the summer vacations he did not return home, but accompanied this artist on sketching tours along the coast of Maine. His style improved immensely the moment he abandoned flat studies and began to work directly from Nature. He drew figures well, showed a feeling for desolate landscapes, and even gave promise of a good eye for colour. But he allowed his fondness for art to interfere constantly with his college work. By the middle of his senior year he was so loaded with conditions that it was only Geary's unwearied coaching that pulled him through at all — as Vandover knew it would, for that matter.

Vandover returned to San Francisco when he was twenty-two. It was astonishing; he had gone away a pimply, overgrown boy, raw and callow as a fledgling, constrained in society, diffident, awkward. Now he returned, a tall, well-formed Harvardian, as careful as a woman in the matter of dress, very refined in his manners. Besides, he was a delightful conversationalist. His father was rejoiced; every one declared he was a charming fellow.

They were right. Vandover was at his best at this time; it was undeniable that he had great talent, but he was so modest about it that few knew how clever he really was.

He went out to dinners and receptions and began to move a little in society. He became very popular: the men liked him because he was so unaffected, so straightforward, and the women because he was so respectful and so deferential.

He had no vices. He had gone through the ordeal of college life and had come out without contracting any habit more serious than a vague distaste for responsibility, and an inclination to shirk disagreeable duties. Cards he never thought of. It was rare that he drank so much as a glass of beer.

However, he had come back to a great disappointment. Business in San Francisco had entered upon a long period of decline, and values were decreasing; for ten years rents had been sagging lower and lower. At the same time the interest on loans and insurances had increased, and real estate was brought to a standstill; one spoke bitterly of a certain great monopoly that was ruining both the city and state. Vandover's father had suffered with the rest, and now told his son that he could not at this time afford to send him to Paris. He would have to wait for better times.

At first this was a sharp grief to Vandover; for years he had looked forward to an artist's life in the Quarter. For a time he was inconsolable, then at length readjusted himself good-naturedly to suit the new order of things with as little compunction as before, when he had entered Harvard. He found that he could be contented in almost any environment, the weakness, the certain pliability of his character easily fitting itself into new grooves, reshaping itself to suit new circumstances. He prevailed upon his father to allow him to have a downtown studio. In a little while he was perfectly happy again.

Vandover's love for his art was keen. On the whole he kept pretty steadily to his work, spending a good six hours at his easel every day, very absorbed over the picture in hand. He was working up into large canvases the sketches he had made along the Maine coast, great, empty expanses of sea, sky, and sand-dune, full of wind and sun. They were really admirable. He even sold one of them. The Old Gentleman was delighted, signed him a check for twenty dollars, and told him that in three years he could afford to send him abroad.

In the meanwhile Vandover set himself to enjoy the new life. Little by little his "set" formed around him;

Geary and young Haight, of course, and some half dozen young men of the city: young lawyers, medical students, and clerks in insurance offices. As Vandover thus began to see the different phases of that life which lay beyond the limits of the college, he perceived more and more clearly that he was an exception among men for his temperance, his purity, and his clean living.

At their clubs and in their smoking-rooms he heard certain practices, which he had always believed to be degrading and abominable, discussed with shouts of laughter. Those matters which until now he had regarded with an almost sacred veneration were subjects for immense jokes. A few years ago he would have been horrified at it all, but the fine quality of this first sensitiveness had been blunted since his experience at college. He tolerated these things in his friends now.

Gradually Vandover allowed his ideas and tastes to be moulded by this new order of things. He assumed the manners of these young men of the city, very curious to see for himself the other lower side of their life that began after midnight in the private rooms of fast cafés and that was continued in the heavy musk-laden air of certain parlours amid the rustle of heavy silks.

Slowly the fascination of this thing grew upon him until it mounted to a veritable passion. His strong artist's imagination began to be filled with a world of charming sensuous pictures.

He commenced to chafe under his innate respect and deference for women, to resent and to despise it. As the desire of vice, the blind, reckless desire of the male, grew upon him, he set himself to destroy this barrier that had so long stood in his way. He knew that it was the wilful and deliberate corruption of part of that which was best in him; he was sorry for it, but persevered, nevertheless, ashamed of his old-time timidity, his ignorance, his boyish purity.

For a second time the animal in him, the perverse evil brute, awoke and stirred. The idea of resistance hardly occurred to Vandover; it would be hard, it would be disagreeable to resist, and Vandover had not accustomed himself to the performance of hard, disagreeable duties. They were among the unpleasant things that he shirked. He told himself that later on, when he had grown older and steadier and had profited by experience and knowledge of the world, when he was stronger, in a word, he would curb the thing and restrain it. He saw no danger in such a course. It was what other men did with impunity.

In company with Geary and young Haight he had come to frequent a certain one of the fast cafés of the city. Here he met and became acquainted with a girl called Flossie. It was the opportunity for which he was waiting, and he seized it at once.

This time there was no recoil of conscience, no shame, no remorse; he even felt a better estimation of himself, that self-respect that comes with wider experiences and with larger views of life. He told himself that all men should at one time see certain phases of the world; it rounded out one's life. After all, one had to be a man of the world. Those men only were perverted who allowed themselves to be corrupted by such vice.

Thus it was that Vandover, by degrees, drifted into the life of a certain class of the young men of the city. Vice had no hold on him.   The brute had grown larger in him, but he knew that he had the creature in hand.   He was its master, and only on rare occasions did he permit himself to gratify its demands, feeding its abominable hunger from that part of him which he knew to be the purest, the cleanest, and the best.

Three years passed in this fashion.

CHAPTER THREE

Vandover had decided at lunch that day that he would not go back to work at his studio in the afternoon, but would stay at home instead and read a very interesting story about two men who had bought a wrecked opium ship for fifty thousand dollars, and had afterward discovered that she contained only a few tins of the drug. He was curious to see how it turned out; the studio was a long way downtown, the day was a little cold, and he felt that he would enjoy a little relaxation. Anyhow, he meant to stay at home and put in the whole afternoon on a good novel.

But even when he had made up his mind to do this he did not immediately get out his book and settle down to it. After lunch he loitered about the house while his meal digested, feeling very comfortable and contented. He strummed his banjo a little and played over upon the piano the three pieces he had picked up: two were polkas, and the third, the air of a topical song; he always played the three together and in the same sequence. Then he strolled up to his room, and brushed his hair for a while, trying to make it lie very flat and smooth. After this he went out to look at Mr. Corkle, the terrier, and let him run a bit in the garden; then he felt as though he must have a smoke, and so went back to his room and filled his pipe. When it was going well, he took down his book

31

and threw himself into a deep leather chair, only to jump
up again to put on his smoking-jacket. All at once he
became convinced that he must have something to eat
while he read, and so went to the kitchen and got himself
some apples and a huge slice of fresh bread. Ever since
Vandover was a little boy he had loved fresh bread and
apples. Through the windows of the dining-room he saw
Mr. Corkle digging up great holes in the geranium beds.
He went out and abused him and finally let him come
back into the house and took him upstairs with him.

Then at last he settled down to his novel, in the very
comfortable leather chair, before a little fire, for the last
half of August is cold in San Francisco. The room was
warm and snug, the fresh bread and apples were delicious,
the good tobacco in his pipe purred like a sleeping kitten,
and his novel was interesting and well written. He felt
calm and soothed and perfectly content, and took in the
pleasure of the occasion with the lazy complacency of a
drowsing cat.

Vandover was self-indulgent — he loved these sensuous
pleasures, he loved to eat good things, he loved to be warm,
he loved to sleep. He hated to be bored and worried —
he liked to have a good time.

At about half-past four o'clock he came to a good
stopping-place in his book; the two men had got to quarrelling, and his interest flagged a little. He pushed Mr.
Corkle off his lap and got up yawning and went to the
window.

Vandover's home was on California Street not far from
Franklin. It was a large frame house of two stories; all
the windows in the front were bay. The front door was

directly in the middle between the windows of the parlour and those of the library, while over the vestibule was a sort of balcony that no one ever thought of using. The house was set in a large well-kept yard. The lawn was pretty; an enormous eucalyptus tree grew at one corner. Nearer to the house were magnolia and banana trees growing side by side with pines and firs. Humming-birds built in these, and one could hear their curious little warbling mingling with the hoarse chirp of the English sparrows which nested under the eaves. The back yard was separated from the lawn by a high fence of green latticework. The hens and chickens were kept here and two roosters, one of which crowed every time a cable-car passed the house. On the door cut through the lattice-fence was a sign, "Look Out for the Dog." Close to the unused barn stood an immense windmill with enormous arms; when the wind blew in the afternoon the sails whirled about at a surprising speed, pumping up water from the artesian well sunk beneath. There was a small conservatory where the orchids were kept. Altogether, it was a charming place. However, adjoining it was a huge vacant lot with cows in it. It was full of dry weeds and heaps of ashes, while around it was an enormous fence painted with signs of cigars, patent bitters, and soap.

Vandover stood at a front window and looked out on a rather dreary prospect. The inevitable afternoon trades had been blowing hard since three, strong and brisk from the ocean, driving hard through the Golden Gate and filling the city with a taint of salt. Now the fog was coming in; Vandover could see great patches of it sweeping

along between him and the opposite houses. All the
eucalyptus trees were dripping, and occasionally there
came the faint moan of the fog-horn out at the heads.   He
could see up the street for nearly two miles as it climbed
over Nob Hill.   It was almost deserted; a cable-car now
and then crawled up and down its length, and at times a
delivery wagon rattled across it; but that was about all.
On the opposite sidewalk two boys and a girl were coasting
downhill on their roller-skates and their brake-wagons.
The cable in its slot kept up an incessant burr and clack.
The whole view was rather forlorn, and Vandover turned
his back on it, taking up his book again.

About five o'clock his father came home from his office.
"Hello!" said he, looking into the room; "aren't you home
a little early to-day?   Ah, I thought you weren't going
to bring that dog into the house any more.   I wish you
wouldn't, son; he gets hair and fleas about everywhere."

"All right, governor " answered Vandover.   "I'll take
him out.   Come along, Cork."

"But aren't you home earlier than usual to-day?" persisted his father as Vandover got up.

"Yes," said Vandover, "I guess I am, a little."

After supper the same evening when Vandover came
downstairs, drawing on his gloves, his father looked over
his paper, saying pleasantly:

"Well, where are you going to-night?"

"I'm going to see my girl, ' said Vandover, smiling; then
foreseeing the usual question, he added, "I'll be home
about eleven, I guess."

"Got your latch-key?" asked the Old Gentleman, as he
always did when Vandover went out.

"Yep," called back Vandover as he opened the door. "I'll not forget it again. Good-night, governor."

Vandover used to call on Turner Ravis about twice a week; people said they were engaged. This was not so.

Vandover had met Miss Ravis some two years before. For a time the two had been sincerely in love with each other, and though there was never any talk of marriage between them, they seemed to have some sort of tacit understanding. But by this time Vandover had somehow outgrown the idea of marrying Turner. He still kept up the fiction, persuaded that Turner must understand the way things had come to be. However, he was still very fond of her; she was a frank, sweet-tempered girl and very pretty, and it was delightful to have her care for him.

Vandover could not shut his eyes to the fact that young Haight was very seriously in love with Turner. But he was sure that Turner preferred him to his chum. She was too sincere, too frank, too conscientious to practise any deception on him.

There was quite a party at the Ravises' house that evening when Vandover arrived. Young Haight was there, of course, and Charlie Geary. Besides Turner herself there was Henrietta Vance, a stout, pretty girl, with pop eyes and a little nose, who laughed all the time and who was very popular. These were all part of Vandover's set; they called each other by their first names and went everywhere together. Almost every Saturday evening they got together at Turner's house and played whist, or euchre, or sometimes even poker. "Just for love," as Turner said.

When Vandover came in they were all talking at the same time, disputing about a little earthquake that had occurred the night before. Henrietta Vance declared that it had happened early in the morning.

"*Wasn't* it just about midnight, Van?" cried Turner.

"I don't know," answered Vandover. "It didn't wake me up. I didn't even know there was one."

"Well, I know I heard our clock strike two just about half an hour afterward," protested young Haight.

"Oh, it was almost five o'clock when it came," cried Henrietta Vance.

"Well, now, you're *all* off," said Charlie Geary. "I know just when she quaked to the fraction of a minute, because it stopped our hall clock at just a little after three."

They were silent. It was an argument which was hard to contradict. By and by, young Haight declared, "There must have been two of them then, because ——"

"How about whist or euchre or whatever it is to be?" said Charlie Geary, addressing Turner and interrupting in an annoying way that was peculiar to him. "Can't we start in now that Van has come?" They played euchre for a while, but Geary did not like the game, and by and by suggested poker.

"Well — if it's only just for love," said Turner, "because, you know, mamma doesn't like it any other way."

At ten o'clock Geary said, "Let's quit after this hand round — what do you say?" The rest were willing and so they all took account of their chips after the next deal. Geary was protesting against his poor luck. Honestly he hadn't held better than three tens more than twice during the evening. It was Henrietta Vance who took in everything; did one ever *see* anything to beat her luck? "the funniest thing!"

They began to do tricks with the cards. Young Haight showed them a very good trick by which he could make the pack break every time at the ace of clubs. Vandover exclaimed: "Lend me a silk hat and ninety dollars and I'll show you the queerest trick you ever saw," which sent Henrietta Vance off into shrieks of laughter. Then Geary took the cards out of young Haight's hands, asking them if they knew *this* trick.

Turner said yes, she knew it, but the others did not, and Geary showed it to them. It was interminable. Henrietta Vance chose a card and put it back into the deck. Then the deck was shuffled and divided into three piles. After this Geary made a mental calculation, selected one of these piles, shuffled it, and gave it back to her, asking her if she saw her card in it; then more shuffling and dividing until their interest and patience were quite exhausted. When Geary finally produced a jack of hearts and demanded triumphantly if that was her card, Henrietta began to laugh and declared she had forgotten *what* card she chose. Geary said he would do the trick all over for her. At this, however, they all cried out, and he had to give it up, very irritated at Henrietta's stupidity.

Vexed at the ill success of this first trick, he retired a little from their conversation, puzzling over the cards, thinking out new tricks. Every now and then he came back among them, going about from one to another, holding out the deck and exclaiming, "Choose any card —choose any card."

After a while they all adjourned to the dining-room and Turner and Vandover went out into the kitchen, foraging among the drawers and shelves. They came back bringing with them a box of sardines, a tin of *paté*, three quart bottles of blue-ribbon beer, and what Vandover called "devilish-ham" sandwiches.

"Now do we want *tamales* to go with these?" said Turner, as she spread the lunch on the table. Henrietta Vance cried out joyfully at this, and young Haight volunteered to go out to get them. "Get six," Turner cried out after him. "Henrietta can always eat two. Hurry up, and we won't eat till you get back."

While he was gone Turner got out some half-dozen glasses for their beer. "Do you know," she said as she set the glasses on the table, "the funniest thing happened this morning to mamma. It was at breakfast; she had just drunk a glass of water and was holding the glass in her hand like this" — Turner took one of the thin beer glasses in her hand to show them how — "and was talking to pa, when all at once the glass broke right straight around a ring, just below the brim, you know, and fell all ——" On a sudden Turner uttered a shrill exclamation; the others started up; the very glass she held in her hand at the moment cracked and broke in precisely the manner she was describing. A narrow ring snapped from the top, dropping on the floor, breaking into a hundred bits.

Turner drew in a long breath, open-mouthed, her hand in the air still holding the body of the glass that remained in her fingers. They all began to exclaim over the wonder.

"Well, did you ever in all your *life?*" shouted Miss

Vance, breaking into a peal of laughter. Geary cried out, "Cæsar's ghost!" and Vandover swore under his breath.

"If that isn't the strangest thing I ever saw!" cried Turner. "*Isn't* that funny — why — oh! I'm going *to try it with another glass!*" But the second glass remained intact. Geary recovered from his surprise and tried to explain how it could happen.

"It was the heat from your fingers and the glass was cold, you know," he said again and again.

But the strangeness of the thing still held them. Turner set down the glass with the others and dropped into a chair, letting her hands fall in her lap, looking into their faces, nodding her head and shutting her lips:

"Ah, *no*," she said after a while. "That *is* funny. It kind of scares one." She was actually pale.

"Oh, there's Dolly Haight!" cried Henrietta Vance as the door bell rang. They all rushed to the door, running and scrambling, eager to tell the news. Young Haight stood bewildered on the door mat in the vestibule, his arms full of brown-paper packages, while they recounted the marvel. They all spoke at once, holding imaginary beer glasses toward him in their outstretched hands. Geary, however, refused to be carried away by their excitement, and one heard him from time to time repeating, between their ejaculations, "It was the heat from her fingers, you know, and the glass was cold."

Young Haight was confused, incredulous; he could not at first make out what *had* happened.

"Well, just come and *look* at the broken *glass* on the *floor*," shouted Turner decisively, dragging him into the dining-room. They waited, breathless, to hear what he would say. He looked at the broken glass and then into their faces. Then he suddenly exclaimed:

"Ah, you're joking me."

"No, honestly," protested Vandover, "that was just the way it happened."

It was some little time before they could get over their impression of queerness, but by and by Geary cried out that the *tamales* were getting cold. They settled down to their lunch, and the first thing young Haight did was to cut his lip on the edge of the broken glass. Turner had set it down with the others and he had inadvertently filled it for himself.

It was a trifling cut. Turner fetched some court-plaster, and his lip was patched up. For all that, it bled quite a little. He was very embarrassed; he kept his handkerchief to his mouth and told them repeatedly to go on with their lunch and not to mind him.

As soon as they were eating and drinking they began to be very jolly, and Vandover was especially good-humoured and entertaining. He made Henrietta Vance shout with laughter by pretending that the olive in his *tamale* was a green hen's egg.

About half-past ten young Haight rose from the table saying he thought it was about time to say good-night. "Don't be in a hurry," said Turner. "It's early yet." After that, however, they broke up very quickly.

Before he left Vandover saw Turner in the dining-room alone for a minute.

"Will I see you at church to-morrow?" he asked, as she held his overcoat for him.

"I don't know, Van," she answered. "You know Henrietta is going to stay all night with me, and I think she will want me to go home with her to-morrow morning and then stay to dinner with her. But I'm going to early communion to-morrow morning; why can't you meet me there?"

"Why, I can," answered Vandover, settling his collar. "I should like to very much."

"Well, then," she replied, "you can meet me in front of the church at half-past seven o'clock."

"Hey, break away there!" cried Geary from the front door. "Come along, Van, if you are going with us."

Turner let Vandover kiss her before they joined the others. "I'll see you at seven-thirty to-morrow morning," he said as he went away.

The three young men went off down the street, arm in arm, smoking their cigars and cigarettes. As soon as they were alone, Charlie Geary began to tell the other two of everything he had been doing since he had last seen them.

"Well, sir," he said as he took an arm of each, "well, sir, I had a fine sleep last night; went to bed at ten and never woke up till half-past eight this morning. Ah, you bet I needed it, though. I've been working like a slave this week. You know I take my law-examinations in about ten days. I'll pass all right. I'm right up to the handle in everything. I don't believe the judge could stick me anywhere in the subject of torts."

"Say, boys," said Vandover, pausing and looking at his watch, "it isn't very late; let's go downtown and have some oysters."

"That's a good idea," answered young Haight.   "How about you, Charlie?"

Geary said he was willing.   "Ah," he added, "you ought to have seen the beefsteak I had this evening at the Grillroom."   And as they rode downtown he told them of the steak in question.   "I had a little mug of ale with it, too, and a dish of salad.   Ah, it went great."

They decided after some discussion that they would go to the Imperial.

CHAPTER FOUR

THE Imperial was a resort not far from the corner of Sutter and Kearney streets, a few doors below a certain well-known drug store, in one window of which was a showcase full of live snakes.

The front of the Imperial was painted white, and there was a cigar-stand in the vestibule of the main entrance. At the right of this main entrance was another smaller one, a ladies' entrance, on the frosted pane of which one read, "Oyster Café."

The main entrance opened directly into the barroom· It was a handsome room, paved with marble flags. To the left was the bar, whose counter was a single slab of polished redwood. Behind it was a huge, plate-glass mirror, balanced on one side by the cash-register and on the other by a statuette of the Diving Girl in tinted bisque. Between the two were pyramids of glasses and bottles, liqueur flasks in wicker cases, and a great bouquet of sweet-peas.

The three bartenders, in clean linen coats and aprons, moved about here and there, opening bottles, mixing drinks, and occasionally turning to punch the indicator of the register.

On the other side of the room, facing the bar, hung a large copy of a French picture representing a *Sabbath*, witches, goats, and naked girls whirling through the air. Underneath it was the lunch counter, where clam-fritters, the specialty of the place, could be had four afternoons in the week.

Elsewhere were nickel-in-the-slot machines, cigar-lighters, a vase of wax flowers under glass, and a racing chart setting forth the day's odds, weights, and entries. On the end wall over the pantry-slides was a second "barroom" picture, representing the ladies of a harem at their bath.

But its "private rooms" were the chief attraction of the Imperial. These were reached by going in through the smaller door to the right of the main vestibule. Any one coming in through this entrance found himself in a long and narrow passage. On the right of this passage were eight private rooms, very small, and open at the top as the law required. Half-way down its length the passage grew wider. Here the rooms were on both sides and were much larger than those in front.

It was this part of the Imperial that was most frequented, and that had made its reputation. In the smaller rooms in front one had beer and Welsh rabbits; in the larger rooms, champagne and terrapin.

Vandover, Haight, and Geary came in through the ladies' entrance of the Imperial at about eleven o'clock, going slowly down the passage, looking into each of the little rooms, searching for one that was empty. All at once Vandover, who was in the lead, cried out:

"Well, if here isn't that man Ellis, drinking whisky by himself. Bah! a man that will drink whisky all *alone!* Glad to see you just the same, Bandy; move along, will you—give a man some room."

"Hello, hello, Bandy!" cried Geary and young Haight,

hitting him in the back, while Geary added: "How long have you been down here? *I've* just come from making a call with the boys. Had a fine time; what are you drinking, whisky? *I'm* going to have something to eat. Didn't have much of a lunch to-day, but you ought to have seen the steak I had at the Grillroom — as thick as that, and tender! Oh, it went great! Here, hang my coat up there on that side, will you?"

Bancroft Ellis was one of the young men of the city with whom the three fellows had become acquainted just after their return from college. For the most part, they met him at downtown restaurants, in the foyers and vestibules of the theatres, on Kearney Street of a Saturday afternoon, or, as now, in the little rooms of the Imperial, where he was a recognized habitué and where he invariably called for whisky, finishing from three to five "ponies" at every sitting. On very rare occasions they saw him in society, at the houses where their "set" was received. At these functions Ellis could never be persuaded to remain in the parlours; he slipped up to the gentlemen's dressing-rooms at the earliest opportunity, and spent the evening silently smoking the cigars and cigarettes furnished by the host. When Vandover and his friends came up between dances, to brush their hair or to rearrange their neckties, they found him enveloped in a blue haze of smoke, his feet on a chair, his shirt bosom broken, and his waistcoat unbuttoned. He would tell them that he was bored and thirsty and ask how much longer they were going to stay. He knew but few of their friends; his home was in a little town in the interior and he prided himself on being a "Native Son of the Golden West."

He was a clerk in an insurance office on California Street, and had never been out of the state.

For the rest he was a good enough fellow and the three others liked him very much. He had a curious passion for facts and statistics, and his pockets were full of little books and cards to which he was constantly referring. He had one of those impossible pocket-diaries, the first half dozen pages loaded with information of every kind printed in blinding type, postal rates to every country in the world, statistics as to population and rates of death, weights and measures, the highest mountains in the world, the greatest depths of the ocean. He kept a little book in his left-hand vest pocket that gave the plan and seating capacity of every theatre in the city, while in the right-hand pocket was a tiny Webster's dictionary which was his especial pride. The calendar for the current year was pasted in the lining of his hat, together with the means to be employed in the resuscitation of a half-drowned person. He also carried about a "Vest Pocket Edition of Popular Information," which had never been of the slightest use to him.

The room in which they were now seated was very small and opened directly upon the passage. On either side of the table was a seat that would hold two, and on the wall opposite the door hung a mirror, its gilt frame enclosed in pink netting. The table itself was covered with a tolerably clean cloth, though it was of coarse linen and rather damp.

There were the usual bottles of olives and pepper sauce, a plate of broken crackers, and a ribbed match-safe of china. The sugar bowl was of plated ware and on it were scratched numberless dates together with the first names of a great many girls, "Nannie," "Ida," "Flossie."

Between the castor bottles was the bill of fare, held by a thin string between two immense leather covers which were stamped with wine merchants' advertisements. Geary reached for this before any of the others, saying at the same time, "Well, what are you going to have? *I'm* going to have a Welsh rabbit and a pint of ale." He looked from one to the other as if demanding whether or no they approved of his choice. He assumed the management of what was going on, advising the others what to have, telling Vandover not to order certain dishes that he liked because it took so long to cook them. He had young Haight ring for the waiter, and when he had come, Geary read off the entire order to him twice over, making sure that he had taken it correctly. "That's what we want all right, all right — isn't it?" he said, looking around at the rest.

The waiter, whose eyes were red from lack of sleep, put down before them a plate of limp, soft shrimps.

"Hello, Toby!" said Vandover.

"Good evening, gentlemen," answered Toby. "Why, good evening, Mr. Vandover; haven't seen you 'round here for some time." He took their order, and as he was going away, Vandover called him back:

"Say, Toby," said he, "has Flossie been around to-night?"

"No," answered Toby, "she hasn't shown up yet. Her running-mate was in about nine, but she went out again right away."

"Well," said Vandover, smiling, "if Flossie comes 'round show her in here, will you?"

The others laughed, and joked him about this, and Vandover settled back in his seat, easing his position.

"Ah," he exclaimed, "I like it in here. It's always pleasant and warm and quiet and the service is good and you get such good things to eat."

Now that the young fellows were by themselves, and could relax that restraint, that good breeding and delicacy which had been natural to them in the early part of the evening at the Ravises', their manners changed: they lounged clumsily upon their seats, their legs stretched out, their waistcoats unbuttoned, caring only to be at their ease. Their talk and manners became blunt, rude, unconstrained, the coarser masculine fibre reasserting itself. With the exception of young Haight they were all profane enough, and it was not very long before their conversation became obscene.

Geary told them how he had spent the afternoon promenading Kearney and Market streets and just where he had gone to get his cocktail and his cigar. "Ah," he added, "you ought to have seen Ida Wade and Bessie Laguna. Oh, Ida was rigged up to beat the band; honestly her *hat* was as broad across as that. You know there's no use talking, she's an awfully handsome girl."

A discussion arose over the girl's virtue. Ellis, Geary, and young Haight maintained that Ida was only fast; Vandover, however, had his doubts.

"For that matter," said Ellis after a while, "I like Bessie Laguna a good deal better than I do Ida."

"Ah, yes," retorted young Haight, "you like Bessie Laguna too much anyhow."

Young Haight had a theory that one should never care

in any way for that kind of a girl nor become at all intimate with her.

"The matter of liking her or not liking her," he said, "ought not to enter into the question at all. You are both of you out for a good time and that's all; you have a jolly flirtation with her for an hour or two, and you never see her again. That's the way it ought to be! This idea of getting intimate with that sort of a piece, and trying to get her to care for you, is all wrong."

"Oh," said Vandover deprecatingly, "you take all the pleasure out of it; where does your good time come in if you don't at least pretend that you like the girl and try to make her like you?"

"But don't you see," answered Haight, "what a dreadful thing it would be if a girl like that came to care for you seriously? It isn't the same as if it were a girl of your own class."

"Ah, Dolly, you've got a bean," muttered Ellis, sipping his whisky.

Meanwhile, the Imperial had been filling up; at about eleven the theatres were over, and now the barroom was full of men. They came in by twos and threes and sometimes even by noisy parties of a half dozen or more. The white swing doors of the main entrance flapped back and forth continually, letting out into the street puffs of tepid air tainted with the smell of alcohol. The men entered and ordered their drinks, and leaning their elbows upon the bar continued the conversation they had begun outside. Afterward they passed over to the lunch counter and helped themselves to a plate of stewed tripe or potato salad, eating it in a secluded corner, leaning over so as not to stain their coats. There was a continual clinking of glasses and popping of corks, and at every instant the cash-register clucked and rang its bell.

Between the barroom and the other part of the house was a door hung with blue plush curtains, looped back; the waiters constantly passed back and forth through this, carrying plates of oysters, smoking rarebits, tiny glasses of liqueurs, and goblets of cigars.

All the private rooms opening from either passage were full; the men came in, walking slowly, looking for their friends; but more often, the women and girls passed up and down with a chatter of conversation, a rattle of stiff skirts and petticoats, and a heavy whiff of musk. There was a continual going and coming, a monotonous shuffle of feet and hum of talk. A heavy odorous warmth in which were mingled the smells of sweetened whisky, tobacco, the fumes of cooking, and the scent of perfume, exhaled into the air. A gay and noisy party developed in one of the large back rooms; at every moment one could hear gales of laughter, the rattle of chairs and glassware, mingled with the sounds of men's voices and the little screams and cries of women. Every time the waiter opened the door to deliver an order he let out a momentary torrent of noises.

Girls, habitués of the place, continued to pass the door of the room where Vandover and his friends were seated. Each time a particularly handsome one went by, the four looked out after her, shutting their lips and eyes and nodding their heads.

Young Haight had called for more drinks, ordering, however, mineral water for himself, and Vandover was

just telling about posing the female models in a certain
life-class to which he belonged, when he looked up and
broke off, exclaiming:

"Well, well, here we are at last! How are you, Flossie?
Come right in."

Flossie stood in the doorway smiling good-humouredly
at them, without a trace of embarrassment or of confusion
in her manner. She was an immense girl, quite six feet
tall, broad and well-made, in proportion. She was very
handsome, full-throated, heavy-eyed, and slow in her
movements. Her eyes and mouth, like everything about
her, were large, but each time she spoke or smiled, she
disclosed her teeth, which were as white, as well-set, and
as regular as the rows of kernels on an ear of green corn.
In her ears were small yellow diamonds, the only jewellery
she wore. There was no perceptible cosmetic on her face,
which had a clean and healthy look as though she had
just given it a vigorous washing.

She wore a black hat with a great flare to the brim on
one side. It was trimmed very dashingly with black
feathers, imitation jet, and a little puff of plush — robin's-
egg blue. Her dress was of rough, black camel's hair,
tailor-made, and but for the immense balloon sleeves,
absolutely plain. It was cut in such a way that from
neck to waist there was no break, the buttons being
on the shoulder and under the arm. The skirt was full
and stiff, and without the least trimming. Everything
was black — hat, dress, gloves — and the effect was of a
simplicity and severity so pronounced as to be very
striking.

However, around her waist she wore as a belt a thick

rope of oxidized silver, while her shoes, or rather walking slippers, were of white canvas.

She belonged to that class of women who are not to know one's last name or address, and whose hate and love are equally to be dreaded. There was upon her face the unmistakable traces of a ruined virtue and a vanished innocence. Her slightest action suggested her profession; as soon as she removed her veil and gloves it was as though she were partially undressed, and her uncovered face and hands seemed to be only portions of her nudity.

The general conception of women of her class is a painted and broken wreck. Flossie radiated health; her eyes were clear, her nerves steady, her flesh hard and even as a child's. There hung about her an air of cleanliness, of freshness, of good nature, of fine, high spirits, while with every movement she exhaled a delicious perfume that was not only musk, but that seemed to come alike from her dress, her hair, her neck, her very flesh and body.

Vandover was no longer the same as he had been during his college days. He was familiar now with this odour of abandoned women, this foul sweet savour of the great city's vice, that quickened his breath and that sent his heart knocking at his throat. It was the sensitive artist nature in him that responded instantly to anything sensuously attractive. Each kind and class of beautiful women could arouse in Vandover passions of equal force, though of far different kind. Turner Ravis influenced him upon his best side, calling out in him all that was cleanest, finest, and most delicate. Flossie appealed only to the animal and the beast in him, the evil, hideous brute that made instant answer.

"What will you take, Flossie?" asked Vandover, as she settled herself among them. "We are all drinking beer except Ellis. *He's* filling up with whisky." But Flossie never drank. It was one of the peculiarities for which she was well known.

"I don't want either," she answered, and turning to the waiter, she added, "You can bring me some Apollinaris water, Toby."

Flossie betrayed herself as soon as she spoke, the effect of her appearance was spoiled. Her voice was hoarse, a low-pitched rasp, husky, throaty, and full of brutal, vulgar modulations.

"Smoke, Flossie?" said Geary, pushing his cigarette case across to her. Flossie took a cigarette, rolled it to make it loose, and smoked it while she told them how she had once tried to draw up the smoke through her nose as it came out between her lips.

"And honestly, boys," she growled, "it made me that sick that I just had to go to bed."

"Who is the crowd out back?" asked Geary for the sake of saying something. Flossie embarrassed them all a little, and conversation with girls of her class was difficult.

"Oh, that's May and Nannie with some men from a banquet at the Palace Hotel," she answered.

The talk dragged along little by little and Flossie began badgering young Haight. "Say, you over there," she exclaimed, "what's the matter with you? You don't say anything."

Young Haight blushed and answered very much embarrassed: "Oh, I'm just listening." He was anxious to get away. He got up and reached for his hat and coat, saying with a good-natured smile: "Well, boys and girls, I think I shall have to leave you."

"Don't let me frighten you away," said Flossie, laughing.

"Oh, no," he answered, trying to hide his embarrassment, "I have to go anyhow."

While the others were saying good night to him and asking when they should see him again, Flossie leaned over to him, crying out, "Good night!" All at once, and before he knew what she was about, she kissed him full on the mouth. He started sharply at this, but was not angry, simply pulling away from her, blushing, very embarrassed, and more and more anxious to get away. Toby, the waiter, appeared at their door:

"That last was on me, you know," said young Haight, intercepting Vandover and settling for the round of drinks.

"Hello!" exclaimed Toby, "what's the matter with your lip?"

"I cut it a little while ago on a broken glass," answered young Haight. "Is it bleeding again?" he added, putting two fingers on his lips.

"It is sure enough," said Geary. "Here," he went on, wetting the corner of a napkin from the water bottle, "hold that on it."

The others began to laugh. "Flossie did that," Vandover explained to Toby. Ellis was hastily looking through his pockets, fumbling about among his little books.

"I had something here," he kept muttering, "if I can only *find* it, that told just what to do when you cut yourself with glass. There may be glass *in* it, you know."

"Oh, that's all right, that's all right," exclaimed young

Haight, now altogether disconcerted. "It don't amount to anything."

"I tell you what," observed Geary; "get some court-plaster at the snake doctor's just above here."

"No, no, that's all right," returned young Haight, moving off. "Good night. I'll see you again pretty soon."

He went away. Ellis, who was still searching through his little books, suddenly uttered an exclamation. He leaned out into the passage, crying: "The half of a hot onion; tie it right on the cut." But Haight had already gone. "You see," explained Ellis, "that draws out any little particles of glass. Look at this," he added, reading an item just below the one he had found. "You can use cigar ashes for eczema."

Flossie nodded her head at him, smiling and saying: "Well, the next time I have eczema I will remember that."

Flossie left them a little after this, joining Nannie and May in the larger room that held the noisy party. The three fellows had another round of drinks.

All the evening Ellis had been drinking whisky. Now he astonished the others by suddenly calling for beer. He persisted in drinking it out of the celery glass, which he emptied at a single pull. Then Vandover had claret-punches all round, protesting that his mouth felt dry as a dust-bin. Geary at length declared that he felt pretty far gone, adding that he was in the humour for having "a high old time."

"Say, boys," he exclaimed, bringing his hand down on the table, "what do you say that we all go to every

joint in town, and wind up at the Turkish baths? We'll
have a regular *time*. Let's see now how much money I
have."

Thereat they all took account of their money. Vandover
had fourteen dollars, but he owed for materials at his art
dealer's, and so put away eight of it in an inside pocket.
The others followed his example, each one reserving five
dollars for immediate use.

"That will be one dollar for the Hammam," said Geary,
"and four dollars apiece for drinks. You can get all we
want on four dollars." They had a last claret-punch and,
having settled with Toby, went out.

Coming out into the cold night air from the warm interior of the Imperial affected Vandover and Geary in a
few minutes. But apparently nothing could affect Ellis,
neither whisky, claret-punch nor beer. He walked steadily
between Vandover and Geary, linking an arm in each
of theirs.

These two became very drunk almost at once. At
every minute Vandover would cry out, "Yee-ee-*ow!*
Thash way I feel, jush like that." Geary made a "Josh"
that was a masterpiece, the success of the occasion. It
consisted in exclaiming from time to time, "Cherries are
ripe!" This was funny. It seemed to have some ludicrous, hidden double-meaning that was irresistible. It
stuck to them all the evening; when a girl passed them on
Kearney Street and Geary cried out at her that "Cherries
were ripe!" it threw them all into spasms of laughter.

They went first to the Palace Garden near the Tivoli
Theatre, where Geary and Vandover had beer and Ellis
a whisky cocktail. The performance was just finishing,

and they voted that they were not at all amused at a lean, overworked girl whom they saw performing a song and dance through a blue haze of tobacco smoke; so they all exclaimed, "Cherries are ripe!" and tramped out again to visit the Luxembourg. The beer began to go against Vandover's stomach by this time, but he forced it down his throat, shutting his eyes. Then they said they would go to the toughest place in town, "Steve Casey's"; this was on a side-street. The walls were covered with yellowed photographs of once-famous pugilists and old-time concert-hall singers. There was sand on the floor, and in the dancing room at the back, where nobody danced, a jaded young man was banging out polkas and quick-steps at a cheap piano.

At the Crystal Palace, where they all had shandy-gaff, they met one of Ellis's friends, a young fellow of about twenty. He was stone deaf, and in consequence had become dumb; but for all that he was very eager to associate with the young men of the city and would not hear of being separated and set apart with the other deaf mutes. He was very pleased to meet them and joined them at once. They all knew him pretty well and called him the "Dummy."

In the course of the evening the party was seen at nearly every bar and saloon in the neighbourhood of Market and Kearney streets. Geary and Vandover were very drunk indeed. Vandover was having a glorious time; he was not silent a minute, talking, laughing, and singing, and crying out continually, "Cherries are ripe!" When he could think of nothing else to say he would exclaim, "Yee-ee-*ow !*   Thash way I feel."

For two hours they drank steadily. Vandover was in a dreadful condition; the Dummy got so drunk that he could talk, a peculiarity which at times had been known to occur to him. As will sometimes happen, Geary sobered up a little and at the "Grotto" bathed his head and face in the washroom. After this he became pretty steady, he stopped drinking, and tried to assume the management of the party, ordering their drinks for them, and casting up the amount of the check.

About two o'clock they returned toward the Luxembourg, staggering and swaying. The Luxembourg was a sort of German restaurant under a theatre where one could get some very good German dishes. There Vandover had beer and sauerkraut, but Ellis took more whisky. The Dummy continued to make peculiar sounds in his throat, half-noise, half-speech, and Geary gravely informed the waiter that cherries were ripe.

All at once Ellis was drunk, collapsing in a moment. The skin around his eyes was purple and swollen, the pupils themselves were contracted, and their range of vision seemed to stop at about a yard in front of his face. Suddenly he swept glasses, plates, castor, knives, forks, and all from off the table with a single movement of his arm.

They all jumped up, sober in a minute, knowing that a scene was at hand. The waiter rushed at Ellis, but Ellis knocked him down and tried to stamp on his face. Vandover and the Dummy tried to hold his arms and pull him off. He turned on the Dummy in a silent frenzy of rage and brought his knuckles down upon his head again and again. For the moment Ellis could neither

hear, nor see, nor speak; he was blind, dumb, fighting
drunk, and his fighting was not the fighting of Vandover.

"Get in here and help, will you?" panted Vandover to
Geary, as he struggled with Ellis. "He can kill people
when he's like this. Oh, damn the whisky anyhow!
Look out — don't let him get that knife! Grab his other
arm, there! now, kick his feet from under him! Oh, kick
hard! Sit on his legs; there now. Ah! Hell! he's bitten
me! Look out! here comes the bouncer!"

The bouncer and three other waiters charged into them
while they were struggling on the floor. Vandover was
twice knocked down and the Dummy had his lip split.
Ellis struggled to his feet again and, still silent, fought
them all alike, a fine line of froth gathering at the corners
of his lips.

When they were finally ejected, and pulled themselves
together in the street outside, Geary had disappeared.
He had left them during the struggle with Ellis and had
gone home. Ah, you bet he wasn't going to stay any
longer with the crowd when they got like that. If Ellis
was fool enough to get as drunk as that it was his own
lookout. *He* wasn't going to stay and get thrown out of
any saloon; ah, no, you bet he was too clever for that.
He was sober enough now and would go home to bed and
get a good sleep.

The fight in the saloon had completely sobered the
rest of them. Ellis was tractable enough again, and very
sorry for having got them into such a row. Vandover
was horribly sick at his stomach.

The three locked arms and started slowly toward the

Turkish baths. On their way they stopped at an all-night drug store and had some seltzer.

Vandover had about three hours' sleep that night. He was awakened by the attendant shaking his arm and crying:

"Half-past six, sir."

"Huh!" he exclaimed, starting up. "What about half-past six? I don't want to get up."

"Told me to call you, sir, at half-past six; quarter to seven now."

"Oh, all right, very well," answered Vandover. He turned away his face on the pillow, while a wretched feeling of nausea crept over him; every movement of his head made it ache to bursting. Behind his temples the blood throbbed and pumped like the knocking of hammers. His mouth would have been dry but for a thick slime that filled it and that tasted of oil. He felt weak, his hands trembled, his forehead was cold and seemed wet and sticky.

He could recall hardly anything of the previous night. He remembered, however, of going to the Imperial and of seeing Flossie, and he *did* remember at last of leaving word to be called at half-past six.

He got up without waking the other two fellows and took a plunge in the cold tank, dressed very slowly, and went out. The stores were all closed, the streets were almost deserted. He walked to the nearest uptown car-line and took an outside seat, feeling better and steadier for every moment of the sharp morning air.

Van Ness Avenue was very still. It was about half-past seven. The curtains were down in all the houses; here and there a servant could be seen washing down the front steps. In the vestibules of some of the smaller houses were loaves of French bread and glass jars of cream, while near them lay the damp twisted roll of the morning's paper. There was everywhere a great chittering of sparrows, and the cable-cars, as yet empty, trundled down the cross streets, the conductors cleaning the windows and metal work. From far down at one end of the avenue came the bells of the Catholic Cathedral ringing for early mass; and a respectable-looking second girl hurried past him carrying her prayer-book. At the other end of the avenue was a blue vista of the bay, the great bulk of Mount Tamalpais rearing itself out of the water like a waking lion.

In front of the little church Turner was waiting for him. She was dressed very prettily and the cold morning air had given her a fine colour.

"You don't look more than half awake," she said, as Vandover came up. "It was awfully good of you to come. Oh, Van, you look dreadfully. It is too bad to make you get up so early."

"No, no," protested Vandover. "I was only too glad to come. I didn't sleep well last night. I hope I haven't kept you waiting."

"I've only just come," answered Turner. "But I think it is time to go in."

The little organ was muttering softly to itself as they entered. It was very still otherwise. The morning sun struck through the stained windows and made pretty lights about the altar; besides themselves there were some half dozen other worshippers. The little organ ceased with a long droning sigh, and the minister in his white robes turned about, facing his auditors, and in the midst of a great silence opened the communion service with the words: "Ye who do truly and earnestly repent you of your sins and are in love and charity with your neighbours ——"

As Vandover rose with the rest the blood rushed to his head and a feeling of nausea and exhaustion, the dregs of his previous night's debauch, came over him again for a moment, so that he took hold of the back of the pew in front of him to steady himself.

CHAPTER FIVE

In the afternoons Vandover worked in his studio, which was on Sacramento Street, but in the mornings he was accustomed to study in the life-class at the School of Design.

This was on California Street over the Market, an immense room partitioned by enormous wooden screens into alcoves, where the still-life classes worked, painting carrots, grapes, and dusty brown stone-jugs.

All about were a multitude of casts, the fighting gladiator, the discobulus, the Venus of Milo, and hundreds of smaller pieces, masks, torsos, and the heads of the Parthenon horses. Flattened paint-tubes and broken bits of charcoal littered the floor and cluttered the chairs and shelves. A strong odour of turpentine and fixative was in the air, mingled with the stronger odours of linseed oil and sour, stale French bread.

Every afternoon a portrait class of some thirty-odd assembled in one of the larger alcoves near the door. Several of the well-known street characters of the city had posed for this class, and at one time Father Elphick, the white-haired, bareheaded vegetarian, with his crooked stick and white clothes, had sat to it for his head.

Vandover was probably the most promising member of the school. His style was sketchy, conscientious, and full of strength and decision. He worked in large lines,

63

broad surfaces and masses of light or shade. His colour
was good, running to purples, reds, and admirable greens,
full of bitumen and raw sienna.

Though he had no idea of composition, he was clever
enough to acknowledge it. His finished pictures were
broad reaches of landscape, deserts, shores, and moors in
which he placed solitary figures of men or animals in a
way that was very effective — as, for instance, a great
strip of shore and in the foreground the body of a drowned
sailor; a lion drinking in the midst of an immense Sahara;
or, one that he called "The Remnant of an Army," a
dying war horse wandering on an empty plain, the saddle
turned under his belly, his mane and tail snarled with
burrs.

Some time before there had come to him the idea for a
great picture. It was to be his first masterpiece, his salon
picture when he should get to Paris. A British cavalry-
man and his horse, both dying of thirst and wounds, were
to be lost on a Soudanese desert, and in the middle distance on a ridge of sand a lion should be drawing in upon
them, crouched on his belly, his tail stiff, his lower jaw
hanging. The melodrama of the old English "Home
Book of Art" still influenced Vandover. He was in love
with this idea for a picture and had determined to call it
"The Last Enemy." The effects he wished to produce
were isolation and intense heat; as to the soldier, he was
as yet undecided whether to represent him facing death
resignedly, calmly, or grasping the barrel of his useless
rifle, determined to fight to the last.

Vandover loved to paint and to draw. He was perfectly contented when his picture was "coming right,"

and when he felt sure he was doing good work. He often did better than he thought he would, but never so well as he thought he *could*.

However, it bored him to work very hard, and when he did not enjoy his work he stopped it at once. He would tell himself on these occasions that one had to be in the mood and that he should wait for the inspiration, although he knew very well how absurd such excuses were, how false and how pernicious.

That certain little weakness of Vandover's character, his self-indulgence, had brought him to such a point that he thought he *had* to be amused. If his painting amused him, very good; if not, he found something else that would.

On the following Monday as he worked in the life-class, Vandover was thinking, or, rather, trying not to think, of what he had done the Sunday morning previous when he had gone to communion with Turner Ravis. For a long time he evaded the thought because he knew that if he allowed it to come into his mind it would worry and harass him. But by and by the effort of dodging the enemy became itself too disagreeable, so he gave it up, and allowed himself to look the matter squarely in the face.

Ah, yes; it was an ugly thing he had done there, a really awful thing. He must have been still drunk when he had knelt in the chancel. Vandover shuddered as he thought of this, and told himself that one could hardly commit a worse sacrilege, and that some time he would surely be called to account for it. But here he checked himself suddenly, not daring to go further. One would have no peace of mind left if one went on brooding over such things in this fashion. He realized the enormity of what he had done. He had tried to be sorry for it. It was perhaps the worst thing he had ever done, but now he had reached the lowest point. He would take care never to do such a thing again. After this he would be better.

But this was not so. Unconsciously, Vandover had shut a door behind him; he would never again be exactly the same, and the keeping of his appointment with Turner Ravis that Sunday morning was, as it were, a long step onward in his progress of ruin and pollution.

He shook himself as though relieving his shoulders of a weight. The model in the life-class had just been posed for the week, and the others had begun work. The model for that week was a woman, a fact that pleased Vandover, for he drew these nude women better than any one in the school, perhaps better than any one in the city. Portrait work and the power to catch subtle intellectual distinctions in a face were sometimes beyond him, but his feeling for the flesh, and for the movement and character of a pose, was admirable.

He set himself to work. Holding his stick of charcoal toward the model at arm's-length, he measured off the heads, five in all, and laid off an equal number of spaces upon his paper. After this, by aid of his mirror, he studied the general character of the pose for nearly half an hour. Then, with a few strokes of his charcoal he laid off his larger construction lines with a freedom and a precision that were excellent. Upon these lines he made a second drawing a little more detailed, though as yet everything was blocked in, angularly and roughly. Then, putting a thin flat edge upon his charcoal, he started the careful and finished outline.

By the end of an hour the first sketch of his drawing was complete. It was astonishingly good, vigorous and solid; better than all, it had that feeling for form that makes just the difference between the amateur and the genuine artist.

By this time Vandover's interest began to flag. Four times he had drawn and redrawn the articulation of the model's left shoulder. As she stood, turned sideways to him, one hand on her hip, the deltoid muscle was at once contracted and foreshortened. It was a difficult bit of anatomy to draw. Vandover was annoyed at his ill success — such close attention and continued effort wearied him a little — the room was overheated and close, and the gas stove, which was placed near the throne to warm the model, leaked and filled the room with a nasty brassy smell. Vandover remembered that the previous week he had been looking over some old bound copies of *l'Art* in the Mechanics Library and had found them of absorbing interest. There was a pleasant corner and a huge comfortable chair near where they were in the reading-room, and from the window one could occasionally look out upon the street. It was a quiet spot, and he would not be disturbed all the morning. The idea was so attractive that he put away his portfolio and drawing things and went out.

For an hour he gave himself up to the enjoyment of *l'Art*, excusing his indolence by telling himself that it was all in his profession and was not time lost. A reproduction of a picture by Gérome gave him some suggestions for the "Last Enemy," which he noted very carefully.

He was interrupted by a rustle of starched skirts and a voice that said:

"Why, hello, Van!"

He looked up quickly to see a young girl of about twenty dressed in a black close-fitting bolero jacket of imitation astrakhan with big leg-of-mutton sleeves, a striped silk skirt, and a very broad hat tilted to one side. Her hair was very blond, though coarse and dry from being bleached, and a little flat curl of it lay very low on her forehead. She was marvellously pretty. Vandover was delighted.

"Why, *Ida!*" he exclaimed, holding her hand; "*it's* awfully nice to see you here; won't you sit down?" and he pushed his chair toward her.

But Ida Wade said no, she had just come in after a new book, and of course it had to be out. But where had he kept himself so long? That was the way he threw off on her; ah, yes, he was going with Miss Ravis now and wouldn't look at any one else.

Vandover protested against this, and Ida Wade went on to ask him why he couldn't come up to call on her that very night, adding:

"We might go to the Tivoli or somewhere." All at once she interrupted herself, laughing, "Oh, I heard all about you the other night. *'Cherries are ripe!'* You and the boys painted the town red, didn't you? Ah, Van, I'm right on to *you!*"

She would not tell him how she heard, but took herself off, laughing and reminding him to come up early.

Ida Wade belonged to a certain type of young girl that was very common in the city. She was what men, among each other, called "gay," though that was the worst that could be said of her. She was virtuous, but the very fact that it was necessary to say so was enough to cause the statement to be doubted.   When she was younger and had been a pupil at the Girls' High School, she had known and had even been the companion of such girls as Turner Ravis and Henrietta Vance, but since that time girls of that class had ignored her.   Now, almost all of her acquaintances were men, and to half of these she had never been introduced.   They had managed to get acquainted with her on Kearney Street, at theatres, at the Mechanics' Fair, and at baseball games.   She loved to have a "gay" time, which for her meant to drink California champagne, to smoke cigarettes, and to kick at the chandelier.   She was still virtuous and meant to stay so; there was nothing vicious about her, and she was as far removed from Flossie's class as from that of Turner Ravis.

She was very clever; half of her acquaintances, even the men, did not know how very "gay" she was.   Only those — like Vandover — who knew her best, knew her for what she was, for Ida was morbidly careful of appearances, and as jealous of her reputation as only fast girls are.

Bessie Laguna was her counterpart.   Bessie was "the girl she went with," just as Henrietta Vance was Turner's "chum" and Nannie was Flossie's "running-mate."

Ida lived with her people on Golden Gate Avenue not far from Larkin Street.   Her father had a three-fourths interest in a carpet-cleaning establishment on Howard Street, and her mother gave lessons in painting on china and on velvet.   Ida had just been graduated from the normal school, and often substituted at various kindergartens in the city.   She hoped soon to get a permanent place.

Vandover arrived at Ida's house that night at about eight o'clock in the midst of a drenching fog. The parlour and front room on the second floor were furnished with bay windows decorated with some meaningless sort of millwork. The front door stood at the right of the parlour windows. Two Corinthian pillars on either side of the vestibule supported a balcony; these pillars had iron capitals which were painted to imitate the wood of the house, which in its turn was painted to imitate stone. The house was but two stories high, and the roof was topped with an iron cresting. There was a microscopical front yard in which one saw a tiny gravel walk, two steps long, that led to a door under the front steps, where the gas-meter was kept. A few dusty and straggling calla-lilies grew about.

Ida opened the door for Vandover almost as soon as he rang, and pulled him into the entry, exclaiming: "Come in out of the wet, as the whale said to Jonah. *Isn't* it a nasty night?" Vandover noticed as he came in that the house smelt of upholstery, cooking, and turpentine. He did not take off his overcoat, but went with her into the parlour.

The parlour was a little room with tinted plaster walls shut off from the "back-parlour" by sliding doors. A ply carpet covered the floor, a cheap piano stood across one corner of the room, and a greenish sofa across another. The mantelpiece was of white marble with gray spots; on one side of it stood an Alaskan "grass basket" full of photographs, and on the other an inverted section of a sewer-pipe painted with daisies and full of gilded cat-tails tied with a blue ribbon. Near the piano straddled a

huge easel of imitation brass upholding the crayon picture
of Ida's baby sister enlarged from a photograph. Across
one corner of this picture was a yellow "drape." There
were a great many of these "drapes" all about the room,
hanging over the corners of the chairs, upon an edge of the
mantelpiece, and even twisted about the chandelier. In
the exact middle of the mantelpiece itself was the clock,
one of the chief ornaments of the room, almost the first
thing one saw upon entering; it was a round-faced timepiece perversely set in one corner of an immense red plush
palette; the palette itself was tilted to one side, and was
upheld by an easel of twisted brass wire. Out of the
thumb-hole stuck half a dozen brushes wired together in
a round bunch and covered with gilt paint. The clock
never was wound. It went so fast that it was useless as
a timepiece. Over it, however, hung a large and striking
picture, a species of cheap photogravure, a lion lying in
his cage, looking mildly at the spectator over his shoulder.
In front of the picture were real iron bars, with real
straw tucked in behind them.

Ida sat down on the piano stool, twisting back and forth,
leaning her elbows on the keys.

"All the folks have gone out to a whist-party, and I'm
left all alone in the house with Maggie," she said. Then
she added: "Bessie and Bandy Ellis said they would come
down to-night, and I thought we could all go downtown
to the Tivoli or somewhere, in the open-air boxes, you
know, way up at the top." Hardly had she spoken the
words when Bessie and Ellis arrived.

Ida went upstairs to get on her hat at once, because it
was so late, and Bessie went with her.

Ellis and Vandover laughed as soon as they saw each other, and Ellis exclaimed mockingly, "Ye-e-ow, thash jush way I feel." Vandover grinned:

"That's so," he answered. "I *do* remember now of having made that remark several times. But *you* — oh, you were fearful. Do you remember the row in the Luxembourg? Look there where you bit me."

Ellis was incensed with Geary because he had forsaken their party.

"Oh, that's Charlie Geary, all over," answered Vandover.

As they were speaking there came a sudden outburst of bells in various parts of the city and simultaneously they heard the hoarse croaking of a whistle down by the water-front.

"Fire," said Vandover indifferently.

Ellis was already fumbling in his pockets, keeping count of the strokes.

"That's one," he exclaimed, pulling out and studying his list of alarm-boxes, "and one-two-three, that's three and one-two-three-*four*, one thirty-four. Let's see now! That's Bush and Hyde streets, not very far off," and he returned his card to the inside pocket of his coat as though he had accomplished a duty.

He lit a cigar. "I wonder now," he said, hesitating. "I guess I better not smoke in here. I'll go outside and get a mouthful of smoke before the girls come down." He went out and Vandover sat down to the cheap piano and played his three inevitable pieces, the two polkas and the air of the topical song; but he was interrupted by Ellis, who opened the door, crying out:

"Oh, come out here and see the *fire*, will you? Devil of a blaze!" Vandover ran out and saw a great fan-shaped haze of red through the fog over the roofs of the houses.

"Oh, say, girls," he shouted, jumping back to the foot of the stairs; "Ida, Bessie, there's a fire. Just look out of your windows. Hark, there go the engines."

Bessie came tearing down the stairs and out on the front steps, where the two fellows were standing hatless.

"Where? Oh, show me where! O-o-oh, sure enough! That's a *big* fire. Just *hear* the engines. *Oh, let's go!*"

"Sure; come on, let's go!" exclaimed Vandover. "Tell Ida to hurry up."

"Oh, Ida," cried Bessie up the stairs, "there's an awful big fire right near here, and we're going."

"Oh, wait!" shouted Ida, her mouth full of pins. "I had to change my waist. Oh, *do* wait for me. Where is it *at?* Please wait; I'm coming right down in just a minute."

"Hurry up, hurry up!" cried Vandover. "It will be all out by the time we get there. I'm coming up to help."

"No, no, no!" she screamed. "Don't; you rattle me. I'm all mixed up. Oh, *darn* it, I can't find my czarina!"

But at last she came running down, breathless, shrugging herself into her bolero jacket. They all hurried into the street and turned in the direction of the blaze. Other people were walking rapidly in the same direction, and there was an opening and shutting of windows and front doors. A steamer thundered past, clanging and smoking, followed by a score of half-exhausted boys. It took them longer to reach the fire than they expected, and by the time they had come within two blocks of it they were quite out of breath.   Here the excitement was lively; the sidewalks were full of people going in the same direction; on all sides there were guesses as to where the fire was.   On the front steps of many houses stood middle-aged gentlemen, still holding their evening papers and cigars, very amused and interested in watching the crowd go past.   One heard them from time to time calling to their little sons, who were dancing on the sidewalks, forbidding them to go; in the open windows above could be seen the other members of the family, their faces faintly tinged with the glow, looking and pointing, or calling across the street to their friends in the opposite houses.   Every one was in good humour; it was an event, a fête for the entire neighbour-hood.

Vandover and his party came at last to the first engines violently pumping and coughing, the huge gray horses standing near by, already unhitched and blanketed, in-differently feeding in their nosebags.   Some of the crowd preferred to watch the engines rather than the fire, and there were even some who were coming away from it, exclaiming "false alarm" or "all out now."

The party had come up quite close; they could smell the burning wood and could see the roofs of the nearer houses beginning to stand out sharp and black against the red glow beyond.   It was a barn behind a huge frame house that was afire, the dry hay burning like powder, and by the time they reached it the flames were already dwindling. The hose was lying like a python all about the streets, while upon the neighbouring roofs were groups of firemen with helmets and axes; some were shouting into the street below, and others were holding the spouting nozzles of the hose. "Ah," exclaimed an old man, standing near to Ida and Vandover, "ah, *I* was here when it first broke out; you ought to have seen the flames then! Look, there's a tree catching!"

The crowd became denser; policemen pushed it back and stretched a rope across the street. There was a world of tumbling yellow smoke that made one's eyes smart, and a great crackling and snapping of flames. Terribly excited little boys were about everywhere whistling and calling for each other as the crowd separated them.

They watched the fire for some time, standing on a pile of boards in front of a half-built house, but as it dwindled they wearied of it.

"Want to go?" asked Vandover at last.

"Yes," answered Ida, "we might as well. Oh, where's Bessie and Ellis?" They were nowhere to be seen. Vandover whistled and Ida even called, but in vain. The little boys in the crowd mimicked Ida, crying back, "Hey! Bessie! Oh, *Bes-see*, mommer wants you!" The men who stood near laughed at this, but it annoyed Vandover much more than it did Ida.

"Ah, well, never mind," she said at length. "Let them go. Now shall *we* go?"

It was too late for the theatre, but to return home was out of the question. They started off aimlessly downtown.

While he talked Vandover was perplexed. Ida was gayly dressed and was one of those girls who cannot open their mouths nor raise a finger in the street without attracting attention. Vandover was not at all certain that he cared to be seen on Kearney Street as Ida Wade's escort;

one never knew who one was going to meet.   Ida was not
a bad girl, she was not notorious, but, confound it, it
would look queer; and at the same time, while Ida was the
kind of girl that one did not want to be seen with, she was
not the kind of girl that could be told so.   In an upper
box at the Tivoli it would have been different — one could
keep in the background; but to appear on Kearney Street
with a girl who wore a hat like that and who would not
put on her gloves — ah, no, it was out of the question.

Ida was talking away endlessly about a kindergarten
in which she had substituted the last week.

She told him about the funny little nigger girl, and about
the games and songs and how they played birds and hopped
around and cried, "Twit, twit," and the game of the
butterflies visiting the flowers.   She even sang part of a
song about the waves.

> "Every little wave had its night-cap on;
>   Its white-cap, night-cap, white-cap on."

"It's more *fun* than enough," she said.

"Say, Ida," interrupted Vandover at length, "I'm
pretty hungry.   Can't we go somewhere and eat something?   I'd like a Welsh rabbit."

"All right," she answered.   "Where do you want to
go?"

"Well," replied Vandover, running over in his mind the
places he might reach by unfrequented streets.   "There's
Marchand's or Tortoni's or the Poodle Dog."

"Suits *me*," she answered, "any one you like.   Say,
Van," she added, "weren't you boys at the Imperial the
other night?   What kind of a place is that?"

On the instant Vandover wondered what she could mean. Was it possible that Ida would go to a place like that with him?

"The Imperial?" he answered. "Oh, I don't know; the Imperial is a sort of a nice place. It has private rooms, like all of these places. The cooking is simply out of sight. I think there is a bar connected with it." Then he went on to talk indifferently about the kindergarten, though his pulse was beating fast, and his nerves were strung taut. By and by Ida said:

"I didn't know there was a bar at the Imperial. I thought it was just some kind of an oyster joint. Why, I heard of a very nice girl, a swell girl, going in there."

"Oh, yes," said Vandover, "they do. I say, Ida," he went on, "what's the matter with going down *there?*"

"The *Imperial?*" exclaimed Ida. "Well, I guess *not!*"

"Why, it's all right, if I'm with you," retorted Vandover, "but if you don't like it we can go anywhere else."

"Well, I guess we *will* go anywhere else," returned Ida, and for the time the subject was dropped.

They took a Sutter Street car and got off at Grant Avenue, having decided to go to Marchand's.

"That's the Imperial down there, isn't it?" asked Ida as they reached the sidewalk. Vandover made a last attempt:

"I say, Ida, come on, let's go there. It's all right if I'm with you. Ah, come along; what's the odds?"

"*No — no — NO*," she answered decisively. "What kind of a girl do you think I am, anyway?"

"Well, I tell you what," answered Vandover, "just come down *by* the place, and if you don't like the looks of it you needn't go in. I want to get some cigarettes, anyhow. You can walk down with me till I do *that*."

"I'll walk down with you," replied Ida, "but I shan't go in."

They drew near to the Imperial. The street about was deserted, even the usual hacks that had their stand there were gone.

"You see," explained Vandover as they passed slowly in front of the doors, "this is all quiet enough. If you pulled down your veil no one would know the difference, and here's the ladies' entrance, you see, right at the side."

"All right, come along, let's go in," exclaimed Ida suddenly, and before he knew it they had swung open the little door of the ladies' entrance with its frosted pane of glass and had stepped inside.

It was between nine and ten o'clock, and the Imperial was quiet as yet; a few men were drinking in the barroom outside, and Toby, the red-eyed waiter, was talking in low tones to a girl under one of the electric lights.

Vandover and Ida went into one of the larger rooms in the rear passage and shut the door. Ida pushed her bolero jacket from her shoulders, saying, "This seems nice and quiet enough."

"Well, of course," answered Vandover, as though dismissing the question for good. "Now, what are we going to have? I say we have champagne and oysters."

"Let's have Cliquot, then," exclaimed Ida, which was the only champagne she had ever heard of besides the California brands.

She was very excited. This was the kind of "gay" time she delighted in, tête-à-tête champagne suppers with

men late at night. She had never been in such a place
as the Imperial before, and the daring and novelty of
what she had done, the whiff of the great city's vice caught
in this manner, sent a little tremor of pleasure and excitement over all her nerves.

They did not hurry over their little supper, but ate and
drank slowly, and had more oysters to go with the last
half of their bottle. Ida's face was ablaze, her eyes flash-
ing, her blond hair disordered and falling about her cheeks.

Vandover put his arm about her neck and drew her
toward him, and as she sank down upon him, smiling and
complaisant, her hair tumbling upon her shoulders and
her head and throat bent back, he leaned his cheek against
hers, speaking in a low voice.

"No — no," she murmured, smiling; "never — ah, if
I hadn't come — no, Van — please ——" And then with
a long breath she abandoned herself.

About midnight he left her at the door of her house on
Golden Gate Avenue. On their way home Ida had grown
more serious than he had ever known her to be. Now she
began to cry softly to herself. "Oh, Van," she said, putting her head down upon his shoulder, "oh, I am so *sorry*.
You don't think any less of me, do you? Oh, Van, you
must be true to me now!"

CHAPTER SIX

EVERYBODY in San Francisco knew of the Ravises and always made it a point to speak of them as one of the best families of the city. They were not new and they were not particularly rich. They had lived in the same house on California Street for nearly twenty years and had always been comfortably well off. As things go in San Francisco, they were old-fashioned. They had family traditions and usages and time-worn customs. Their library had been in process of collection for the past half century and the pictures on the walls were oil paintings of steel engravings and genuine old-fashioned chromos, beyond price to-day.

Their furniture and ornaments were of the preceding generation, solid, conservative. They were not chosen with reference to any one style, nor all bought at the same time. Each separate piece had an individuality of its own. The Ravises kept their old things, long after the fashion had gone out, preferring them to the smarter "art" objects on account of their associations.

There were six in the family, Mr. and Mrs. Ravis, Turner, and her older brother, Stanley, Yale '88, a very serious young gentleman of twenty-seven, continually professing an interest in economics and finance. Besides these were the two children, Howard, nine years old, and his sister, aged fourteen, who had been christened Virginia.

They were a home-loving race. Mr. Ravis, senior,

belonged to the Bohemian Club, but was seldom seen
there.   Stanley was absorbed in his law business, and
Turner went out but little.   They much preferred each
other's society to that of three fourths of their acquaintances, most of their friends being "friends of the family,"
who came to dinner three or four times a year.

It was a custom of theirs to spend the evenings in the
big dining-room at the back of the house, after the table
had been cleared away, Mr. Ravis and Stanley reading
the papers, the one smoking his cigar, the other his pipe;
Mrs. Ravis, with the magazines and Turner with the
Chautauquan.   Howard and Virginia appropriated the
table to themselves where they played with their soldiers
and backgammon board.

The family kept two servants, June the "China boy,"
who had been with them since the beginning of things, and
Delphine the cook, a more recent acquisition.   June was,
in a way, butler and second boy combined; he did all the
downstairs work and the heavy sweeping, but it was
another timeworn custom for Mrs. Ravis and Turner to
spend part of every morning in putting the bedrooms to
rights, dusting and making up the beds.   Besides this,
Turner exercised a sort of supervision over Howard and
Virginia, who were too old for a nurse but too young to
take care of themselves.   She had them to bed at nine,
mended some of their clothes, made them take their baths
regularly, reëstablished peace between them in their hourly
quarrels, and, most arduous task of all, saw that Howard
properly washed himself every morning, and on Wednesday and Saturday afternoons that he was suitably dressed
in time for dancing school.

It was Sunday afternoon. Mrs. Ravis was reading to her husband, who lay on the sofa in the back-parlour smoking a cigar. Stanley had gone out to make a call, while Howard and Virginia had forgathered in the bath-room to sail their boats and cigar boxes in the tub. Toward half-past three, as Turner was in her room writing letters, the door-bell rang. She stopped, with her pen in the air, wondering if it might be Vandover. It was June's afternoon out. In a few minutes the bell rang again, and Turner ran down to answer it herself, inter-cepting Delphine, who took June's place on these occa-sions, but who was hopelessly stupid.

Mrs. Ravis had peered out through the curtains of the parlour window to see who it was, and Turner met her and Mr. Ravis coming upstairs, abandoning the parlour to Turner's caller.

"Mamma and I are going upstairs to read," explained Mr. Ravis. "It's some one of your young men. You can bring him right in the parlour."

"I think it's Mr. Haight," said Turner's mother. "Ask him to stay to tea."

"Well, "said Turner doubtfully, as she paused at the foot of the stairs, "I will, but you know we never have anything to speak of for Sunday evening tea. June is out, and you know how clumsy and stupid Delphine is when she waits on the table."

It *was* young Haight. Turner was very glad to see him, for next to Vandover she liked him better than any of the others. She was never bored by being obliged to entertain him, and he always had something to say and some clever way of saying it.

About half-past five, as they were talking about amateur photography, Mrs. Ravis came in and called them to tea.

Tea with the Ravises was the old-fashioned tea of twenty years ago. One never saw any of the modern "delicacies" on their Sunday evening table, no enticing cold lunch, no spices, not even catsups or pepper sauces. The turkey or chicken they had had for dinner was served cold in slices; there was canned fruit, preserves, tea, crackers, bread and butter, a large dish of cold pork and beans, and a huge glass pitcher of ice-water.

In the absence of June, Victorine the cook went through the agony of waiting on the table, very nervous and embarrassed in her clean calico gown and starched apron. Her hands were red and knotty, smelling of soap, and they touched the chinaware with an over-zealous and constraining tenderness as if the plates and dishes had been delicate glass butterflies. She stood off at a distance from the table making sudden and awkward dabs at it. When it came to passing the plates, she passed them on the wrong side and remembered herself at the wrong moment with a stammering apology. In her excess of politeness she kept up a constant murmur as she attended to their wants. Another fork? Yes, sir. She'd get it right away, sir. Did Mrs. Ravis want another cuppa tea? No? No more tea? Well, she'd pass the bread. Some bread, Master Howard? Nice French bread, he always liked that. Some more preserved pears, Miss Ravis? Yes, miss, she'd get them right away; they were just over here on the sideboard. Yes, here they were. No more? Now she'd go and put them back. And at last when she had set the nerves of all of them in a jangle, was dismissed to the kitchen and retired with a gasp of unspeakable relief.

Somewhat later in the evening young Haight was alone with Turner, and their conversation had taken a very unusual and personal turn. All at once Turner exclaimed:

"I often wonder what good I am in the world to anybody. I don't *know* a thing, I can't *do* a thing. I couldn't cook the plainest kind of a meal to *save* me, and it took me all of two hours yesterday to do just a little buttonhole stitching. I'm not good for anything. I'm not a help to anybody."

Young Haight looked into the blue flame of the gas-log, almost the only modern innovation throughout the entire house, and was silent for a moment; then he leaned his elbows on his knees and, still looking at the flame, replied:

"I don't know about that. You have been a considerable help to *me*."

"To *you!*" exclaimed Turner, surprised. "A help to *you?* Why, how do you mean?'

"Well," he answered, still without looking at her, "one always has one's influence, you know."

"Ah, lots of influence *I* have over anybody," retorted Turner, incredulously.

"Yes, you have," he insisted. "You have plenty of influence over the people that care for you. You have plenty of influence over me."

Turner, very much embarrassed, and not knowing how to answer, bent down to the side of the mantelpiece and turned up the flame of the gas-log a little. Young Haight continued, almost as embarrassed as she:

"I suppose I'm a bad lot, perhaps a little worse than

most others, but I think — I hope — there's some good
in me. I know all this sounds absurd and affected, but
really I'm not posing; you won't mind if I speak just as I
think, for this once. I promise," he went on with a half
smile, "not to do it again. You know my mother died
when I was little and I have lived mostly with men. You
have been to me what the society of women has been to
other fellows. You see, you are the only girl I ever knew
very well — the only one I ever wanted to know. I have
cared for you the way other men have cared for the different women that come into their lives; as they have cared
for their mothers, their sisters — and their wives. You
have already influenced me as a mother or sister should
have done; what if I should ever ask you to be — to be
the *other* to me, the one that's best of all?"

Young Haight turned toward her as he finished and
looked at her for the first time. Turner was still very
much embarrassed.

"Oh, I'm very glad if I've been a help to — to anybody
— to you," she said, confusedly. "But I never knew that
you cared — that you thought about me — in that way.
But you mustn't, you know, you mustn't care for me in
that way. I ought to tell you right away that I never
could care for you more than — I always have done; I
mean care for you only as a very, very good friend. You
don't know, Dolly," she went on eagerly, "how it hurts
me to tell you so, because I care so much for you in every
other way that I wouldn't hurt your feelings for anything;
but then you know at the same time it would hurt you a
great deal more if I *shouldn't* tell you, but encourage you,
and let you go on thinking that perhaps I liked you more

than any one else, when I *didn't*. Now wouldn't that be
wrong? You don't know how glad it makes me feel that
I have been of some good to you, and that is just why I
want to be sincere *now* and not make you think any less
of me — think any worse of me."

"Oh, *I* know," answered young Haight. "I know I
shouldn't have said anything about it. I knew before-
hand, or thought I knew, that you didn't care in that
way."

"Maybe I have been wrong," she replied, "in not seeing
that you cared so much, and have given you a wrong impression. I thought you knew how it was all the time."

"Knew how what was?" he asked, looking up.

"Why," she said, "knew how Van and I were."

"I knew that Van cared for you a great deal."

"Yes, but you know," she went on, hesitating and confused, "you know we are engaged. We have been engaged for nearly two years."

"But *he* don't consider himself as engaged!" The
words were almost out of Haight's mouth, but he shut
his teeth against them and kept silence — he hardly knew
why.

"Suppose Vandover were out of the question," he said,
getting up and smiling in order not to seem as serious as
he really was.

"Ah," she said, smiling back at him. "I don't know;
that's a hard question to answer. I've never *asked* myself
that question."

"Well, I'm saving you the trouble, you see," he answered, still smiling. "I am asking it *for* you."

"But I don't want to answer such a question off-hand

like that; how can I tell?   It would only be *perhaps*, just now."

Young Haight answered quickly that "just now" he would be contented with that "perhaps"; but Turner did not hear this.   She had spoken at the same time as he, exclaiming, "But what is the good of talking of that? Because no matter what happened I feel as though I could not break my promise to Van, even if I should want to. Because I have talked like this, Dolly," she went on more seriously, "you must not be deceived or get a wrong impression.   You understand how things are, don't you?"

"Oh, yes," he answered, still trying to carry it off with a laugh.   "I know, I know.   But now I hope you won't let anything I have said bother you, and that things will go on just as if I hadn't spoken, just as if nothing had happened."

"Why, of course," she said, laughing with him again. "Of *course*, why shouldn't they?"

They were both at their ease again by the time young Haight stood at the door with his hat in his hand ready to go.

He raised his free hand over her head, and said, with burlesque, dramatic effect, trying to keep down a smile:

"Bless you both; go, go marry Vandover and be happy; I forgive you."

"Ah — don't be so *utterly* absurd," she cried, beginning to laugh.

CHAPTER SEVEN

On a certain evening about four months later Ellis and
Vandover had a "date" with Ida Wade and Bessie Laguna
at the Mechanics' Fair. Ellis, Bessie, and Ida were to
meet Vandover there in the Art Gallery, as he had to
make a call with his father, and could not get there until
half-past nine. They were all to walk about the Fair until
ten, after which the two men proposed to take the girls
out to the Cliff House in separate coupés. The whole
thing had been arranged by Ellis and Bessie, and Vandover
was irritated. Ellis ought to have had more sense; rushing the girls was all very well, but everybody went to the
Mechanics' Fair, and he didn't like to have nice girls like
Turner or Henrietta Vance see him with chippies like that.
It was all very well for Ellis, who had no social position,
but for *him*, Vandover, it would look too confounded
queer. Of course he was in for it now, and would have to
face the music. You can't tell a girl like that that you're
ashamed to be seen with her, but very likely he would get
himself into a regular box with it all.

When he arrived at the Mechanics' Pavilion, it was
about twenty minutes of ten, and as he pushed through
the wicket he let himself into a huge amphitheatre full of
colour and movement.

There was a vast shuffling of thousands of feet and a
subdued roar of conversation like the noise of a great

mill; mingled with these were the purring of distant
machinery, the splashing of a temporary fountain and
the rhythmic clamour of a brass band, while in the piano
exhibit the hired performer was playing a concert-grand
with a great flourish.   Nearer at hand one could catch
ends of conversation and notes of laughter, the creaking
of boots, and the rustle of moving dresses and stiff
skirts.   Here and there groups of school children el-
bowed their way through the crowd, crying shrilly, their
hands full of advertisement pamphlets, fans, picture
cards, and toy whips with pewter whistles on the butts,
while the air itself was full of the smell of fresh popcorn.

Ellis and Bessie were in the Art Gallery upstairs.   Mrs.
Wade, Ida's mother, who gave lessons in hand painting,
had an exhibit there which they were interested to find;
a bunch of yellow poppies painted on velvet and framed
in gilt.   They stood before it some little time hazarding
their opinions and then moved on from one picture to
another; Ellis bought a catalogue and made it a duty to
find the title of every picture.   Bessie professed to be
very fond of painting; she had 'taken it up' at one time
and had abandoned it, only because the oil or turpentine
or something was unhealthy for her.   "Of course," she
said, "I'm no critic, I only know what I like.   Now that
one over there, I like *that*.   I think those ideal heads like
that are lovely, don't you, Bandy?   Oh, there's Van!"

"Hello!" said Vandover, coming up.   "Where's Ida?"

"Hello, Van!" answered Bessie.   "Ida wouldn't come.
Isn't it too mean?   She said she couldn't come because
she had a cold, but she was just talking through her face,
I know.   She's just got kind of a streak on and you can't

get anything out of her. You two haven't had a row, have you? Well, I didn't *think* you had. But she's worried about something or other. I don't believe she's been out of the house this week. But isn't it mean of her to throw cold water on the procession like this? She's been giving me a lecture, too, and says she's going to reform."

"Well," said Vandover, greatly relieved, "that's too bad. We could have had a lot of fun to-night. I'm awfully sorry. Well, what are you two going to do?"

"Oh, I guess we'll follow out our part of the programme," said Ellis. "You are kind of left out, though."

"I don't know," answered Vandover. "Maybe I'll go downtown, and see if I can find some of the boys."

"Oh, Dolly Haight is around here somewheres," said Ellis. "We saw him just now over by the chess machine."

"I guess I'll try and find him, then," responded Vandover. "Well, I hope you two enjoy yourselves." As he was turning away Bessie Laguna came running back, and taking him a little to one side said:

"You'd better go round and see Ida pretty soon if you can. She's all broke up about something, I'm sure. I think she'd like to see you pretty well. Honestly," she said, suddenly very grave, "I never saw Ida so cut up in my life. She's been taking on over something in a dreadful way, and I think she'd like to see you. She won't tell *me* anything. You go around and see her."

"All right," answered Vandover smiling, "I'll go."

As he was going down the stairs on his way to find young Haight it occurred to him what Ida's trouble might be. He was all at once struck with a great fear, so that for an instant he turned cold and weak, and reached out his hand to steady himself against the railing of the stairs.   Ah, what a calamity that would be! What a calamity! What a dreadful responsibility! What a crime! He could not keep the thought out of his mind. He tried to tell himself that Ida had practically given her consent by going into such a place; that he was not the only one, after all; that there was nothing certain as yet. He stood on the stairway, empty for that moment, biting the end of his thumb, saying to himself in a low voice:

"What a calamity, what a horrible calamity that would be! Ah, you scoundrel! You damned fool, not to have thought!" A couple of girls, the counter girls at one of the candy booths, came down the stairs behind him with a great babble of talk. Vandover gave an irritated shrug of his shoulders as if freeing himself from the disagreeable subject and went on.

He could not find young Haight down stairs and so went up into the gallery again. After a long time he came upon him sitting on an empty bench nursing his cane and watching the crowd go past.

"Hello, old man!" he exclaimed. "Ellis told me I would find you around somewhere. I was just going to give you up." He sat down beside his chum, and the two began to talk about the people as they passed. "Ah, get on to the red hat!" exclaimed Vandover on a sudden. "That's the third time she's passed."

"Has Ellis gone off with Bessie Laguna?" asked young Haight.

"Yes," answered Vandover. "They're going to have a time at the Cliff House.'

"That's too bad," young Haight replied. "Ellis has

just thrown himself away with that girl. He might have
known some very nice people when he first came here.
Between that girl and his whisky he has managed to spoil
every chance he might have had."

"There's Charlie Geary," Vandover exclaimed suddenly,
whistling and beckoning. "Hey, there, Charlie! where you
going? Oh," he cried on a sudden as Geary came up,
"oh, get on to his new store clothes, will you?" They
both pretended to be overwhelmed by the elegance of
Geary's new suit.

"O-oh!" cried young Haight. "The bloody, bloomin',
bloated swell. Just let me *touch* them!"

Vandover shaded his eyes and turned away as though
dazzled. "This is *too* much," he gasped. "Such mag-
nificence, such purple and fine linen." Then suddenly he
shouted, "Oh, *oh! look* at the crease in those trousers.
No; it's too much, I can't stand it."

"Oh, shut up," said Geary, irritated, as they had intended he should be. "Yes," he went on, "I thought I'd
blow myself. I've been working like a dog the whole
month. I'm trying to get in Beale's office. Beale and
Storey, you know. I got the promise of a berth last week,
so I thought I'd blow myself for some rags. I've been
over to San Rafael all day visiting my cousins; had a great
time; went out to row. Oh, and had a great feed: lettuce
sandwiches with mayonnaise. Simply out of sight. I
came back on the four o'clock boat and held down the
'line' on Kearney Street for an hour or two."

"Yes?" young Haight said perfunctorily, adding after
a moment, "Isn't this a gay crowd, a typical San Francisco crowd and ——"

"I had a cocktail in the Imperial at about quarter of five," said Geary, "and got a cigar at the Elite; then I went around to get my clothes. Oh, you ought to have heard the blowing up I gave my tailor! I let him have it right straight."

Geary paused a moment, and Vandover said: "Come on, let's walk around a little; don't you want to? We might run on to the red hat again."

"I told him," continued Geary without moving, "that if he wanted to do any more work for me, he'd have to get in front of himself in a hurry, and that *I* wasn't full of bubbles, if *he* was. 'Why,' says he, 'why, Mr. Geary, I've never had a customer talk like this to me before since I've been in the business!' 'Well, Mr. Allen,' says I, 'it's time you *had!*' Oh, sure, I gave it to him straight."

"Vandover has gone daft over a girl in a red hat," said young Haight, as they got up and began to walk. "Have you noticed her up here?"

"I went to the Grillroom after I left the tailor's," continued Geary, "and had supper downtown. Ah, you ought to have seen the steak they gave me! Just about as thick as it was wide. I gave the slavey a four-bit tip. Oh, it's just as well, you know, to keep in with them, if you go there often. I lunch there four or five times a week."

They descended to the ground floor and promenaded the central aisle watching for pretty girls. In front of a candy-counter, where there was a soda fountain, they saw the red hat again. Vandover looked her squarely in the face and laughed a little. When he had passed he looked back; the girl caught his eye and turned away with a droll smile. Vandover paused, grinning, and raising his hat; "I guess that's mine," he said.

"You are not going, are you?" exclaimed young Haight, as Vandover stopped. "Oh, for goodness' sake, Van, do leave the girls alone for one hour in the day. Come on! Come on downtown with us."

"No, no," answered Vandover. "I'm going to chase it up. Good-bye. I may see you fellows later," and he turned back and went up to the girl.

"Look at that!" said young Haight, exasperated. "He knows he's liable to meet his acquaintances here, and yet there he goes, almost arm in arm with a girl like that. It's too bad; why *can't* a fellow keep straight when there are such a lot of *nice* girls?"

Geary never liked to see anything done better than he could do it himself. Just now he was vexed because Vandover had got in ahead of him. He looked after the girl a moment and muttered scornfully:

"Cheap meat!" adding, "Ah, you bet *I* wouldn't do that. I flatter myself that I'm a little too clever to cut my own throat in that fashion. I look out after my interests better than that. Well, Dolly," he concluded, "*I've* got a thirst on. Van and Ellis have gone off with their girls; let's you and I go somewhere and have something wet."

"All right. What's the matter with the Luxembourg?" answered young Haight.

"Luxembourg goes, then," assented Geary, and they turned about and started for the door. As they were passing out some one came running up behind them and took an arm of each: it was Vandover.

"Hello," cried Geary, delighted, "your girl shook you, didn't she?"

"Not a bit of it," answered Vandover. "Oh, but say, she is out of sight! Says her name is Grace Irving. No, she didn't shake me. I made a date with her for next Wednesday night. I didn't want to be seen around here with her, you know."

"Of *course* she will keep that date!" said Geary.

"Well, now, I think she will," protested Vandover.

"Well, come along," interrupted young Haight. "We'll all go down to the Luxembourg and have something cold and wet."

"Ah, make it the Imperial instead," objected Vandover. "We may find Flossie."

"Say," cried Geary, "can't you *live* without trailing around after some kind of petticoats?"

"You're right," admitted Vandover, "I can't," but he persuaded them to go to the Imperial for all that.

At the Imperial, Toby, the red-eyed waiter, came to take their order.

"Good evening, gentlemen," he said. "Haven't seen you around here for some time."

"No, no," said Geary. "I've been too busy. I've been working like a dog lately to get into a certain office. You bet I'll make it all right — all right. Bring me a stringy rabbit and a pint of dog's-head."

"You bet I've been working," he continued after they had settled down to their beer and rabbits, "working like a dog. A man's got to rustle if he's going to make a success at law. *I'm* going to make it go, by George, or I'll know the reason why. I'll make my way in this town and my pile. There's money to be made here and *I* might just as well make it as the next man. Every man for himself, that's what *I* say; that's the way to get along. It may be selfish, but you've got to do it. By God! it's human nature. Isn't that right, hey? Isn't that right?"

"Oh, that's right," admitted young Haight, trying to be polite. After this the conversation lagged a little. Young Haight drank his Apollinaris lemonade through a straw, Geary sipped his ale, and Vandover fed himself Welsh rabbit and Spanish olives with the silent enjoyment of a glutton. By and by, when they had finished and had lighted their cigars and cigarettes, they began to talk about the last Cotillon, to which Vandover and Haight belonged.

"Say, Van," said young Haight, tilting his head to one side and shutting one eye to avoid the smoke from his cigar, "say, didn't I see you dancing with Mrs. Doane after supper?"

"Yes," said Vandover laughing; "all the men were trying to get a dance with her. She had an edge on."

"No?" exclaimed Geary, incredulously.

"That's a fact," admitted young Haight. "Van is right."

"She was opposite to me at table," said Vandover, "and *I* saw her empty a whole bottle of champagne."

"Why, I didn't know they got drunk like that at the Cotillons," said Geary. "I thought they were very swell."

"Well, of course, they don't as a rule," returned Vandover. "Of course there are girls like — like Henrietta Vance who belong to the Cotillon and make it what it is,

and what it ought to be. But there are other girls like
Mrs. Doane and Lilly Stannard and the Trafford girls
that like their champagne pretty well now, and don't
you forget it! Oh, you know, I wouldn't call it getting
drunk, though."

"Well, why not?" exclaimed young Haight impatiently.
"Why not call it 'getting drunk?' Why not call things
by their right name? You can see just how bad they
are then; and I think it's shameful that such things can
go on in an organization that is supposed to contain the
very best people in the city. Now, I just want to tell
you what I saw at one of these same Cotillons in the first
part of the season. Lilly Stannard disappeared after
supper and people said she was sick and was going home,
but I knew exactly what was the matter, because I had
seen her at the supper table. Well, I had gone outside
on the steps to get a mouthful of smoke, and my little
cousin, Hetty, who has just come out and who is only
nineteen, was out there with me because it was so warm
inside, and *she* had seen Lilly Stannard filling up with
champagne at supper, and didn't know what to make of
it. Well, we were just talking about it, and I was trying
to make her believe too that Lilly Stannard was sick,
when here comes Lilly herself out to her carriage. Her
maid was supporting her, just about half-carrying her.
Lilly's face was so pale that the powder on it looked like
ashes, her hair was all coming down, and she was hiccoughing. Now," continued young Haight, his eyes
snapping, and his voice raised so as to make itself heard
above the exclamations of his two friends, "now, that's
a *fact;* I give you my word of honour that it actually

happened. It's not hearsay; I saw it myself. It's fine, isn't it?" he went on, wrathfully. "It sounds well, don't it, when it's told *just as it happened?* The girl was dead drunk. Oh, she may have made a mistake; it may have been the first time; but the fact remains that she always drinks a lot of champagne at the Cotillons, and other girls have been drunk there, too. Mrs. Doane, that Van tells about, was *drunk;* that's the word for it. She was dead drunk that night, and there was my little cousin, Hetty, who had never seen even a man the worse for his liquor, standing there and taking it all in. Of course, every one hushed the thing up or else said the poor girl was sick; but Hetty knew, and what effect do you suppose it had upon a little girl like that, who had always been told what nice, irreproachable people went to the Cotillons? Hetty will never be the same little girl now that she was before. Oh, it makes me damned tired."

"Well, I don't see," said Geary, "why the girls should make such a fuss about the men keeping straight. I daresay now that this Stannard girl would cut us all dead if she knew how drunk we were that night about four months ago — that night that you fellows got thrown out of the Luxembourg."

"No, I don't believe she would at all," said young Haight.

"She'd think better of you for it," put in Vandover. "Look here," he went on, "all this talk of women demanding the same moral standard for men as men do for women is fine on paper, but how does it work in real life? The women don't demand it at all. Take the average society girl in a big city like this. The girls that we meet at teas and receptions and functions — don't you suppose they know the life we men lead? Of course they do. They may not know it in detail, but they know in a general way that we get drunk a good deal and go to disreputable houses and that sort of thing, and do they ever cut us for that? No, sir; not much. Why, I tell you, they even have a little more respect for us. They like a man to know things, to be experienced. A man that keeps himself straight and clean and never goes around with fast women, they think is ridiculous. Of course, a girl don't want to know the particulars of a man's vice; what they want is that a man should have the knowledge of good and evil, yes, and lots of evil. To a large extent I really believe it's the women's fault that the men are what they are. If they demanded a higher moral standard the men would come up to it; they encourage a man to go to the devil and then — and then when he's rotten with disease and ruins his wife and has children — what is it — '*spotted toads*' — *then* there's a great cry raised against the men, and women write books and all, when half the time the woman has only encouraged him to be what he is."

"Oh, well now," retorted young Haight, "you know that all the girls are not like that."

"Most of them that you meet in society are."

"But they are the best people, aren't they?" demanded Geary.

"No," answered Vandover and young Haight in a breath, and young Haight continued:

"No; I believe that very few of what you would call the 'best people' go out in society — people like the Ravises, who have good principles, and keep up old-fashioned virtues and all that. You know," he added, "they have family prayers down there every morning after breakfast."

Geary began to smile.

"Well, now, I don't care," retorted young Haight, "I like that sort of thing."

"So do I," said Vandover. "Up home, now, the governor asks a blessing at each meal, and somehow I wouldn't like to see him leave it off. But you can't tell me," he went on, going back to the original subject of their discussion, "you can't tell me that American society girls, city-bred, and living at the end of the nineteenth century, don't know about things. Why, man alive, how can they help but know? Look at those that have brothers — don't you suppose they know, and if they know, why don't they use their influence to stop it? I tell you if any one were to write up the lives that we young men of the city lead after dark, people wouldn't believe it. At that party that Henrietta Vance gave last month there were about twenty fellows there and I knew every one, and I was looking around the supper-table and wondering how many of those young fellows had never been inside of a disreputable house, and there was only *one* beside Dolly Haight!"

Young Haight exclaimed at this, laughing good-naturedly, twirling his thumbs, and casting down his eyes with mock-modesty.

"Well, that's the truth just the same," Vandover went on. "We young men of the cities are a fine lot. I'm not doing the baby act. I'm not laying the blame on the girls altogether, but I say that in a measure the girls are responsible. They want a man to be a *man*, to be up to date, to be a man of the world and to go in for that sort of vice, but they don't know, they don't dream, how rotten and disgusting it is.   Oh, I'm not preaching.   I know I'm just as bad as the rest, and I'm going to have a good time while I can, but sometimes when you stop and think, and as Dolly says 'call things by their right names,' why you feel, don't you know — *queer*."

"I don't believe, Van," responded young Haight, "that it's *quite* as bad as you say.   But it's even wrong, I think, that a good girl should know anything about vice at all."

"Oh, that's nonsense," broke in Geary; "you can't expect nowadays that a girl, an American girl, can live twenty years in a city and not know things.   Do you think the average modern girl is going to be the absolutely pure and innocent girl of, say, fifty years ago?   Not much; they are right on to things to-day.   You can't tell them much.   And it's all right, too; they know how to look out for themselves, then.   It's part of their education; and I think if they haven't the knowledge of evil, and don't know what sort of life the average young man leads, that their mothers ought to tell them."

"Well, I don't agree with you," retorted young Haight. "There's something revolting in the idea that it's necessary a young girl should be instructed in that sort of nastiness."

"Why, not at all," answered Geary.   "Without it she might be ruined by the first man that came along.   It's a protection to her virtue."

"Oh, pshaw!   I don't believe it at all," cried young Haight, impatiently.   "I believe that a girl is born with a natural intuitive purity that will lead her to protect her virtue just as instinctively as she would dodge a blow; if she wants to go wrong she will have to make an effort herself to overcome that instinct."

"And if she don't," cried Vandover eagerly, "if she don't — if she don't protect her virtue, I say a man has a right to go as far with her as he can."

"If *he* don't, some one else will," said Geary.

"Ah, you can't get around it that way," answered young Haight, smiling. "It's a man's duty to protect a girl, even if he has to protect her against herself."

When he got home that night Vandover thought over this remark of young Haight's and in its light reviewed what had occurred in the room at the Imperial. He felt aroused, nervous, miserably anxious. At length he tried to dismiss the subject from his mind; he woke up his drowsing grate fire, punching it with the poker, talking to it, saying, "Wake up there, you!" When he was undressed, he sat down before it in his bathrobe, absorbing its heat luxuriously, musing into the coals, scratching himself as was his custom. But for all that he fretted nervously and did not sleep well that night.

Next morning he took his bath. Vandover enjoyed his bath and usually spent two or three hours over it. When the water was very warm he got into it with his novel on a rack in front of him and a box of chocolates conveniently near. Here he stayed, for over an hour, eating and reading, and occasionally smoking a cigarette, until at length the enervating heat of the steam gradually overcame him and he dropped off to sleep.

On this particular morning between nine and ten Geary called, and as was his custom came right up to Vandover's room. Mr. Corkle, lying on the wolfskin in the bay window, jumped up with a gruff bark, but, recognizing him, came up wiggling his short tail. Geary saw Vandover's clothes thrown about the floor and the closed door of the bathroom.

"Hey, Van!" he called. "It's Charlie Geary. Are you taking a bath?"

"Hello! What? Who is it?" came from behind the door. "Oh, is that you, Charlie? Hello! how are you? Yes, I'm taking a bath. I must have been asleep. Wait a minute; I'll be out."

"No, I can't stop," answered Geary. "I've an appointment downtown; overslept myself, and had to go without my breakfast; makes me feel all broke up. I'll get something at the Grillroom about eleven; a steak, I guess. But that isn't what I came to say. Ida Wade has killed herself! Isn't it fearful? I thought I'd drop in on my way downtown and speak to you about it. It's dreadful! It's all in the morning papers. She must have been out of her head."

"What is it — what has she done?" came back Vandover's voice. "Papers — I haven't seen — what has she done? Tell me — what has she done?"

"Why, she committed suicide last night by taking laudanum," answered Geary, "and nobody knows why. She didn't leave any message or letter or anything of the kind. It's a fearful thing to happen so suddenly, but it seems she has been very despondent and broke up about something or other for a week or two. They found her in her room last night about ten o'clock lying across her table with only her wrapper on. She was unconscious then, and between one and two she died. She was un-

conscious all the time. Well, I can't stop any longer,
Van; I've an appointment downtown. I was just going
past the house and I thought I would run up and speak
to you about Ida. I'll see you again pretty soon and
we'll talk this over."

Mr. Corkle politely attended Geary to the head of the
stairs, then went back to Vandover's room, and after
blowing under the crack of the bathroom door to see if his
master was still there returned to the wolfskin and sat
down on his short tail and yawned. He was impatient
to see Vandover and thought he stayed in his bath an
unnecessarily long time. He went up to the door again
and listened. It was very still inside; he could not hear
the slightest sound, and he wondered again what could
keep Vandover in there so long. He had too much self-
respect to whine, so he went back to the wolfskin and
curled up in the sun, but did not go to sleep.

By and by, after a very long time, the bathroom door
swung open, and Vandover came out. He had not dried
himself and was naked and wet. He went directly to the
table in the centre of the room and picked up the morning
paper, looking for the article of which Geary had spoken.
At first he could not find it, and then it suddenly jumped
into prominence from out the gray blur of the print on an
inside page beside an advertisement of a charity concert for
the benefit of a home for incurable children. There was a
picture of Ida taken from a photograph like one that she
had given him, and which even then was thrust between
the frame and glass of his mirror. He read the article
through; it sketched her life and character and the circumstances of her death with the relentless terseness of

the writer cramped for space. According to this view,
the causes of her death were unknown. It had been remarked that she had of late been despondent and in ill
health.

Vandover threw the paper down and straightened up,
naked and dripping, putting both hands to his head. In
a low voice under his breath he said:

"What have I done?   What have I done now?"

Like the sudden unrolling of a great scroll he saw his
responsibility for her death and for the ruin of that something in her which was more than life. What would become of her now? And what would become of him?   For
a single brief instant he tried to persuade himself that Ida
had consented after all. But he knew that this was not
so. She had consented, but he had forced her consent;
he was none the less guilty. And then in that dreadful
moment when he saw things in their true light, all the
screens of conventionality and sophistry torn away, the
words that young Haight had spoken came back to him.
No matter if she had consented, it was his duty to have
protected her, even against herself.

He walked the floor with great strides, steaming with
the warm water, striking his head with his hands and
crying out, "Oh, this is fearful, fearful! What have I
done now?   I have killed her; yes, and worse!"

He could think of nothing worse that could have happened to him.   What a weight of responsibility to carry —
he who hated responsibility of any kind, who had always
tried to escape from anything that was even irksome, who
loved his ease, his comfort, his peace of mind!

At every moment now he saw the different consequences

of what he had done. Now, it was that his life was ruined, and that all through its course this crime would hang like a millstone about his neck. There could be no more enjoyment of anything for him; all the little pleasures and little self-indulgences which till now had delighted him were spoiled and rendered impossible. The rest of his life would have to be one long penitence; any pleasure he might take would only make his crime seem more abominable.

Now, it was a furious revolt against his mistake that had led him to such a fearful misunderstanding of Ida; a silent impotent rage against himself and against the brute in him that he had permitted to drag him to this thing.

Now, it was a wave of an immense pity for the dead girl that overcame him, and he saw himself as another person, destroying what she most cherished for the sake of gratifying an unclean passion.

Now, it was a terror for himself. What would they do to him? His part in the affair was sure to be found out. He tried to think what the punishment for such crime would be; but would he not be considered a murderer as well? Could he not hang for this? His imagination was never more active; his fear never more keen. At once a thousand plans of concealment or escape were tossed up in his mind.

But worse than all was the thought of that punishment from which there was absolutely no escape, and of that strange other place where his crime would assume right proportions and receive right judgment, no matter how it was palliated or evaded here. Then for an instant it was as if a gulf without bottom had opened under him, and he had to fight himself back from its edge for sheer self-preservation. To look too long in that direction was simple insanity beyond any doubt.

And all this time he threw himself to and fro in his room, his long white arms agitated and shaking, his wet and shining hair streaming far over his face, and the sparse long fell upon his legs and ankles, all straight and trickling with moisture. At times an immense unreasoning terror would come upon him all of a sudden, horrible, crushing, so that he rolled upon the bed groaning and sobbing, digging his nails into his scalp, shutting his teeth against a desire to scream out, writhing in the throes of terrible mental agony.

That day and the next were fearful. To Vandover everything in his world was changed. All that had happened before the morning of Geary's visit appeared to him to have occurred in another phase of his life, years and years ago. He lay awake all night long, listening to the creaking of the house and the drip of the water faucets. He turned from his food with repugnance, told his father that he was sick, and kept indoors as much as he could, reading all the papers to see if he had been found out. To his great surprise and relief, a theory gained ground that Ida was subject to spells of ill-health, to long fits of despondency, and that her suicide had occurred during one of these. If Ida's family knew anything of the truth, it was apparent that they were doing their best to cover up their disgrace. Vandover was too thoroughly terrified for his own safety to feel humiliated at this possible explanation of his security. There was as yet not even a guess that implicated him.

He thought that he was bearing up under the strain well enough, but on the evening of the second day, as he was pretending to eat his supper, his father sent the servant out and turning to him, said kindly:

"What is it, Van? Aren't you well nowadays?"

"Not very, sir," answered Vandover. "My throat is troubling me again."

"You look deathly pale," returned his father. "Your eyes are sunken and you don't eat."

"Yes, I know," said Vandover. "I'm not feeling well at all. I think I'll go to bed early to-night. I don't know" — he continued, after a pause, feeling a desire to escape from his father's observation — "I don't know but what I'll go up now. Will you tell the cook to feed Mr. Corkle for me?"

His father looked at him as he pushed back from the table.

"What's the matter, Van?" he said. "Is there anything wrong?"

"Oh, I'll be all right in the morning," he replied nervously. "I feel a little under the weather just now."

"Don't you think you had better tell me what the trouble is?" said his father, kindly.

"There *isn't* any trouble, sir," insisted **Vandover**. "I just feel a little under the weather."

But as he was starting to undress in his room a sudden impulse took possession of him, an overwhelming childish desire to tell his father all about it. It was beginning to be more than he was able to bear alone. He did not allow himself to stop and reason with this impulse, but slipped on his vest again and went downstairs. He found his father in the smoking-room, sitting unoccupied in the huge leather chair before the fireplace.

As Vandover came in the Old Gentleman rose and without a word, as if he had been expecting him, went to the door and shut and locked it. He came back and stood before the fireplace watching Vandover as he approached and took the chair he had just vacated. Vandover told him of the affair in two or three phrases, without choosing his words, repeating the same expressions over and over again, moved only with the desire to have it over and done with.

It was like a burst of thunder. The worst his father had feared was not as bad as this. He had expected some rather serious boyish trouble, but this was the crime of a man. Still watching his son, he put out his hand, groping for the edge of the mantelpiece, and took hold of it with a firm grasp. For a moment he said nothing; then:

"And — and you say you seduced her."

Without looking up, Vandover answered, "Yes, sir," and then he added, "It is horrible; when I think of it I sometimes feel as though I should go off my head. I ——"

But the Old Gentleman interrupted him, putting out his hand:

"Don't," he said quickly, "don't say anything now — please."

They were both silent for a long time, Vandover gazing stupidly at a little blue and red vase on the table, wondering how his father would take the news, what next he would say; the Old Gentleman drawing his breath short, occasionally clearing his throat, his eyes wandering vaguely about the walls of the room, his fingers dancing upon the

edge of the mantelpiece. Then at last he put his hand
to his neck as though loosening his collar and said, looking
away from Vandover:

"Won't you — won't you please go out — go away for a
little while — leave me alone for a little while."

When Vandover closed the door, he shut the edge of a
rug between it and the sill; as he reopened it to push the
rug out of the way he saw his father sink into the chair and,
resting his arm upon the table, bow his head upon it.

He did not see his father again that night, and at breakfast next morning not a word was exchanged between
them, but his father did not go downtown to his office
that forenoon, as was his custom. Vandover went up
to his room immediately after breakfast and sat down
before the window that overlooked the little garden in the
rear of the house.

He was utterly miserable, his nerves were gone, and at
times he would feel again a touch of that hysterical, unreasoning terror that had come upon him so suddenly the
other morning.

Now there was a new trouble: the blow he had given
his father. He could see that the Old Gentleman was
crushed under it, and that he had never imagined that his
son could have been so base as this. Vandover wondered
what he was going to do. It would seem as if he had
destroyed all of his father's affection for him, and he trembled lest the Old Gentleman should cast him off, everything. Even if his father did not disown him, he did not
see how they could ever be the same. They might go on
living together in the same house, but as far apart from
each other as strangers. This, however, did not seem

natural; it was much more likely that his father would send him away, anywhere out of his sight, forwarding, perhaps through his lawyer or agents, enough money to keep him alive. The more Vandover thought of this, the more he became convinced that such would be his father's decision. The Old Gentleman had spent the night over it, time enough to make up his mind, and the fact that he had neither spoken to him nor looked at him that morning was only an indication of what Vandover was to expect. He fancied he knew his father well enough to foresee how this decision would be carried out, not with any imprecations or bursts of rage, but calmly, sadly, inevitably.

Toward noon his father came into the room, and Vandover turned to face him and to hear what he had to say as best he could. He knew he should not break down under it, for he felt as though his misery had reached its limit, and that nothing could touch or affect him much now.

His father had a decanter of port in one hand and a glass in the other; he filled the glass and held it toward Vandover, saying gently:

"I think you had better take some of this: you've hardly eaten anything in three days. Do you feel pretty bad, Van?"

Vandover put the glass down and got upon his feet. All at once a great sob shook him.

"Oh, governor!" he cried.

It was as if it had been a mother or a dear sister. The prodigal son put his arms about his father's neck for the first time since he had been a little boy, and clung to him and wept as though his heart were breaking.

CHAPTER EIGHT

"We will begin all over again, Van," his father said later that same day. "We will start in again and try to forget all this, not as much as we *can*, but as much as we *ought*, and live it down, and from now on we'll try to do the thing that is right and brave and good."

"Just try me, sir!" cried Vandover.

That was it, begin all over again. He had never seen more clearly than now that other life which it was possible for him to live, a life that was above the level of self-indulgence and animal pleasures, a life that was not made up of the society of lost women or fast girls, but yet a life of keen enjoyment.

Whenever he had been deeply moved about anything, the power and desire of art had grown big within him, and he turned to it now, instinctively and ardently.

It was all the better half of him that was aroused — the better half that he had kept in check ever since his college days, the better half that could respond to the influences of his father and of Turner Ravis, that other Vandover whom he felt was his real self, Vandover the true man, Vandover the artist, not Vandover the easy-going, the self-indulgent, not Vandover the lover of women.

From this time forward he was resolved to give up the world that he had hitherto known, and devote himself with all his strength to his art. In the first glow of that

112

resolution he thought that he had never been happier; he wondered how he could have been blind so long; what was all that life worth compared with the life of a great artist, compared even with a life of sturdy, virile effort and patient labour even though barren of achievement?

And then something very curious happened: The little picture of Turner Ravis that hung over his mantelpiece caught his glance, looking out at him with her honest eyes and sweet smile. In an instant he seemed to love her as he had never imagined he could love any one. All that was best in him went out toward her in a wave of immense tenderness; the tears came to his eyes, he could not tell why. Ah, he was not good enough for her now, but he would love her so well that he would grow better, and between her and his good father and his art, the better Vandover, the real Vandover, would grow so large and strong within him that there should be no room for the other Vandover, the Vandover of Flossie and of the Imperial, the Vandover of the brute.

During the course of talk that day between himself and his father, it was decided that Vandover should go away for a little while. He was in a fair way to be sick from worry and nervous exhaustion, and a sea trip to San Diego and back seemed to be what he stood most in need of. Besides this, his father told him, it was inevitable that his share in Ida's death would soon be known; in any case it would be better for him to be away from the city.

"You take whatever steamer sails next," said his father, "and go down to Coronado and stay there as long as you like, three weeks anyway; stay there until you get well, and when you get back, Van, we'll have a talk about Paris again. Perhaps you would like to get away this winter, maybe as soon as next month. You think it over while you are away, and when you want to go, why, we'll go over together, Van. What do you think? Would you like to have your old governor along for a little while?"

The *Santa Rosa* cast off the company's docks the next day about noon in the midst of a thick, cold mist that was half rain. The Old Gentleman came to see Vandover off.

The steamer, which seemed gigantic, was roped and cabled to the piers, feeling the water occasionally with her screw to keep the hawsers taut. About the forward gangway a band of overworked stevedores were stowing in the last of the cargo, aided by a donkey engine, which every now and then broke out into a spasm of sputtering coughs. At the passenger gangway a great crowd was gathered, laughing and exchanging remarks with the other crowd that leaned over the railings of the decks.

There was a smell of pitch and bilge in the air mingled with the reek of hot oil from the engines. About twelve o'clock an odour of cooking arose, and the steward went about the decks drumming upon a snoring gong for dinner.

Half an hour later the great whistle roared interminably, drowning out the chorus of "good-byes" that rose on all sides. Long before it had ceased, the huge bulk had stirred, almost imperceptibly at first, then, gathering headway, swung out into the stream and headed for the Golden Gate.

Vandover was in the stern upon the hurricane deck, shaking his hat toward his father, who had tied his hand-

kerchief to his cane and was waving it at him as he stood
upon an empty packing-case.   As the throng of those who
were left behind dwindled away, one by one, Vandover
could see him standing there, almost the last of all, and
long after the figure itself was lost in the blur of the background he still saw the tiny white dot of the handkerchief
moving back and forth, as if spelling out a signal to him
across the water.

The fog drew a little higher as they passed down the
bay.   To the left was the city swarming upon its hills, a
dull gray mass, cut in parallel furrows by the streets;
straggling and uneven where it approached the sand-
dunes in the direction of the Presidio.   To the right the
long slope of Tamalpais climbed up and was lost in the
fog, while directly in front of them was the Golden Gate,
a bleak prospect of fog-drenched headlands on either
side of a narrow strip of yellow, frothy water.   Beyond
that, the open Pacific.

A brisk cannonade was going on from the Presidio and
from Black Point, and both forts were hidden behind a great
curtain of tumbling white smoke that rolled up to mingle
with the fog.   Everybody was on that side of the deck
watching and making guesses as to the reason of it.   It
was perhaps target practice.   Ah, it was a good thing that
the steamer was not in line with the target.   Perhaps,
though, that was the safest place to be.   Some one told
about a derelict that was anchored as a target off the heads,
and shot at for fifteen hours without being touched once.
Oh, they were great gunners at the Presidio!   But just
the same the sound of cannon was a fine thing to hear; it
excited one.   A noisy party of gentlemen already in-

stalled in the smoking-room came out on deck for a moment with their cards in their hands, and declared laughingly that the whole thing was only a salute in the *Santa Rosa's* honour.

By the middle of the afternoon, Vandover began to see that for him the trip was going to be tedious. He knew no one on board and had come away so hurriedly that he had neglected to get himself any interesting books. He spent an hour or two promenading the upper deck until the cold wind that was blowing drove him to the smoking-room, where he tried to interest himself in watching some of the whist games that were in progress.

It surprised him that he could find occasion to be bored so soon after what had happened; but he no longer wished to occupy his mind by brooding over anything so disagreeable and wanted some sort of amusement to divert and entertain him. Vandover had so accustomed himself to that kind of self-indulgence that he could not go long without it. It had become a simple necessity for him to be amused, and just now he thought himself justified in seeking it in order to forget about Ida's death. He had dwelt upon this now for nearly four days, until it had come to be some sort of a formless horror that it was necessary to avoid. He could get little present enjoyment by looking forward to the new life that he was going to begin and in which his father, his art, and Turner Ravis were to be the chief influences. The thought of this prospect did give him pleasure, but he had for so long a time fed his mind upon the more tangible and concrete enjoyments of the hour and minute that it demanded them now continually.

He sat for a long time upon the slippery leather cushions of the smoking-room trying desperately to become interested in the whist game, or gazing awestruck at the man at his elbow who was smoking black Perrique in a pipe, inhaling the smoke and blowing it out through his nose. After a while he returned to the deck.

There it was cold and wet and a strong wind was blowing from the ocean. Four miles to the east an endless procession of brown, bare hills filed slowly past under the fog. The sky was a dreary brown and the leagues of shifting water a melancholy desert of gray. Besides these there was nothing but the bleached hills and the drifting fog; the wind blew continually, passing between the immense reaches of sea and sky with prolonged sighs of infinite sadness.

Three seagulls followed the vessel, now in a long line, now abreast, and now in a triangle. They sailed slowly about, dipping and rising in the vast hollows between the waves, turning their heads constantly from side to side.

Vandover went to the stern and for a time found amusement in watching the indicator of the patent log, and listening for its bell. But his interest in this was soon exhausted, and he returned to the smoking-room again, reflecting that this was only the first afternoon and that there still remained two days that somehow had to be gone through with.

About five o'clock, as he was on his way to get a glass of seltzer, he saw Grace Irving, the girl of the red hat whom he had met at the Mechanics' Fair, sitting on a camp-stool just inside of her stateroom eating a banana. The sight of her startled him out of all composure for the min-

ute. His first impulse was to speak to her, but he reflected that he was done with all that now and that it was
better for him to pass on as though he had not seen her,
but as he came in front of her she looked up quickly and
nodded to him very pleasantly in such a way that it was
evident she had already known he was on board. It was
impossible for Vandover to ignore her, and though he did
not stop, he looked back at her and smiled as he took off his
hat.

He went down to supper in considerable agitation, marvelling at the coincidence that had brought them together again. He wondered, too, how she could be so
pleasant to him now, for as a matter of course he had not
kept the engagement he had made with her at the Fair.
At the same time, he felt that she must think him a great
fool not to have stopped and spoken to her; either he
should have done that or else have ignored her little bow
entirely. He was firmly resolved to have nothing to do
with her, yet it chafed him to feel that she thought him
diffident. It seemed now as though he owed it to himself
to speak to her if only for a minute and make some sort
of an excuse. By the time he had finished his supper, he
had made up his mind to do this, and then to avoid her for
the rest of the trip.

As he was leaving the dining saloon he met her coming
down the stairs alone, dressed very prettily in a checked
travelling ulster with a gray velvet collar, and a little fore
and aft cap to match. He stopped her and made his
excuses; she did not say much in reply and seemed a little
offended, so that Vandover could not refrain from adding
that he was very glad to see her on board.

"Ah, you don't seem as if you were, very," she said, putting out her chin at him prettily and passing on.   It was an awkward and embarrassing little scene and Vandover was glad that it was over.   But the thing had been done now, he had managed to show the girl that he did not wish to keep up the acquaintance begun at the Fair, and from now on she would keep out of his way.

He took a few turns on the upper deck, smoking his pipe, walking about fast, while his dinner digested.   The sun went down behind the black horizon in an immense blood-red nebula of mist, the sea turned from gray to dull green and then to a lifeless brown, and the *Santa Rosa's* lights began to glow at her quarters and at her masthead; in her stern the screw drummed and threshed monotonously, a puff of warm air reeking with the smell of hot oil came from the engine hatch, and in an instant Vandover saw again the curved roof of the immense iron-vaulted depot, the passengers on the platform staring curiously at the group around the invalid's chair, the repair gang in spotted blue overalls, and the huge white cat dozing on an empty baggage truck.

The wind freshened and he returned to the smoking-room to get warm.   The same game of whist was going on, and the man with the Perrique tobacco had filled another pipe and continued to blow the smoke through his nose.

After a while Vandover went back to the main deck and wandered aft, where he stood a long time looking over the stern, interested in watching the receding water. It was dark by this time, the wind had increased and had blown the fog to landward, and the ocean had changed to a deep blue, the blue of the sky at night; here and there a wave broke, leaving a line of white on the sea like the trail of a falling star across the heavens, while the white haze of the steamer's wake wandered vaguely across the intense blue like the milky way across the zenith.

Vandover was horribly bored. There seemed to be absolutely nothing to amuse him, unless, indeed, he should decide to renew his acquaintance with Grace Irving. But this was out of the question now, for he knew what it would lead to. Even if he should yield to the temptation, he did not see how he could take any great pleasure in that sort of thing again, after what had happened.

Of all the consequences of what he had done, the one which had come to afflict him the most poignantly was that his enjoyment of life was spoiled. At first he had thought that he never could take pleasure in anything again so long as he should live, that his good times were gone. But as his pliable character rearranged itself to suit the new environment, he began to see that there would come a time when he would grow accustomed to Ida's death and when his grief would lose its sharpness. He had even commenced to look forward to this time and to long for it as a sort of respite and relief. He believed at first that it would not be for a great many years; but even so soon after the suicide as this, he saw with a little thrill of comfort that it would be but a matter of months. At the same time Vandover was surprised and even troubled at the ease with which he was recovering from the first shock. He wondered at himself, because he knew he had been sincere in his talk with his father. Vandover was not given to self-analysis, but now for a minute he was wondering if this reaction were due to his youth, his good health and his good spirits, or whether there was something wrong with him.   However, he dismissed these thoughts with a shrug of his shoulders as though freeing himself from some disagreeable burden. Ah, he was no worse than the average; one could get accustomed to almost anything; it was only in the books that people had their lives ruined; and to brood over such things was unnatural and morbid.   Ah! what a dreadful thing to become morbid!   He could not bring Ida back, or mitigate what he had done, or be any more sorry for it by making himself miserable.   Well, then!   Only he would let that sort of thing alone after this, the lesson had been too terrible; he would try and enjoy himself again, only it should be in other ways.

Later in the evening, about nine o'clock, when nearly all the passengers were in bed, and Vandover was leaning over the side of the boat finishing his pipe before turning in himself, Grace Irving came out of her stateroom and sat down at a little distance from him, looking out over the water, humming a little song.   She and Vandover were the only people to be seen on the deserted promenade.

Vandover saw her without moving, only closing his teeth tighter on his pipe.   It was evident that Grace expected him to speak to her and had given him a chance for an admirable little tête-à-tête.   For a moment Vandover's heart knocked at his throat; he drew his breath once or twice sharply through his nose.   In an instant all the old evil instincts were back again, urging and clamouring never so strong, never so insistent.   But Vandover set his face against them, honestly, recalling his resolution, telling

himself that he was done with that life.   As he had said,
the lesson had been too terrible.

He turned about resolutely, and walked slowly away
from her.   The girl looked after him a moment, surprised,
and then called out:

"Oh, Mr, Vandover!"

Vandover paused a moment, looking back.

"Where are you going?" she went on.   "Didn't you
see me here?   Don't you want to come and talk to me?"

"No," answered Vandover, smiling good-humouredly,
trying to be as polite as was possible.   "No, I don't."
Then he took a sudden resolution, and added gravely,
"I don't want to have anything to do with you."

In his stateroom, as he sat on the edge of his berth
winding his watch before going to bed, he thought over
what he had said.   "That was a mean way to talk to a
girl," he told himself, "but," he added, "it's the only
thing to do.   I simply couldn't start in again after all
that's happened.   Oh, yes, that was the right thing to
do!"

He felt a glow of self-respect for his firmness and his
decision, a pride in the unexpected strength, the fine
moral rigour that he had developed at the critical moment.   He *could* turn sharp around when he wanted to,
after all.   Ah, yes, that was the only thing to do if one
was to begin all over again and live down what had happened.   He wished that the governor might know how
well he had acted.

CHAPTER NINE

VANDOVER stayed for two weeks at Coronado Beach and managed to pass the time very pleasantly. He was fortunate enough to find a party at the hotel whom he knew very well. In the morning they bathed or sailed on the bay, and in the afternoon rode out with a pack of greyhounds and coursed jack-rabbits on the lower end of the island. Vandover's good spirits began to come back to him, his appetite returned, his nerves steadied themselves, he slept eight hours every night. But for all that he did not think that things were the same with him. He said to himself that he was a changed man; that he was older, more serious.

During this time he received several letters from his father which he answered very promptly. In the course of their correspondence it was arranged that they should both leave for Europe on the twenty-fifth of that month, and that consequently, Vandover should return to the city not later than the fifteenth. Vandover was having such a good time, however, that he stayed over the regular steamer in order to go upon a moonlight picnic down on the beach. The next afternoon he took passage for San Francisco on a second-class boat.

This homeward passage turned out to be one long misery for Vandover. He had never been upon a second-class boat before and had never imagined that anything could be so horribly uncomfortable or disagreeable.   The *Maz-atlan* was overcrowded, improperly ballasted, and rolled continually.   The table was bad, the accommodations inadequate, the passengers hopelessly uncongenial.   Cold and foggy weather accompanied the boat continually. The same endless procession of bleached hills still filed past under the mist, going now in the opposite direction, and the same interminable game of whist was played in the smoking-room, only with greasier, second-class cards, amidst the acrid smoke of second-class tobacco.   At supper, the first day out, a little Jew who sat next to Vandover, and who invariably wore a plush skull-cap with ear-laps, tried to sell him two flawed and yellow diamonds.

The evening after leaving Port Hartford the *Mazatlan* ran into dirty weather.   It was not stormy — simply rough, disagreeable, the wind and sea directly ahead. Half an hour after supper Vandover began to be sick. For a long time he sat on the slippery leather cushions in the nasty smoking-room, sucking limes, drinking seltzer, and trying to be interested in the card games.   He dozed a little and awoke, feeling wretched, covered with a cold sweat, racked by a pain in the back of his head, and tortured by an abominable nausea.   He groped his way out upon the swaying, gusty deck, descended to his cabin, and went to bed.

The *Mazatlan* had booked more passengers than could be accommodated, the steward being obliged to make up beds on the floor of the dining saloon and even upon some of the tables.   Vandover had not been able to get a stateroom, and so had put up with a bunk in the common cabin at the stern of the vessel.

About two o'clock in the morning he woke up in this place frightfully sick at the stomach and wretched in body and mind. He had an upper bunk, and for a long time he lay on his back rolling about with the rolling of the steamer, vaguely staring straight above him at the roof of the cabin, hardly a hand's-breadth above his face. The roof was iron, painted with a white paint very thick and shiny, and was studded with innumerable bolt-heads and enormous nuts. By and by, for no particular reason, he rose on his elbow and, leaning over the side of his berth, looked about him.

The light streaming from two strong-smelling ship's lanterns showed the cabin, long and narrow. There were two cramped passageways, on either side of which the tiers of bunks, mere open racks filled with bedding, rose to the roof, those occupied by women hung with spotted turkey-red calico.

The cabin was two decks below the open air and every berth was occupied, the only ventilation being through the door. The air was foul with the stench of bilge, the reek of the untrimmed lamps, the exhalation of so many breaths, and the close, stale smell of warm bedding.

A vague murmur rose in the air, the sound of deep breathing, the moving of restless bodies between the coarse sheets, the momentary noise of the scratching of blunt finger-tips, a subdued cough, the moan of a sleeping child. All the while the shaft of the screw, seemingly close beneath the floor, pounded and rumbled without a moment's stop.

Immediately underneath Vandover two men, saloon-keepers, awoke and lit their cigars and began a long dis-

cussion on the question of license. Two or three bunks
distant, a woman, a Salvation Army lassie, one of a large
party of Salvationists who were on board, began to cough
violently, choking for breath. Across the aisle the little
Jew of the plush skull-cap with ear-laps snored monotonously in alternate keys, one a guttural bass, the other a
rasping treble. The *Mazatlan* was rolling worse than
ever, now up and down, now from side to side, and now
with long forward lurches that combined the other two
motions. During one of these latter the little Jew was
half awakened. He stopped snoring, leaving an abrupt
silence in the air. Then Vandover could hear him thresh-
ing about uneasily; still half asleep he began to mutter
and swear: "Dat's it, r-roll; I woult if I were you; r-roll,
dat's righd — dhere, soh — ah, geep it oop — r-roll, you
damnt ole tub, yust *r-r-roll*."

The continued pitching, the foul air, and the bitter
smoke from the saloonkeepers' cigars became more than
Vandover could stand. His stomach turned, at every instant he gagged and choked. He suddenly made up his
mind that he could stand it no longer, and determined to
go on deck, preferring to walk the night out rather than
spend it in the cabin. He drew on his shoes without lacing
them, and dressed himself hurriedly, omitting his collar
and scarf; he put his hat on his tumbled hair, swung into
his overcoat, and, wrapping his travelling-rug around
him, started up toward the deck. On the stairs he was
seized with such a nausea that he could hardly keep from
vomiting where he stood, but he rushed out upon the lower
deck, gaining the rail with a swimming head.

He sank back upon an iron capstan with a groan, weak

and trembling, his eyes full of tears, a bursting feeling in
his head. He was utterly miserable.

It was about half-past two in the morning, and a cold
raw wind was whistling through the cordage and flinging
the steamer's smoke down upon the decks and upon the
water like a great veil of crêpe. A sickly half-light was
spread out between the sea and the heavens. By its
means he could barely distinguish great, livid blotches of
fog or cloud whirling across the black sky, and the unnum-
bered multitude of white-topped waves rushing past,
plunging and rising like a vast herd of black horses galloping on with shaking white manes. Low in the northeast horizon lay a long pale blur of light against which the
bow of the steamer, inky black, rose and fell and heaved
and sank incessantly. To the landward side and very near
at hand, so near that he could hear the surf at their feet,
the long procession of hills continually defiled, vague and
formless masses between the sea and sky. The wind, the
noise of the waves rushing past, the roll of the breakers and
the groaning of the cordage all blended together and filled
the air with a prolonged minor note, lamentable beyond
words. The atmosphere was cold and damp, the spray flying like icy bullets. The sombre light that hung over the
sea reflected itself in long blurred streaks upon the wet
decks and slippery iron rods. Here and there about the
rigging a tremulous ball of orange haze showed where the
ship's lanterns were swung. Directly under him in the
stern the screw snarled incessantly in a vortex of boiling
water that forever swirled away and was lost in the darkness. From time to time the indicator of the patent log,
just beside him, rang its tiny bell.

Vandover drew his rug about him and went up to the main deck, dragging his shoelaces after him.   The wind was stronger here, but he bent his head against it and went on toward the smoking-room, for the idea had occurred to him that he could shut himself in there and pass the rest of the night upon the cushions; anything was better than returning to the cabin downstairs.

The deck was jerked away from beneath his feet, and he was hurled forward, many times his own length, against a companionway, breaking his thumb as he fell.   A second shock threw him down again as he rose; everything about him shook and danced like glassware upon a jarred table.   Then the whole ship rose under his feet as no wave had ever lifted it, and fell again, not into yielding water, but upon something that drove through its sides as if they had been paper.   A deafening, crashing noise split the mournful howl of the wind, and far underneath him Vandover heard a rapid series of blows, a dreadful rumbling and pounding that thrilled and quivered through all the vessel's framework up to her very mast-tips.   On all fours upon the deck, holding to a cleat with one hand, he braced himself, watching and listening, his senses all alive, his muscles tense.   In the direction of the engine-room he heard the furious ringing of a bell.   The screw stopped.   The *Mazatlan* wallowed helplessly in the trough of the sea.

Vandover's very first impulse was a wild desire of saving himself; he had not the least thought for any one else.   Every soul on board might drown, so only he should be saved.   It was the primitive animal instinct, the blind adherence to the first great law, an impulse that in this first moment of excitement could not be resisted. He ran forward and snatched a life-preserver from the pile that was stored beneath the bridge.

As he was fastening it about him, the passengers began to pour out upon the deck, from their staterooms, from the companionways, and from the dining saloon. In an instant the deck was crowded. Men and women ran about in all directions, pushing and elbowing each other, calling shrilly over one another's heads. Near to Vandover a woman, clothed only in her night-dress, clung to the arm of a half-dressed man, crying again and again for a certain "August." She wrung her hands in her excitement; at times the man shouted "August!" in a quavering bass voice. "August, here we are over *here!*" "Oh, where *is* Gussie?" wailed the woman. "Here, here I am," another voice answered at length; "here I am, I'm all right." "Oh," exclaimed the woman with a sob of relief, "here's Gussie; now let's all keep together whatever happens."

All about the decks just such scenes were going on; most of the women wore only their night-gowns or dressing-gowns, their hair tumbling down and blowing about their cheeks, their bare feet slipping and sliding on the heaving wet decks. The men were in shirt and drawers, standing in the centre of their family groups, silent, excited, very watchful; others of them ran about searching for life-preservers, shouting hoarsely, talking to themselves, speaking all their thoughts aloud.

But there was no panic; there was excitement, confusion, bewilderment, but no excess of fear, no unreasoning terror, deaf, blind, utterly reckless.

All at once a man parted the crowd with shoulders and

elbows, passing along the deck with great strides.   It was the captain.   The next instant Vandover saw him on the bridge, hatless, without his vest or his coat, just as he had sprung from his berth.   From time to time he shouted his orders, leaning over the rail, gesturing with his arm. The crew ran about, carrying out his directions, jostling the men out of the way, knocking over women and children, speaking to no one, intent only upon their work.

In a few moments the deck steward and one of the officers appeared amid the crowd of passengers.   They were very calm, and at every instant shouted, "There is no danger; every one go back to his berth; clear the deck, please; no danger, gentlemen; everybody be quiet; go back to your berths!"   The steward even came up to Vandover and pulled at the straps of his life-preserver, exclaiming, "Take this off! there is no danger; you're only exciting the other passengers.   Come on, take it off and go back to your berth."

Vandover obeyed him, slowly loosening the buckles, looking around him, bewildered, but still holding the preserver in his hands.

Best of all, however, was the example of a huge old fellow wearing the cap and clothes of a boatswain's mate of a United States battleship; he seemed to dominate the excited throng in a moment, going about from group to group, quieting them all, spreading a feeling of confidence and courage throughout the whole ship.   He was an inspiration to Vandover, who began to be ashamed of having yielded to the first selfish instinct of preservation.

Just as the boatswain's mate was offering his flask to the woman whom Vandover had heard calling for "August," the *Mazatlan* lurched heavily once or twice, and then slowly listed to the port side, going over farther and farther every instant. Vandover heard a renewed rumbling and smashing noise far beneath him, and in some way knew that the cargo was shifting. Instead of righting herself, the ship began to heave over more and more. The whole sea on the port side seemed to rise up to meet the rail; under Vandover's feet the incline of the deck grew steeper and steeper. All at once his excitement came back upon him with the sharpness of a blow, and he caught at the brass grating of a skylight exclaiming: "By God! we're going *over*." The women screamed with terror; one heard the men shouting, "Look out! hold on! catch hold there!" An old man, wearing only a gray flannel shirt, lost his footing; he fell, and rolled over and over down the deck stupidly, inertly, without making the slightest effort to save himself, without uttering the least cry; he brought up suddenly against the rail, with a great jar, the shock of his soft, withered body against the hard wood sounding like the sodden impact of a bundle of damp clothes. There was a cry; they thought him killed — Vandover had seen his head gashed against a sharp angle of iron — but he jumped up with sudden agility, clambering up the slope of the deck with the strength and rapidity of an acrobat.

There had been a great rush to the other side of the ship, a wild scrambling up the steep deck, over skylights and between masts and ventilators. People clung to anything, to cleats, to steamer chairs, to the brass railings, to the person who stood next to them. They no longer listened to the protestations of the brave boatswain mate; that last long roll had terrified them.   The sense of a great catastrophe began to spread and widen all about like the rising of some fearful invisible mist.   "*What* had happened?   What was to become of them?"

While Vandover clung to the starboard rail, rolling his eyes wildly, trying to control himself again, a young man, a waiter in the dining saloon, rushed up to him from out of the crowd, holding out his hand.   "It's all up!" he shouted.

Vandover grasped his extended palm, shaking hands with him fervently, without knowing why.   The two looked straight into each other's eyes, their hands gripped close; then the waiter turned away, and dropping on his knees began to pray silently to himself.

Vandover saw a great many others praying; there was even a large group gathered about the band of Salvationists trying to raise a hymn.   Every now and then their voices could be heard, singing all out of tune, a medley of discords.

At one time Vandover caught sight of the little Jew of the plush cap with the ear-laps; he was grovelling upon the deck, huddling a small black satchel to his breast; without a moment's pause he screamed, "God 'a' mercy!   God 'a' mercy!"

The sight revolted Vandover and in a great measure helped to calm him.   In a few moments he had himself in hand again, cool and self-collected, resolved not to act like a fool before the others, but to help them if he could.

Near to him a Salvation Army lassie was down upon her knees trying to cord up a huge bundle wrapped in sailcloth.   "Here," exclaimed Vandover coming up to her,

"let me help. I'll tie this for you — you put *this* on."
He took the wet, stiff ropes from between her fingers and
held the life-preserver toward her; but she refused it.

"No," she cried enthusiastically, "I'm going to be
saved anyhow; I ain't going to drown; Jesus is watching
over me. Oh!" she suddenly exclaimed with a burst of
fervor, "Jesus is going to save me. I *know* I'm going to
be saved. I feel it, I feel it *here*," and she struck her palm
on the breast of the man's red jersey she was wearing.

"Well, I wish *I* could have such a confidence," answered
Vandover, sincerely envying the plain little woman under
the ugly blue bonnet.

She seemed as if inspired, her face glowing. "Only *believe;* that's all," she told him. "It isn't too late for you
now. Ah," she went on, smiling, "ah, you don't know
what it is in a time like this! What a comfort! What a
support! Oh, *look, look!*" she cried, breaking off and starting to her feet. "That man is going to jump!"

It was the boatswain's mate, the hero who had filled all
the passengers with his own coolness and courage, who
had been Vandover's inspiration. Some strange reaction
seemed to have seized upon him. Of a sudden he rushed
to the rail, the starboard rail that was heaved so high out
of the water, stood upon it for a moment, and then with a
great shout jumped over the side. His folly was as in-
fectious as his courage. Four more men followed him,
three going over all at the same time, and a fourth a little
later, hanging an instant upon the outside of the rail, then
dropping down feet first, disappearing with a great splash
that made itself heard in the great silence that had suddenly fallen upon the throng.

Every one had seen what had happened; a thrill of fear and apprehension passed over them all like a cold breath. They were silent, struck dumb, feeling the presence of death close by.

Suddenly a long flash of yellow upon the bridge made a momentary streak on the darkness, and there was the report of a gun. A minute later it was fired again, and alternating with it the *Mazatlan's* whistle began to roar, like a hoarse shout for help. Between these sounds could be heard the renewed clamour upon the decks, the shouting, the screaming, and the rush of many feet; the little children clung about the knees of their mothers, shrieking and wailing monotonously, "Oh, ma*ma* — oh, ma*ma!*" rolling their eyes fearfully behind them.

But many of the children, even some of the older passengers, were absolutely silent, dazed, stupefied with terror and excitement, their eyes vague and distended, looking slowly about them, scarcely daring to move a limb.

Meanwhile the *Mazatlan* was settling forward, and already the spray was beginning to fly over the decks. Little by little the terror increased; people threw themselves down upon the deck, rising up again, their arms raised to heaven, praying aloud, screaming the same things over and over again. The Salvationists tried to raise another hymn, but the sound of their voices was drowned out by the tumult, the roaring of the whistle, the barking of the minute guns, the straining and snapping of the cordage, and the sound of waves drawing closer and closer. Prone upon the deck, his arms still clasped about his black satchel, the little Jew of the plush cap went into some kind of fit, his eyes rolled back, his teeth grinding

upon each other.   Vandover turned from him in disgust.
Then he looked around and above him, drawing a long
breath, saying aloud to himself:

"It looks as though it were the end — well!"

All at once Vandover knew that the water had reached
the boilers; there came a noise of hissing: deafening,
stunning; white billows of steam poured up over the deck.

It was no longer the *Mazatlan*, no longer a thing of wood
and iron, but some strange huge living creature that was
dying there under his feet, some enormous brute that was
plunging and writhing in its last agony, its belly ripped
open by a hidden enemy that struck from beneath, its
entrails torn out, its life-breath going from it in great
gasps of steam.   Suddenly its bellow collapsed; the great
bulk was sinking lower; the enemy was in its very vitals.
The great hoarse roar dwindled to a long death rattle,
then to a guttural rasp; all at once it ceased; the brute was
dead — the *Mazatlan* was a wreck.

Almost at the moment, he heard an order shouted twice
from the bridge, where he could see the shadowy figures
of the captain and officers moving about through the
clouds of steam and smoke and mist.   Immediately there
followed the shrill piping of the boatswain's whistle; one
of the officers, the first engineer, and some half dozen of
the crew came dashing through the crowd, and there was a
great shout of "The boats!   The boats!"

The crowd broke up, rushing here and there about the
ship, reforming again in smaller bands by the boats and
life-rafts.   Vandover followed the first engineer, running
forward toward one of the boats in the bow.

"Come on!" he shouted to the little Salvationist lassie, pausing a moment to help her with her heavy canvas-covered bundle. "Come on! they're going to lower the boats."

She started up to follow him and the boom of the foremast, which the accident had in some way loosened, swung across the deck at the same moment. Vandover was already out of its path but it struck the young woman squarely across the back. She dropped in a heap upon the deck, then her body slowly straightened out, stiff and rigid, her eyes rapidly opened and shut, and a great puff of white froth slowly started from her mouth. Vandover ran forward and lifted her up, but her back was broken; she was already dead. He rose to his feet exclaiming to himself, "But she was so sure — she *knew* she was going to be saved," then suddenly fell silent again, gazing wonderingly at the body, disturbed, very thoughtful.

When Vandover finally reached the lifeboat, he found a great crowd gathered there; three people were already in the boat itself. The first engineer, who commanded that boat, and three of the crew stood by the falls preparing to cast off. Just below on the deck of the *Mazatlan* stood two sailors keeping the crowd in order, continually shouting, "Women and children first!" As the women passed their children forward, the sailors lifted them into the boats, some shrieking, others silent and stupid as if stunned. Then the women were helped up; the men, Vandover among them, climbing in afterward. The davits were turned out and the boat was swung clear of the ship's side.

Vandover looked out and below him and then made an involuntary movement to regain the ship's deck. Far below him, or so at least it seemed, were mountains of tumbling green water, huge, relentless, irresistible, rushing on by thousands, to shatter themselves with dreadful force against the ship's side.   It seemed simple madness to attempt to launch the boat; even the sinking wreck would be safer than this chance.   Vandover was terrified, again deserted by all his calmness and self-restraint.

The sailors standing in the bow and the stern let out the ropes little by little, the vast black hulk of the ship began to loom up above them all, higher and higher, and to their eyes the lifeboat began to grow smaller and smaller, more and more frail, more and more pitiful.

All at once it struck the water with a crash, in an instant it was tossed up again in the air, heaving on the crest of a wave, was carried in and dashed up against the ship, all the oars on that side snapping in an instant.   It was a fearful moment; the little boat was unmanageable in an instant, leaping and plunging among the waves like a terrified horse, banged and battered between the heaving water and the hull of the steamer itself.   Vandover believed that all was over; he partially rose from his seat preparing to jump before the boat should swamp.

There was an interval of shouting and confusion, the first engineer and the crew leaning over the sides fending off the boat with the stumps of the oars and with long boathooks.   Some oars were shipped to the other side to take the place of the broken ones, and a score of hands tugging at them, the boat was at length pulled away out of danger.

The lifeboat had been built to hold thirty-five people; more than forty had crowded into it, and it needed all

prudence and care to keep it afloat in the heavy seas that
were running. The sailors and two of the passengers
were at the oars, while the first engineer took command,
standing in the stern at the steering-oar. He was dressed
in a suit of oilskins, a life-preserver strapped under his
arms; he wore no hat, and at every gust his drenched hair
and beard whipped across his face.

Just as the boat was pulling away from the wreck, Vandover and the others saw the little Jew of the plush cap
with the ear-laps standing upon the rail of the steamer,
holding to a stanchion. He believed that he had been
abandoned, and screamed after them, stretching out his
hands. The engineer turned and saw him, but shook his
head. "Give way there!" he commanded the men;
"there's no more room."

The Jew flung his satchel from him and jumped; for a
moment he disappeared, then suddenly came up on the
crest of a wave, quite close to them, gasping and beating
his hands, the water running out of his mouth, and his
plush cap, glossy with wet, all awry and twisted so that
one ear-lap hung over his eye like a shade. In another
moment he had grasped one of the oar-blades. Every one
was watching and there was a cry, "Draw him in!"
But the engineer refused.

"It's too late!" he shouted, partly to the Jew and partly
to the boat. "One more and we are swamped. Let go
there!"

"But you can't let him drown," cried Vandover and the
others who sat near. "Oh, take him in anyhow; we must
risk it."

"Risk hell!" thundered the engineer. "Look here,

you!" he cried to Vandover and the rest. "I'm in command here and am responsible for the lives of all of you. It's a matter of his life or ours; one life or forty. One more and we are swamped. Let go there!"

"Yes, yes," cried some. "It's too late! there's no more room!"

But others still protested. "It's too horrible; don't let him drown; take him in." They threw him their life-preservers and the stumps of the broken oars. But the Jew saw nothing, heard nothing, clinging to the oar-blade, panting and stupid, his eyes wide and staring.

"Shake him off!" commanded the engineer. The sailor at the oar jerked and twisted it, but the Jew still held on, silent and breathing hard. Vandover glanced at the fearfully overloaded boat and saw the necessity of it and held his peace, watching the thing that was being done. The sailor still attempted to tear the oar from the Jew's grip, but the Jew held on, panting, almost exhausted; they could hear his breathing in the boat. "Oh, don't!" he gasped, rolling his eyes.

"Unship that oar and throw it overboard," shouted the engineer.

"Better not, sir," answered the sailor. "Extra oars all broken." The Jew was hindering the progress of the boat and at every moment it threatened to turn broad on to the seas.

"God damn you, let go there!" shouted the engineer, himself wrenching and twisting at the oar. "Let go or I'll shoot!"

But the Jew, deaf and stupid, drew himself along the oar, hand over hand, and in a moment had caught hold of the gunwale of the boat. It careened on the instant. There was a great cry. "Push him off! We're swamping! Push him off!" And one of the women cried to the mate, "Don't let my little girls drown, sir! Push him away! Save my little girls! Let him drown!"

It was the animal in them all that had come to the surface in an instant, the primal instinct of the brute striving for its life and for the life of its young.

The engineer, exasperated, caught up the stump of one of the broken oars and beat on the Jew's hands where they were gripped whitely upon the boat's rim, shouting, "Let go! let go!" But as soon as the Jew relaxed one hand he caught again with the other. He uttered no cry, but his face as it came and went over the gunwale of the boat was white and writhing. When he was at length beaten from the boat he caught again at the oar; it was drawn in, and the engineer clubbed his head and arms and hands till the water near by grew red. The little Jew clung to the end of the oar like a cat, writhing and grunting, his mouth open, and his eyes fixed and staring. When his hands were gone, he tried to embrace the oar with his arms. He slid off in the hollow of a wave, his body turned over twice, and then he sank, his head thrown back, his eyes still open and staring, and a silver chain of bubbles escaping from his mouth.

"Give way, men!" said the engineer.

"Oh, God!" exclaimed Vandover, turning away and vomiting over the side.

A little while later some one on the bow of the boat called to the engineer asking why it was they were not heading for the shore. The engineer did not answer, but

Vandover in some way understood that it was too danger-
ous to attempt to run the breakers in such heavy weather,
and that they must keep in the open, holding the boat
head on to the seas until either the wind fell or they were
picked up by some other vessel.

It was still very dark, and seen under the night from the
little boat, the ocean and the sky seemed immense and
terrible; the great waves grew out of the obscurity ahead
of them, rushing down upon the boat, big, swelling, silent,
their crests occasionally hissing and breaking into irruptions
of cold white froth.   As one of them would draw near, the
boat would rise upon it as though it would never stop,
would hang a moment upon its summit and then topple
into the black gulf that followed, sending the bitter icy
spray high into the air.   The wind blew steadily.   Suddenly toward three o'clock it began to rain.

Vandover, the engineer, all the five sailors, and two of
the passengers were clothed.   The rest of the passengers
were little better than naked.   Here and there a man had
snatched a blanket from his berth, and one or two of them
were wearing their trousers, but the rest were clothed for
the most part only with their shirts and drawers.   There
were eighteen women and five little girls in the boat.
The little girls were well looked after.   Two were wrapped
in Vandover's travelling-rug and a couple of men had
put their coats around the third.   But there were not
wraps enough to go around among the women, by far the
larger part of them were covered only by their night-dresses
or their bed-gowns.

It was abominably cold; the rain fell continually, and the
wind blew in long gusts, piercing, cutting.   Every plunge

of the boat threw icy bullets of spray into the air, which
the wind caught up and flung down broad upon the boat.
Sometimes even a huge wave would break just upon their
quarter, and then great torrents of bitter, freezing water
would fall over them in a deluge, leaving a sediment of
salt that cracked the skin.   The women were huddled
upon the bottom of the boat near the waist, where they
had been placed for greater safety.   They were fouled
with the muddy water that gathered there, their long hair
dishevelled, dripping with sleet, clinging to their wet
cheeks and throats, their bodies showing pink with cold,
through their thin, soaked coverings, their limbs racked
with long incessant shudderings, a wretched group, miserable beyond words.   One of them close by Vandover's feet,
he noticed particularly, had but a single garment to cover
her.   She was drenched through and through, her bare
feet were blue with the cold, her head was thrown back,
her eyes closed.   She was silent except when an unusual
gust of wind whipped the rain and spray across her body
like the long, fine lash of a whip.   Then with every breath
she moaned, drawing in her breath between her teeth
with a little whistling gasp, too weak, too exhausted,
too nearly unconscious to attempt to shield herself in
any way.

Vandover could do nothing; he had almost stripped
himself to help clothe the others.   Nothing more could be
done.   The suffering had to go on, and he began to wonder
how human beings could endure such stress and yet live.

But Vandover himself suffered too keenly to take much
thought for the sufferings of the others, while besides that
anguish which he shared with the whole boat, the pain in

his broken thumb gnawed incessantly like a rat. From time to time he stared listlessly about him, looking at the dark sky, the tumbling ocean, and the crowded groups in the plunging, rolling lifeboat.

There was nothing picturesque about it all, nothing heroic. It was unlike any pictures he had seen of lifeboat rescues, unlike anything he had ever imagined. It was all sordid, miserable, and the sight of the half-clad women, dirty, sodden, unkempt, stirred him rather to disgust than to pity.

At last the dawn came and grew white over a world of tumbling green billows and scudding wrack. Some three miles distant, seen only when the boat topped a higher wave, the same procession of bleached hills moved gradually to the south under the fog, their feet covered by the white line of the surf. Not far behind in the wake of the boat the stern of the *Mazatlan* rose out of a ring of white foam, the waves breaking over her as if she had been there for ages, the screw writhing its flanges into the air like some enormous starfish already fastened upon the hulk.

One of the other boats could be seen now and then between them and the shore, a momentary dot of black on the vast blur of green and gray.

There was no conversation; the men relieved each other at the oars or bailed out the water with their caps and hands, scarcely interchanging a word. The only utterance was an occasional moaning from among the women and children. There was nothing to eat; long since the two whisky flasks had been exhausted. The rain fell steadily into the sea with a prolonged rippling noise.

Vandover was leaning upon the gunwale of the boat, his

head buried in his arms, when suddenly he raised himself
and asked of the man who sat next to him:

"What was the matter last night? What caused the
accident?"

The other shook his head, wearily, turning away again.
However, the engineer answered:

"We couldn't carry coal enough to keep up the right
pressure of steam and drifted in upon a reef. I said once
before that it would happen some time."

About an hour later Vandover dropped off to sleep, in
spite of the cold, the wet, and the torment in his thumb.
He dozed and woke, and dozed again all through the morning. About noon he was awakened by a more violent
rolling of the boat, the sound of voices, and a stir among
the other passengers.

It was still raining; the boat was no longer cutting the
waves with her nose, but was being rowed seaward flank
on; a sailor stood in the bow holding a coil of rope. Close
in and seen over the tops of the waves were the shaking
and slatting sails of a pilot-boat, lying to. One of the
sails bore an enormous number six.

Vandover slept all that day and the night following,
rolled in hot blankets. The next morning he awoke with
a strange sense of unreality and of having dropped a day
somewhere. As he lay in his stuffy little bunk between
decks, and felt the rolling of the pilot-boat under him, he
still fancied himself upon the *Mazatlan*; he felt the pain
in his bandaged thumb and wondered how it came there.
Then his fall on the deck came back to him, the wreck
of the steamer, the excitement on board, the reports of
the rifle fired as a minute gun, the clouds of steam that

smelt of a great laundry, and the drowning of the little
Jew of the plush cap with the ear-laps. He shuddered
and grew sick again for a minute, telling himself that he
would never forget that scene.

Such of the passengers as could get about breakfasted
as best they could in the cabin with the boatkeeper and
four of the pilots. Here they were informed as to what
was to be done with them. The schooner would not go
in for two weeks, and it was out of the question to keep the
castaways on board for that length of time. However, at
that moment the pilots were cruising in the neighbourhood
on the lookout for two Cape Horners that were expected
to be up at any moment. It was decided that when the
first of these should be met with the party should be transferred.

An hour after they had been picked up, the wind had
begun to freshen. By noon of the second day it had come
on to blow half a gale. One could hope only for the best
as regarded the rest of the *Mazatlan's* boats and rafts.
Not another sign of the wreck was seen by the schooner.

The castaways filled the little schooner to overflowing,
hindering her management, and getting in the way at
every step. The pilot crew hustled them about without
ceremony, and after dinner one had to intervene to prevent a fight between one of them and a sailor from the
Mazatlan over the question of a broken pipe. The women
of the *Mazatlan* kept in their berths continually, rolled in
hot blankets, dosed with steaming whisky punches. In
the afternoon, however, Vandover saw two of them in the
lee of the house attempting to dry their hair; one of them
was the woman he had particularly noticed in the life-

boat clad in a night-dress, and he wondered vaguely where the dress had come from she now was wearing.

About three o'clock of the afternoon of the following day Vandover was sitting on the deck near the stern, fastening on his shoes with a length of tarred rope, the laces which he had left trailing having long before broken and pulled out. By that time the wind was blowing squally out of the northeast. The schooner was put under try sails, "a three-reefed mitten with the thumb brailed up," as he heard the boatkeeper call it. This latter was at the wheel for a moment, but in a little while he called up a young man dressed in a suit of oilskins and a pea jacket and gave him the charge. For a long time Vandover watched the boy turning the spokes back and forth, his eyes alternating between the binocle and the horizon.

In the evening about half-past ten, the lookout in the crow's nest sang out: "Smoke — oh!" sounding upon his fish horn. The boatkeeper ran aft and lit a huge calcium flare, holding it so as to illuminate the big number on the mainsail. Suddenly, about a quarter of a mile off their weather-bow, a couple of rockets left a long trail of yellow against the night. It was the *Cape Horner*, and presently Vandover made out her lights, two glowing spots moving upon the darkness, like the eyes of some nocturnal sea-monster. In a few minutes she showed a blue light on the bridge; she wanted a pilot.

The schooner approached and was laid to, and the towering mass of the great deep-sea tramp began to be dimly seen through the darkness. There was little confusion in making the transfer of the castaways. Most of them seemed still benumbed with their recent terrible exposure.

They docilely allowed themselves to be pushed into the pilot tender and again endured the experience of being lowered to the shifting waves below. Silently, like frightened sheep, they stood up in turn in the rocking tender and allowed the life preserver to be fitted about their shoulders to protect them from the bite of the rope's noose beneath their arms. There followed a sickening upward whirl between sea and sky, and then the comforting grasp of many welcoming hands from the deck above. By three o'clock in the morning the transfer had been made.

Vandover boarded the *Cape Horner* in company with the pilot and the rest and reached San Francisco late on the next day, which happened to be a Sunday.

CHAPTER TEN

About ten o'clock Vandover went ashore in the ship's yawl and landed in the city on a literally perfect day in early November. It seemed many years since he had been there. The drizzly morning upon which the *Santa Rosa* had cast off was already too long ago to be remembered. The city itself as he walked up Market Street toward Kearney seemed to have taken on a strange appearance.

It was Sunday, the downtown streets were deserted except for the cable-cars and an occasional newsboy. The stores were closed and in their vestibules one saw the peddlers who were never there on week-days, venders of canes and peddlers of glue with heavy weights attached to mended china plates.

Vandover had had no breakfast and was conscious of feeling desperately hungry. He determined to breakfast downtown, as he would arrive home too late for one meal and too early for the other.

Almost all of his money had been lost with the *Mazatlan;* he found he had but a dollar left. He would have preferred breakfasting at the Grillroom, but concluded he was too shabby in appearance, and he knew he would get more for his money at the Imperial.

It was absolutely quiet in the Imperial at the hour when he arrived. The single bartender was reading a paper, and

in the passage between the private rooms a Chinese with
a clean napkin wound around his head was polishing
the brass and woodwork. In the passage he met Toby,
the red-eyed waiter, just going off night duty, without his
usual apron or white coat, dressed very carefully, wearing a brown felt hat.

"Why, how do you do, Mr. Vandover?"exclaimed Toby.
"Haven't seen you round here for some time." Vandover
was about to answer when the other interrupted:

"Well, what's happened to *you*?   Look as though you'd
been drawn through hell backward and beaten with a cat!"

In fact Vandover's appearance was extraordinary. His
hat was torn and broken, and his clothes, stained with
tar and dirt, shrunken and wrinkled by sea-water. His
shoes were fastened with bits of tarred rope; he was wearing a red flannel shirt with bone buttons which the boatkeeper on the pilot boat had given him, tied at the neck
with a purple handkerchief of pongee silk; his hair was
long, and a week's growth of beard was upon his lip and
cheeks.

"That's a fact," he answered grimly. "I do look
queer. I was in a wreck down the coast," he added hastily.

"The *Mazatlan!*" exclaimed Toby. "That's a fact;
the papers have been full of it. That's so, you were one
of the survivors."

"The survivors!" echoed Vandover with wondering
curiosity. "Tell me — you know I haven't heard a word
yet — were there many lives lost?" He marvelled at the
strangeness of the situation, that this bar waiter should
know more of the wreck than he himself who had been
upon it.

"You bet there were!" answered Toby. "Twenty-three altogether; one boat capsized; Kelly, 'Bug' Kelly, son of that fellow that runs the Crystal Grotto, *he* was drowned, and one of Hocheimer's — Hocheimer, the jeweller, you know — one of his travelling salesmen was drowned; a little Jew named Brann, a diamond expert; he jumped overboard and ——"

"Don't!" said Vandover with a sharp gesture. "I saw him drown — it was sickening."

"Were *you* in that boat?" exclaimed Toby. "Well, wait till I tell you; the authorities here are right after that first engineer with a sharp stick, and some of the passengers, too, for not taking him in. A woman in one of the other boats saw it all and gave the whole thing away. A thing like that is regular murder, you know." Vandover shut his teeth against answering, and after a little Toby went on, willing to talk. "You know, we've got a new man for the day-work down here now — George isn't here any more. No, he's going to start a roadhouse out on the almshouse drive in a few months; swell place, you know. I'll have him send you cards for the opening."

Vandover ordered oysters, an omelette, and a pint of claret from the new waiter who did the day-work, and ate and drank the meal — the like of which he had not tasted since leaving Coronado — with delicious enjoyment.

He delayed over it long, taking a great pleasure in satisfying the demands of the animal in him. The wine made him heavy, warm, stupid; he felt calm, soothed, and perfectly contented, and had to struggle against a desire to go to sleep where he was. The atmosphere of the Imperial was warm and there was a tepid languor in the air as of the traces of many past debauches, a stale odour of sweetened whisky and of musk.   After the roughness and hardships of the last week he felt a pleasant sense of quiet, of relaxation, of enervation.   He even began to wish that Flossie would come in.   This, however, made him rouse himself; he shook himself, and started home, paying his carfare with his last nickel.

He sat on the outside of the car, wondering if any one he knew would see him, half hoping that such a thing might happen, realizing the dramatic interest that would centre about him now in his present condition as a survivor of a wreck.   The idea soon attracted him immensely and he began to look out for any possible acquaintance as the car began to climb over Nob Hill.

At the crossing of Polk Street he saw Ida Wade's mother in deep mourning, standing near a grocery store holding a little pink parcel.

It was like a blow between the eyes.   Vandover caught his breath and started violently, feeling again for an instant the cold grip of the hysterical terror that had so nearly overcome him on the morning after Ida's death. It slowly relaxed, however, and by the time he had reached the house on California Street he was almost himself again.

It was about church time when Vandover arrived at home once more.   There was a Sunday quiet in the air. The bells were ringing, and here and there family groups on their way to church, the children walking in front, very sedate in their best clothes, carrying the prayer-books carefully, by special privilege.

The butler was working in the garden, as he sometimes did of a Sunday morning, pottering about a certain bed

of sweet-peas, and it was the housekeeper who answered
his ring. She recognized him with a prolonged exclamation, raising her hands to heaven.

"O-oh, and is it you, Mr. Vandover, sir? Ah, how
we've been upset about you and all, and it's glad to see
you back again your father will be! Oh, such times as
we had when we heard about the wreck and knowing you
were on it! Yes, sir, your father's *pretty* well, though he
was main poorly yesterday morning. But he's better now.
You'll find him in the smoking-room now, sir."

Vandover pushed open the door of the smoking-room
quietly. His father was sitting unoccupied in the huge
leather chair before the fireplace. He was dead, and must
have died some considerable time before, as he was already
cold. He could have suffered no pain, hardly a muscle
had moved, and his attitude was quite natural, the legs
crossed, the right hand holding the morning's paper. However, as soon as Vandover touched the body it collapsed
and slid down into a heap in the depth of the chair, the jaw
dropping open, the head rolling sidewise upon his shoulder.

Vandover ran out into the hall, waving his arms,
shouting for the servants. "Oh, why didn't you tell me?"
he cried to the housekeeper "Why did you let me find
him so? When did he die?" The housekeeper was dis-
traught. She couldn't believe it. Only a little while ago
he had called her to say there were no more matches in
the little brass matchsafe. She began to utter long cries
and lamentations like a hen in distress, raising her hands
to heaven. All at once they heard some one rushing up
the stairs. It was the butler, in his shirt-sleeves and his
enormous apron of ticking, still carrying his trowel in his

hand. He was bewildered, his eyes protruding, while all
about him he spread the smell of fresh earth. At every
instant he exclaimed:

"What? What? What's the matter?"

"Oh, my dear old governor — and all alone!" cried
Vandover through shut teeth.

"Oh, oh, the good God!" exclaimed the housekeeper,
crossing herself and rolling her eyes. "And him asking
for matches in the little brass box only a minute since.
Oh, the good, kind master!"

Suddenly Vandover rushed down the stairs and through
the front hall, snatching his hat from the hatrack as he
passed. He ran to call the family doctor, who lived some
two blocks below on the same street. He caught him
just as he was getting into the carry-all with his family,
bound for church.

Vandover and the physician rode back together in the
carry-all, the two gray horses going up the steep hill at a
trot. The doctor was dressed for church; he wore red
gloves with thick white seams, a spray of lilies-of-the-
valley in his lapel.

"I'm afraid we can do nothing," he said warningly.
"It's your father's old enemy, I suppose. This was —
it was sure to happen sooner or later. Any sudden shock,
you know."

Vandover scarcely listened, holding the door of the
carry-all open with one hand, ready to jump out, beating
the other hand upon his knee.

"Go back and take the rest of them to church now,"
said the doctor to his coachman when the carry-all stopped
in front of Vandover's house.

The whole house was in the greatest agitation all the rest of the day. The curtains were drawn, the door bell rang incessantly, strange faces passed the windows, and the noise of strange footsteps continually mounted and descended the staircase. The hours for meals were all deranged, the table stood ready all day long, and one ate when there was a chance. The telephone was in constant use, and at every moment messenger boys came and went, people spoke in low tones, walking on tiptoe; the florist's wagon drove to the door again and again, and the house began to smell of tuberoses. Reporters came, waiting patiently for interviews, sitting on the leather chairs in the dining-room, or writing rapidly on a corner of the dining-table, the cloth pushed back. The undertaker's assistants went about in their shirt-sleeves, working very hard, and toward the middle of the afternoon the undertaker himself tied the crêpe to the bell handle.

Little by little a subdued excitement spread throughout the vicinity. The neighbours appeared at their windows, looking down into the street, watching everything that went on. It was a veritable event, a matter of comment and interest for the whole block. Women found excuses to call on each other, talking over what had happened, as they sat near their parlour windows, shaking their heads at each other, peering out between the lace curtains. The people on the cable-cars and the pedestrians looked again and again at the crêpe on the bell handle, and the curtained windows, craning their necks backward when they had passed. The neighbours' children collected in little groups on the sidewalk near the house, looking and pointing, drawn close together, talking in low tones. At last

even a policeman appeared, walking deliberately, casting
the shadow of his huge stomach upon the fence that was
about the vacant lot. He frowned upon the children,
ordering them away. But suddenly he discovered an
acquaintance, the driver of an express-wagon that had just
driven up with an enormous anchor of violets. He paused,
exclaiming:

"Why, hello, Connors!"

"Why, hello, Mister Brodhead!"

Then a long conversation was begun, the policeman
standing on the curbstone, one foot resting upon the hub
of a wheel, the expressman leaning forward, his elbows on
his knees, twirling his whip between his hands. The expressman told some sort of story, pointing with his elbow
toward the house, but the other was incredulous, gravely
shaking his head, putting his chin in the air, and closing
his eyes.

Inside the house itself there was a hushed and subdued bustling that centred about a particular room. The
undertaker's assistants and the barber called in low voices
through the halls for basins of water and towels. There
was a search for the Old Gentleman's best clothes and his
clean linen; bureau drawers were opened and shut, closet
doors softly closed. Relatives and friends called and
departed or stayed to help. A vague murmur arose, a
mingled sound of whispers and light footsteps, the rustle
of silks, and the noise of stifled weeping, and then at last
silence, night, solitude, a single gas-jet burning, and Vandover was left alone.

The suddenness of the thing had stunned and dizzied
him, and he had gone through with all the various affairs

of the day wondering at his calmness and fortitude.
Toward eleven o'clock, however, after the suppressed
excitement of the last hours, as he was going to bed, the
sense of his grief and loss came upon him all of a sudden,
with their real force for the first time, and he threw himself upon the bed face downward, weeping and groaning.
During the rest of the night pictures of his father returned
to him as he had seen him upon different occasions, particularly three such pictures came and went through his
mind.

In one the Old Gentleman stood in that very room,
with the decanter in his hand, asking him kindly if he felt
very bad; in another he was on the pier with his handkerchief tied to his cane, waving it after Vandover as
though spelling out a signal to him across the water. But
in a third, he was in the smoking-room, fallen into the
leather chair, his arm resting on the table and his head
bowed upon it.

After the funeral, which took place from the house,
Vandover drove back alone in the hired carriage to his
home. He would have paid the driver, but the other
told him that the undertaker looked out for that. Vandover watched him a moment as he started his horses
downhill, the brake as it scraped against the tire making
a noise like the yelping of a dog. Then he turned and
faced the house. It was near four o'clock in the afternoon, and everything about the house was very quiet.
All the curtains were down except in one of the rooms upstairs. The butler had already opened these windows
and was airing the room. Vandover could hear him moving about, sweeping up, rearranging the furniture, making

up the bed again.   In front of him, between the horse-
block and the front door, one or two smilax leaves were
still fallen, and a tuberose, already yellow.   Behind him
in the street he had already noticed the marks of the
wheels of the hearse where it had backed up to the curb.

The crêpe was still on the bell handle.   Vandover did
not know whether it had been forgotten, or whether it was
proper to leave it there longer.   At any rate he took it off
and carried it into the house with him.

His father's hat, a stiff brown derby hat, flat on the top,
hung on the hatrack.   This had always been a sign to
Vandover that his father was at home.   The sight was so
familiar, so natural, that the same idea occurred to him
now involuntarily, and for an instant it was as though he
had dreamed of his father's death; he even wondered what
was this terrible grief that had overwhelmed him, and
thought that he must go and tell his father about it.   He
took the hat in his hands, turning it about tenderly,
catching the faint odour of the Old Gentleman's hair oil
that hung about it.   It all brought back his father to him
as no picture ever could; he could almost *see* the kind old
face underneath the broad curl of the brim.   His grief
came over him again keener than ever and he put his
arms clumsily about the old hat, weeping and whispering
to himself:

"Oh, my poor, dear old dad — I'm never going to see
you again, never, never!   Oh, my dear, kind old governor!"

He took the hat up to his room with him, putting it
carefully away.   Then he sat down before the window
that overlooked the little garden in the rear of the house,
looking out with eyes that saw nothing.

CHAPTER ELEVEN

THE following days as they began to pass were miserable. Vandover had never known until now how much he loved his father, how large a place he had filled in his life. He felt horribly alone now, and a veritable feminine weakness overcame him, a crying need to be loved as his father had loved him, and also to love some one as he himself had loved his father. Worst of all, however, was his loneliness. He could think of no one who cared in the least for him; the very thought of Turner Ravis or young Haight wrought in him an expression of scorn. He was sure that he was nothing to them, though they were the ones whom he considered his best friends.

Another cause of misery was the fact that his father's death in leaving him alone had also thrown him upon his own resources. Now he would have to shoulder responsibilities which hitherto his father had assumed, and decide questions which until now his father had answered.

However, he felt that his father's death had sobered him as nothing else, not even Ida's suicide, had done. The time was come at length for him to take life seriously. He would settle down now to work at his art. He would go to Paris as his father had wished, and devote himself earnestly to painting. Yes, the time was come for him to steady himself, and give over the vicious life into which he had been drifting.

But it was not long before Vandover had become accustomed to his father's death, and had again rearranged himself to suit the new environment which it had occasioned. He wondered at himself because of the quickness with which he had recovered from this grief, just as before he had marvelled at the ease with which he had forgotten Ida's death.   Could it be true, then, that nothing affected him very deeply?   Was his nature shallow?

However, he was wrong in this respect; his nature was not shallow.   It had merely become deteriorated.

Two days after his father's death Vandover went into the Old Gentleman's room to get a certain high-backed chair which had been moved there from his own room during the confusion of the funeral, and which, pending the arrival of the trestles, had been used to support the coffin.

As he was carrying it back his eye fell upon a little heap of objects carefully set down upon the bureau.   They were the contents of the Old Gentleman's pockets that the undertaker had removed when the body was dressed for burial.

Vandover turned them over, sadly interested in them. There was the watch, some old business letters and envelopes covered with memoranda, his fountain-pen, a couple of cigars, a bank-book, a small amount of change, his pen-knife, and one or two tablets of chewing-gum.

Vandover thrust the pen and the knife into his own pocket.   The bank-book, letters, and change he laid away in his father's desk, but the cigars and the tablets of gum, together with the crumpled pocket-handkerchief that he found on another part of the dressing-case, he put into the Old Gentleman's hat, which he had hidden on the

top shelf of his clothes closet.   The watch he hung upon a
little brass thermometer that always stood on his centre
table.   He even wound up the watch with the resolve
never to let it run down so long as he should live.

The keys, however, disturbed him, and he kept changing
them from one hand to the other, looking at them very
thoughtfully.   They suggested to him the inquiry as to
whether or no his father had made a will, and how much
money he, Vandover, could now command.   One of the
keys was a long brass key.   Vandover knew that this
unlocked a little iron box that from time out of mind had
been screwed upon the lower shelf of the clothes closet in
his father's room.   It was in this box that the Old Gentleman kept his ready money and a few important papers.

For a long time Vandover stood undecided, changing
the keys about from one hand to the other, hesitating before opening this iron box; he could not tell why.   By and
by, however, he went softly into his father's room, and
into the clothes closet near the head of the bed.   Holding
the key toward the lock, he paused listening; it was impossible to rid his mind of the idea that he was doing
something criminal.   He shook himself, smiling at the
fancy, assuring himself of the honesty of the thing, yet
opening the box stealthily, holding the key firmly in order
that it might not spring back with a loud click, looking
over his shoulder the while and breathing short through
his nose.

The first thing that he saw inside was a loaded revolver,
the sudden view of which sent a little qualm through the
pit of his stomach.   He took it out gingerly, holding it
at arm's length, throwing open the cylinder and spilling

out the cartridges on the bed, very careful to let none of
them fall on the floor lest they should explode.

Next he drew out the familiar little canvas sack. In it
were twenty-dollar gold-pieces, the coin that used to be
"Good for the Masses." Behind that was about thirty
dollars in two rolls, and last of all in an old, oblong tin
cracker-box a great bundle of papers. A list of these papers
was pasted on one end of the box. They comprised
deeds, titles, insurance policies, tax receipts, mortgages,
and all the papers relating to the property. Besides these
there was the will.

He took out this box, laying it on the shelf beside him.
He was closing the small iron safe again very quietly when
all at once, before he could think of what he was doing, he
ran his hand into the mouth of the canvas sack, furtively,
slyly, snatched one of the heavy round coins, and thrust
it into his vest pocket, looking all about him, listening
intently, saying to himself with a nervous laugh, "Well,
isn't it mine anyway?"

In spite of himself he could not help feeling a joy in the
possession of this money as if of some treasure-trove dug
up on an abandoned shore. He even began to plan
vaguely how he should spend it.

However, he could not bring himself to open any of the
papers, but sent them instead to a lawyer, whom he knew
his father had often consulted. A few days later he received a typewritten letter asking him to call at his earliest
convenience.

It was at his residence and not at his office that Vandover saw the lawyer, as the latter was not well at the
time and kept to his bed. However, he was not so sick

but that his doctor allowed him to transact at least some
of his business. Vandover found him in his room, a huge
apartment, one side entirely taken up by book-shelves
filled with works of fiction. The walls were covered with
rough stone-blue paper, forming an admirable background
to small plaster casts of Assyrian *bas-reliefs* and large
photogravures of Renaissance portraits. Underneath
an enormous baize-covered table in the centre of the room
were green cloth bags filled apparently with books, pad-
locked tin chests, and green pasteboard deed-boxes. The
lawyer was sitting up in bed, wearing his dressing-gown
and occasionally drinking hot water from a glass. He was
a thin, small man, middle-aged, with a very round head
and a small pointed beard.

"How do you do, Mr. Vandover?" he said, very pleasantly as Vandover passed by the servant holding open
the door and came in.

"How do you do, Mr. Field?" answered Vandover,
shaking his hand. "Well, I'm sorry to see you like this."

"Yes," answered the lawyer, "I'm — I have trouble
with my digestion sometimes, more annoying than dan-
gerous, I suppose. Take a chair, won't you? You can
find a place for your hat and coat right on the table there.
Well," he added, settling back on the pillows and looking
at Vandover pleasantly, "I think you've grown thinner
since the last time I saw you, haven't you?"

"Yes," answered Vandover grimly, "I guess I have."

"Yes, yes, I suppose so, of course," responded the
lawyer with a vague air of apology and sympathy. "You
have had a trying time of it lately, taking it by and large.
I was *very* painfully shocked to hear of your father's death.

I had met him at lunch hardly a week before; he was a
far heartier man than I was.   Eat?   You should have
seen — splendid appetite.   He spoke at length of you, I remember; told me you expected to go abroad soon to study
painting; in fact, I believe he was to go to Paris with you.
It was very sad and very sudden.   But you know we've
all been expecting — been fearing — that for some time."

They both were silent for a moment, the lawyer looking
absently at the foot-board of the bed, nodding his head
slowly from time to time, repeating, "Yes, sir — yes, sir."
Suddenly he exclaimed, "Well — now, let's see."   He
cleared his throat, coming back to himself again, and
continued in a very businesslike and systematic tone:

"I have looked over your father's papers, Mr. Vandover,
as you requested me to, and I have taken the liberty of
sending for you to let you know exactly how you stand."

"That's the idea, sir," said Vandover, very attentive,
drawing up his chair.

Mr. Field took a great package of oblong papers from
the small table that stood at the head of his bed, and
looked them over, adjusting his eyeglasses.   "Well, now,
suppose we take up the real property first," he continued,
drawing out three or four of these papers and unfolding
them.   "All of your father's money was invested in what
we call 'improved realty.'"

He talked for something over an hour, occasionally
stopping to answer a question of Vandover's, or interrupting himself to ask him if he understood.   At the end it
amounted to this:

The bulk of the estate was residence property in distant quarters of the city.   Some twenty-six houses, very

cheaply built, each, on an average, renting for twenty-eight dollars. When all of these were rented, the gross monthly income was seven hundred and twenty-eight dollars. At this time, however, six were vacant, bringing down the gross receipts per month to five hundred and sixty dollars. The expenses, which included water, commissions for collecting, repairs, taxes, interest on insurance, etc., when expressed in the terms of a monthly average, amounted to one hundred and eighty-six dollars.

"Well, now, let's see," said Vandover, figuring on his cuff, "one hundred and eighty-six from five hundred and sixty leaves me a net monthly income of three hundred and eighty-four — no, seventy-four. Three hundred and seventy-four dollars."

The lawyer shook his head while he drank another glass of hot water:

"You see," he said, wiping his moustache in the hollow of his palm, "you see, we haven't figured on the mortgages yet."

"Mortgages?" echoed Vandover.

"Yes," answered Mr. Field, "when I spoke of expenses I was basing them upon the monthly statements of Adams & Brunt, your father's agents. But they never looked after the mortgages. Your father acted directly with the banks in that matter. I find that there are mortgages that cover the entire property, even the homestead. They are for 6½ and 7 per cent. In some cases there are two mortgages on the same piece of property."

"Well," said Vandover.

"Well," answered the lawyer, "the interest on these foots up to about two hundred and ninety dollars a month."

Vandover made another hasty calculation on his cuff, and leaned back in his chair staring at the lawyer, saying:

"Why, that leaves eighty-four dollars a month, net."

"Yes," assented Field. "I made it that, too."

"Why, the governor used to allow *me* fifty a month," returned Vandover, "just for pocket money."

"I'm afraid you mustn't expect anything like that, now, Mr. Vandover," replied Field, smiling. "You see, when your father was alive and pursuing his profession, he made a comfortable income besides that which he derived from his realty. His law business I consider to have been excellent when you take everything into consideration. He often made five hundred dollars a month at it. Such are the figures his papers show. He could make you a handsome allowance while he was alive, but all that is stopped now!"

"Well, but didn't he — didn't he leave any money, any — any — any lump sum?" inquired Vandover incredulously.

"There was his bank account," answered the other. "You see, he invested most of his savings in this same realty, and since he stopped building he seems to have lived right up to his income."

"But eighty-four dollars!" repeated Vandover; "why, look at the house on California Street where we live. It costs that much to run it, the servants and all."

"Here's your father's domestic-account book," answered Field, taking it up and turning the leaves. "One hundred and seventy-five dollars a month were the average running expenses."

"*One hundred and seventy-five!*" shouted Vandover,

feeling suddenly as if the ground were opening under him. "Why, great heavens! Mr. Field, where am I going to get — what am I going to *do?*"

Mr. Field smiled a little. "Well," he said, "you must make up your mind to live more modestly."

"Modestly?" exclaimed Vandover, scornfully.

"You'll have to rent the house and take rooms."

Vandover gave a gasp of relief.

"I hadn't thought of that," he answered, subsiding at once. "How much would it bring — the house?"

The lawyer hesitated as to this. "That I could hardly tell you definitely," he answered, shaking his head. "Adams & Brunt could give you more exact figures. In fact, I would suggest that you put it into their hands. California near Franklin, isn't it? Yes; the neighbourhood isn't what it used to be, you know. Every one wants to live out on Pacific Heights now. Double house? Yes, well — with the furniture, I suppose — oh, I don't know — say, a hundred and fifty. But, you know, my estimate is only guesswork. Brunt is the man you want to see."

"Well," answered Vandover, solaced, "that makes — two thirty-four; that's more like it. But," he added, hastily, "you say the homestead is mortgaged as well; how about the interest on that?"

"You needn't be bothered about that," answered Mr. Field. "The interest on *that* mortgage is included in the two hundred and ninety that I spoke of, and the insurance interest on the homestead is included in Adams & Brunt's statement. That was on the whole estate *with* the homestead, you understand? But there is another thing you must look out for. Most of the mortgages are for one year, and every time they are renewed there is an expense of between forty and fifty dollars."

"Yes, I see," assented Vandover.

"Now," resumed the lawyer, "here is your father's bank account. He had in the First National to his credit between nine and ten thousand dollars; nine thousand seven hundred and ninety, to be exact. His professional account book shows that there is now due him in bills and notes eight hundred and thirty dollars; on the debit side he owes in all nine hundred; the difference, you see, is seventy. Nine thousand seven hundred and ninety less seventy leaves a balance of nine thousand six hundred and twenty. All clear?" he asked, interrupting himself. Vandover nodded and the other continued:

"Now, your father left a will; here it is. I drew it for him a year ago last September. He has given fifteen hundred dollars to some cousin in the southern part of the state, and six hundred to a few charities here in the city. The remainder, seven thousand five hundred and twenty, and all the rest of the estate is left to you with the wish that you pursue your art studies abroad. Brunt, of Adams & Brunt, and myself are appointed executors. So now, that is just how you stand as far as I can see: seventy-five hundred dollars in ready money and, if we suppose you rent the California Street house, income property that nets you two hundred and thirty-four a month. The will will have to be probated some time next month and you will have to appear; however, I shall let you know about that in time."

During the next two weeks Vandover was plunged into the affairs of business for the first time in his life. It interested and amused him, and he felt a certain self-importance in handling large sums of money, and in figuring interest, rents, and percentages. Three days after his interview with Mr. Field the sale of his father's office effects took place, and the consequent five hundred dollars Vandover turned over into the hands of the lawyer, who was already looking for an investment for the eighty-nine hundred. This matter had given Vandover considerable anxiety.

"I don't want anything fancy," he said to Field. "No big per cents. and bigger risks. If I've got to live economically I want something that's secure. A good solid investment, don't you know, with a fair interest; that's what I'm looking for."

"Yes," answered the lawyer grimly; "I've been looking for that myself ever since I was your age."

They both laughed, and the lawyer added: "Has Brunt found a tenant for the California Street house yet? No? Well, perhaps you had better keep that five hundred for your running expenses until he does. It will probably take some time."

"All right," answered Vandover. "There were a couple of women up to look at the place yesterday, but they wanted to use it for a boarding-house. I won't hear to that. Brunt says they would ruin it, dead sure."

"I suppose you are looking around, yourself, for rooms?" inquired Mr. Field. "Have you found anything to suit you?"

"No," answered Vandover, "I have not. I don't like the idea of living in one of the downtown hotels, and as far as I have looked, the uptown flats are rather steep.

However, I haven't gone around very much as yet. I've been so busy. Oh, how about the paving of the street in front of those Bush Street houses of mine? Brunt says that the supervisors have passed a resolution of intention to that effect. Now shall I let the city contractor have the job or give it to Brunt's man?"

"Better let the city people do it," advised Field. "They may charge more, but you needn't pay *them* for a long time."

By the end of three weeks Vandover had sickened of the whole thing. The novelty was gone, and business affairs no longer amused him. Besides this, he was anxious to settle down in some comfortable rooms. It was now the middle of winter and he had determined that it was not the season for a European trip. He would wait until the summer before going to Paris.

Little by little Vandover turned over the supervision and management of his affairs and his property to Adams & Brunt, declaring that he could not afford to be bothered with them any longer. This course was much more expensive and by no means so satisfactory from a business point of view, but Vandover felt as though the loss in money was more than offset by his freedom from annoyance and responsibility.

He was eager to get settled. The idea of taking rooms that should be all his own and that he could fit up to suit his taste attracted him immensely. Already he saw himself installed in charming bachelor's apartments, the walls covered with rough stone-blue paper forming an admirable background for small plaster casts of Assyrian *bas-reliefs* and photogravures of Velasquez portraits.

There would be a pipe-rack over the mantelpiece, and a window-seat with a corduroy cushion such as he had had in his room in Matthew's.

Very slowly his father's affairs were settled, and by degrees the estate began to adjust itself to the new grooves in which it was to run. By the middle of December everything was beginning to go smoothly, and the day before Christmas Mr. Field announced to Vandover that he had invested his eighty-nine hundred in registered U. S. 4 per cents. They had had several long talks concerning this sum of money, and in the end had concluded that it would be better to invest it in some such fashion rather than to take up any of the mortgages that were on the houses.

During the first weeks of the new year the house on California Street was rented for one hundred and twenty-five dollars to an English gentleman, the president of a fruit syndicate in the southern part of the state. There were but three in the family, and though the rent was below that which Vandover had desired, Brunt advised him to close the transaction at once, as they were desirable tenants and would probably stay in the house a long time.

On the last evening which he was to spend in his home, Vandover cast up his accounts and made out a schedule as to his monthly income.

Rent from realty, net average	$ 84.00
Rent from homestead property on California Street . . .	125.00
Interest on U. S. bonds, 4 per cent.	23.00
Total	$232.00
In small iron safe	$170.00

Received from sale of office effects $500.00

$670.00

Expenses, outstanding bills, lawyer's fees, undertaker's bill,
   expenses for collecting, etc 587.00

Balance, January 16th $83.00

Then with a shrug of the shoulders he dismissed the
whole burdensome business from his mind. Brunt would
manage his property, sending him regularly the monthly
statement in order to keep him informed. The English
gentleman of the fruit syndicate would add his hundred
and twenty-five, and the 4 per cents., faithfully brooding
over his eighty-nine hundred in the dark of the safety deposit drawer, would bring forth their little quota of twenty-
three with absolute certainty. Two thirty-two a month.
Yes, he was comfortably fixed and was free now to do
exactly as he pleased.

His first object now was to settle down for the winter in
some pleasant rooms. He had decided that he would
look for a suite of three — a bedroom, studio, and sitting-
room. The bedroom he was not particular about, the
studio he hoped would have plenty of light from the north,
but the sitting-room *must* be sunny and overlook the
street, else what would be the use of a window-seat? As
to the neighbourhood, he thought he would prefer Sutter
Street anywhere between Leavenworth and Powell.

In the downtown part this street was entirely given
over to business houses; in the far, uptown quarter it was
lined with residences; but between these two undesirable
extremes was an intermediate district where the residences
had given place to flats, and the business blocks to occa-

sional stores.   It was a neighbourhood affected by doctors, dentists, and reputable music-teachers; drug stores occupied many of the corners, here and there a fine residence still withstood the advance of business, there were a number of great apartment houses, and even one or two club buildings.

It was a gay locality, not too noisy, not too quiet. The street was one of the great arteries of travel between the business and the residence portions of the city, and its cable-cars were frequented by ladies going to their shopping or downtown marketing or to and from the matinées.   Acquaintances of Vandover were almost sure to pass at every hour.

He took rooms temporarily at the Palace and at once set about locating on Sutter Street. He had recourse again to Brunt, who furnished him with a long list of vacancies in that neighbourhood. Apartment-hunting was an agreeable pastime to Vandover, though in the end it began to bore him.   Altogether, he visited some fifteen or twenty suites, in each case trying to fit himself into the rooms, imagining how the window-seat would look in such a window, how the pipe-rack would show over such a mantel, just where on such walls the Assyrian *bas-reliefs* could be placed to the best advantage, and if his easel could receive enough steady light from such windows.   Then he considered the conveniences, the baths, the electric light, and the heat.

After a two weeks' search, he had decided upon one of two suites; both of these were in the desired neighbourhood but differed widely in other respects.

The first was reasonable enough in the matter of rent,

and had even been occupied by an artist for some three
or four years previous.   However, the room that Vandover
proposed to use as a sitting-room was small and had no
double windows, thus making the window-seat an impossibility.   There did not seem to be any suitable place for
the Assyrian *bas-reliefs*, and the mantelpiece was of old-
fashioned white marble like the mantelpiece in Mrs.
Wade's front parlour, a veritable horror.   It revolted
Vandover even to think of putting a pipe-rack over it.
These defects were offset by the studio, a large and splendid room with hardwood floors and an enormous north
light, the legendary studio, the dream of an artist, precisely such a studio as Vandover had hoped he would
occupy in the Quarter.

The other suite was in a great apartment house, a hotel
in fact, but very expensive, with electric bulbs and bells,
and with a tiled bathroom connecting with the bedroom.
The room which he would be obliged to use as his studio
was small, dark, the light coming from the west.   But
the sitting-room was perfect.   It had the sun all day long
through a huge bay window that seemed to have been
made for a window-seat; there were admirable, well-
lighted spaces on the walls for casts and pictures, and the
mantelpiece was charming, extremely high, and made of
oak; in a word, the exact sitting-room that Vandover had
in mind.   Already he saw himself settled there as comfortably and snugly as a kernel in a nutshell.   It was
true that upon investigation he found that the grate had
been plastered up and the flue arranged for a stove.
But for that matter there were open-grate stoves to be
had that would permit the fire to be seen and that would

look just as cheerful as a grate. He had even seen such a stove in the window of a hardware store downtown, a tiled stove with a brass fender and with curious flamboyant ornaments of cast-iron — a jewel of a stove.

For two days Vandover hesitated between these two suites, undecided whether he should sacrifice his studio for his sitting-room, or his sitting-room for his studio. At length he came to the conclusion that as he was now to be an artist a good studio ought to be the first consideration, and that since he was to settle down to hard, serious work at last he owed it to himself to have a fitting place in which to paint; yes, decidedly he would take the suite with the studio. He went to the agent, told him of his decision, and put up a deposit to secure the rooms.

The same day upon which he took this decided step he had occasion to pass by both places in question. As he approached the apartment house in which the rejected suite was situated it occurred to him to tell the clerk in the office that he had decided against the rooms; he could take a last look at them at the same time.

He was shown up to the rooms again, and walked about in the sitting-room, asking the same questions about the heat, the plumbing, and the baths. He even went to the window and looked out into the street. It *was* a first-rate berth just the same, and how jolly it would be to lounge in the window-seat of a morning, with a paper, a cigarette, and a cup of coffee, watching the people on their way downtown; the women going to their shopping and morning's marketing. Then all at once he remembered that at most he would only have these rooms for five months, and

reflected that if his whole life was to be devoted to painting
he might easily put up with an inconvenient studio for a
few months.   Once at Paris all would be different.

At that the rooms took on a more charming aspect than
ever; never had they appeared cheerier, sunnier, more
comfortable; never had the oak mantel and the tiled stove
with the flamboyant ornaments been more desirable;
never had a window-seat seemed more luxurious, never
a pipe-rack more delectable, while at the same time, the
other rooms, the rooms of the big studio, presented themselves to his imagination more sombre, uncomfortable,
and forbidding than ever.   It was out of the question to
think of living there; he was angry with himself for having hesitated so long.   But suddenly he remembered the
deposit he had already made; it was ten dollars; for a
moment he paused, then dismissed the matter with an
impatient shrug of the shoulders.   "So much the worse,"
he said.   "What's ten dollars?"   He made up his mind
then and there and went downstairs, walking on his heels,
to tell the clerk that after all he would engage the rooms
from that date.

CHAPTER TWELVE

V<small>ANDOVER</small> took formal possession of his rooms on Sutter Street during the first few days of February. For a week previous they had been in the greatest confusion: the studio filled with a great number of trunks, crates, packing cases, and furniture still in its sacking. In the bedroom was stored the furniture that had been moved out of the sitting-room, while the sitting-room itself was given over to the paperhangers and carpenters. Vandover himself appeared from time to time, inquiring anxiously as to the arrival of his "stuff," or sitting on a packing-case, his hands in his pockets, his hat pushed back, and a cigarette between his lips.

He had passed a delightful week selecting the wall paper and the pattern for the frieze, buying rugs, screens, Assyrian *bas-reliefs*, photogravures of Renaissance portraits, and the famous tiled stove with its flamboyant ornaments. Just after renting his home he had had a talk with the English gentleman of the fruit syndicate and had spoken about certain ornaments and bits of furniture, valuable chiefly to himself, which he wished to keep. The president of the fruit syndicate had been very gracious in the matter, and as soon as Vandover had taken his rooms he had removed two great cases of such articles from the California Street house and had stored them in the studio.

After the workmen were gone away Vandover began the labour of arrangement, aided by one of the paper-hangers he had retained for that purpose. It was a work of three days, but at last everything was in its place, and one evening toward the middle of the month Vandover stood in the middle of the sitting-room in his shirt-sleeves, holding the tweezers and a length of picture-wire in his hand, and looked around him in his new home.

The walls were hung with dull blue paper of a very rough texture set off by a narrow picture moulding of ivory white. A dark red carpet covered with rugs and skins lay on the floor. Upon the left-hand wall, reaching to the floor, hung a huge rug of sombre colours against which were fixed a fencing trophy, a pair of antlers, a little water colour sketch of a Norwegian fjord, and Vandover's banjo; underneath it was a low but very broad divan covered with corduroy. To the right and left of this divan stood breast-high bookcases with olive green curtains, their tops serving as shelves for a multitude of small ornaments, casts of animals by Fremilt and Barye, Donatello's lovely *femme inconnue*, beer steins, a little bronze clock, a calendar, and a yellow satin slipper of Flossie's in which Vandover kept Turkish cigarettes. The writing-desk with the huge blue blotter in a silver frame, the paper-cutter, and the enormous brass inkstand filled the corner to the right of the divan, while drawn up to it was the huge leather chair, the chair in which the Old Gentleman had died. In the drawer of the desk Vandover kept his father's revolver; he never thought of loading it; of late he had only used it to drive tacks with, when he could not find the hammer. Opposite the divan, on the other side of the room, was the famous tiled stove with the flamboyant ornaments; back of this the mantel, and over the mantel a row of twelve grotesque heads in plaster, with a space between each for a pipe.   To the left in the angle of the room stood the Japanese screen in black and gold, and close to this a tea-table of bamboo and a piano-lamp with a great shade of crinkly red paper that Turner Ravis had given to Vandover one Christmas.   The bay window was filled by the window-seat, covered with corduroy like the divan and heaped with cushions, one of them of flaming yellow, the one spot of vivid colour amidst the dull browns and sombre blues of the room.   A great sideboard with decanters and glasses and chafing-dishes faced the window from the end wall.   The entrance to the studio opened to the left of it, which entrance Vandover had hung with curtains of dust-brown plush.

The casts of the Assyrian *bas-reliefs* were against the wall upon either side of the window.   There were three of them, two representing scenes from the life of the king, the third the wounded lioness which Vandover never wearied of admiring.

Upon the wall over the mantel hung two very large photogravures, one of Rembrandt's "Night Watch," the other a portrait of Velasquez representing a young man with a hunting spear.   Above one of the bookcases was an admirable reproduction of the "Mona Lisa"; above the other, a carbon print of a Vandyke, a Dutch lady in a silk gown and very high ruff.

By the side of the "Mona Lisa," however, was a cheap brass rack stuffed with photographs: actresses in tights, French quadrille dancers, high kickers, and chorus girls.

In the studio, Vandover had tacked great squares and stripes of turkey-red cloth against the walls to serve as a background for his sketches.   Some dozen or more portfolios and stretchers were leaned against the baseboard, and a few ornaments and pieces of furniture, such things as Vandover set but little store by, were carelessly arranged about the room.   The throne and huge easel were disposed so as to receive as much light as was possible.

Beyond the studio was the bedroom, but here there was only the regulation furniture.   Some scores of photographs of Vandover's friends were tacked upon the walls, or thrust between the wood and glass of the mirror.

A new life now began for Vandover, a life of luxury and aimlessness which he found charming.   He had no duties, no cares, no responsibilities.   But there could be no doubt that he was in a manner changed; the old life of dissipation seemed to have lost its charm.   For nearly twenty-six years nothing extraordinary had happened to break in upon the uneventful and ordinary course of his existence, and then, suddenly, three great catastrophes had befallen, like the springing of three successive mines beneath his feet: Ida's suicide, the wreck, and his father's death, all within a month.   The whole fabric of his character had been shaken, jostled out of its old shape.   His desire of vice was numbed, his evil habits all deranged; here, if ever, was the chance to begin anew, to commence all over again.   It seemed an easy matter: he would merely have to remain inactive, impassive, and his character would of itself re-form upon the new conditions.

But Vandover made another fatal mistake: the brute in him had only been stunned; the snake was only soothed.

His better self was as sluggish as the brute, and his desire
of art as numb as his desire of vice.   It was not a continued state of inaction and idleness that could help him, but
rather an active and energetic arousing and spurring up
of those better qualities in him still dormant and inert.
The fabric of his nature was shaken and broken up, it
was true, but if he left it to itself there was danger that it
would re-form upon the old lines.

And this was precisely what Vandover did.   As rapidly
as ever his pliable character adapted itself to the new
environment; he had nothing to do; there was lacking both
the desire and necessity to keep him at his easel; he neglected his painting utterly.   He never thought of attend-
ing the life-class at the art school; long since he had given
up his downtown studio.   He was content to be idle, listless, apathetic, letting the days bring whatever they chose,
making no effort toward any fixed routine, allowing his
habits to be formed by the exigencies of the hour.

He rose late and took his breakfast in his room; after
breakfast he sat in his window-seat, reading his paper,
smoking his pipe, drinking his coffee, and watching the
women on their way downtown to their morning's shopping or marketing.   Then, as the fancy moved him, he
read a novel, wrote a few letters, or passed an hour in the
studio dabbling with some sketches for the "Last Enemy."
Very often he put in the whole morning doing pen and inks
of pretty, smartly dressed girls, after Gibson's manner,
which he gave away afterward to his friends.   In the afternoon he read or picked the banjo or, sitting down to the
little piano he had rented, played over his three pieces,
the two polkas and the air of the topical song.   At three

o'clock, especially of Wednesday and Saturday afternoons, he bestirred himself, dressed very carefully, and went downtown to promenade Kearney and Market streets, stopping occasionally at the Imperial, where he sometimes found Ellis and Geary and where he took cocktails in their company.

He rarely went out in the evenings; his father's death had changed all that, at least for a while. He had not seen Turner Ravis nor Henrietta Vance for nearly two months.

Vandover took his greatest pleasure while in his new quarters, delighted to be pottering about his sitting-room by the hour, setting it to rights, rearranging the smaller ornaments, adjusting the calendar, winding the clock and, above all, tending the famous tiled stove.

In his idleness he grew to have small and petty ways. The entire day went in doing little things. He passed one whole afternoon delightfully, whittling out a new banjo bridge from the cover of a cigar-box, scraping it smooth afterward with a bit of glass. The winding of his clock was quite an occurrence in the course of the day, something to be looked forward to. The mixing of his tobacco was a positive event and undertaken with all gravity, while the task of keeping it moist and ripe in the blue china jar, with the sponge attachment, that always stood on the bamboo tea-table by the Japanese screen, was a wearing anxiety that was yet a pleasure.

It became a fad with him to do without matches, using as a substitute "lights," tapers of twisted paper to be ignited at the famous stove. He found amusement for two days in twisting and rolling these "lights," cutting

frills in the larger ends with a pair of scissors, and stacking
them afterward in a Chinese flower jar he had bought for
the purpose and stood on top of the bookcases. The
lights were admirably made and looked very pretty.
When he had done he counted them. He had made two
hundred exactly. What a coincidence!

But the stove, the famous tiled stove with flamboyant
ornaments, was the chiefest joy of Vandover's new life.
He was delighted with it; it was so artistic, so curious, it
kept the fire so well, it looked so cheerful and inviting; a
stove that was the life and soul of the whole room, a
stove to draw up to and talk to; no, never was there
such a stove! There was hardly a minute of the day he
was not fussing with it, raking it down, turning the dam-
per off and on, opening and shutting the door, filling it
with coal, putting the blower on and then taking it off
again, sweeping away the ashes with a little brass-handled
broom, or studying the pictures upon the tiles: the "Punishment of Caliban and His Associates," "Romeo and
Juliet," the "Fall of Phaeton." He even pretended to the
chambermaid that he alone understood how to manage
the stove, forbidding her to touch it, assuring her that it
had to be coaxed and humoured. Often late in the evening as he was going to bed he would find the fire in it
drowsing; then he would hustle it sharply to arouse it,
punching it with the poker, talking to it, saying: "Wake
up there, you!" And then when the fire was snapping he
would sit before it in his bathrobe, absorbing its heat
luxuriously and scratching himself, as was his custom, for
over an hour.

But very often in the evening he would have the boys,

Ellis, Geary, and young Haight, up to a little improvised
supper. They would bring home *tamales* with them,
and Vandover would try to make Welsh rabbits, which
did not always come out well and which they oftentimes
drank instead of ate. Ellis, always very silent, would mix
and drink cocktails continually. Vandover would pick
his banjo, and together with young Haight would listen
to Geary.

"Ah, you bet," this one would say, "I'm going to make
my pile in this town. I can do it. Beale sent me to
court the other morning to get the judge's signature.
He had a grouch on, and wanted to put me off. You
ought to have heard me jolly him. I talked right up to
him! Yes, sir; you bet! Didn't I have the gall? That's
the way you want to do to get along — get right in and not
be afraid. I got his signature, you bet. Ah, I'm right
in it with Beale; he thinks I'm hot stuff."

Now that there was nothing to worry him, and little to
occupy his mind, Vandover gave himself over considerably to those animal pleasures which he enjoyed so much.
He lay abed late in the morning, dozing between the warm
sheets; he overfed himself at table, and drank too much
wine; he ate between meals, having filled his sideboard
with canned patés, potted birds, and devilled meats;
while upon the bamboo table stood a tin box of chocolates out of which he ate whole handfuls at a time. He
would take this box into the bathroom with him and eat
while he lay in the hot water until he was overcome by
the enervating warmth and by the steam and would then
drop off to sleep.

It was during these days that Vandover took up his

banjo-playing seriously, if it could be said that he did anything seriously at this time. He took occasional lessons of a Mexican in a room above a wigmaker's store on Market Street, and learned to play by note. For a little time he really applied himself; after he had mastered the customary style of play he began to affect the more brilliant and fancy performances, playing two banjos at once, or putting nickels under the bridge and picking the strings with a calling-card to imitate a mandolin. He even made up some comical pieces that had a great success among the boys. One of these he called the "Pleasing Pan-Hellenic Production"; another was the imitation of the "Midway Plaisance Music," and a third had for title "A Sailor Robbing a Ship," in which he managed to imitate the sounds of the lapping of the water, the creaking of the oarlocks, the tramp of the sailor's feet upon the deck, the pistol shot that destroyed him, and — by running up the frets on the bass-string — his dying groans, a finale that never failed to produce a tremendous effect.

CHAPTER THIRTEEN

JUST before Lent, and about three months after the death of Vandover's father, Henrietta Vance gave a reception and dance at her house. The affair was one of a series that the girls of the Cotillon had been giving to the men of the same club. Vandover had gone to all but the last, which had occurred while he was at Coronado. He was sure of meeting Geary, young Haight, Turner Ravis, and all the people of his set at these functions, and had always managed to have a very jolly time. He had been very quiet since his father's death and had hardly gone out at all; in fact, since Ida Wade's death and his trip down the coast he had seen none of his acquaintances except the boys. But he determined now that he would go to this dance and in so doing return once more to the world that he knew. By this time he had become pretty well accustomed to his father's death and saw no reason why he should not have a good time.

At first he thought he would ask Turner to go with him, but in the end made up his mind to go alone, instead; one always had a better time when one went alone. Young Haight would have liked to have asked Turner, but did not because he supposed, of course, that Vandover would take her. In the end Turner had Delphine act as her escort.

Vandover arrived at Henrietta Vance's house at about

half-past eight. A couple of workmen were stretching
the last guy ropes of the awning that reached over the
sidewalk; every window of the house was lighted. The
front door was opened for the guest before he could ring,
and he passed up the stairs, catching a glimpse of the parlours through the portières of the doors. As yet they were
empty of guests, the floors were covered with canvas, and
the walls decorated with fern leaves. In a window recess
one of the caterer's men was setting out two punch bowls
and a multitude of glass cups; three or four musicians were
gathered about the piano, tuning up, and one heard the
subdued note of a cornet; the air was heavy with the
smell of pinks and of La France roses.

At the turn of the stairs the Vances' second girl in a
white lawn cap directed him to the gentlemen's dressing-
room, which was the room of Henrietta Vance's older
brother. About a dozen men were here before him, some
rolling up their overcoats into balls and stowing them with
their canes in the corners of the room; others laughing and
smoking together, and still others who were either brush-
ing their hair before the mirrors or sitting on the bed in
their stocking feet, breathing upon their patent leathers,
warming them before putting them on. There were one
or two who knew no one and who stood about unhap-
pily, twisting the tissue paper from the buttons of their
new gloves, and looking stupidly at the pictures on the
walls of the room. Occasionally one of the gentlemen
would step to the door and look out into the hall to see if
the ladies whom they were escorting were yet come out
of their dressing-room, ready to go down.

On the centre table stood three boxes of cigars and a

great many packages of cigarettes, while extra hairbrushes, whiskbrooms, and papers of pins had been placed about the bureau.

As Vandover came in, he nodded pleasantly to such of the men as he knew, and, after hiding his hat and coat under the bed, shook himself into his clothes again and rearranged his dress tie.

The house was filling up rapidly; one heard the deadened roll of wheels in the street outside, the banging of carriage doors, and an incessant rustle of stiff skirts ascending the stairs. From the ladies' dressing-room came an increasing soprano chatter, while downstairs the orchestra around the piano in the back parlour began to snarl and whine louder and louder. About the halls and stairs one caught brief glimpses of white and blue opera cloaks edged with swan's-down alternating with the gleam of a starched shirt bosom and the glint of a highly polished silk hat. Odours of sachet and violets came and went elusively or mingled with those of the roses and pinks. An air of gayety and excitement began to spread throughout the house.

"Hello, old man!" "Hello, Van!" Charlie Geary, young Haight, and Ellis came in together. "Hello, boys!" answered Vandover, hairbrush in hand, turning about from the mirror, where he had been trying to make his hair lie very flat and smooth.

"Look here," said Geary, showing him a dance-card already full, "I've got every dance promised. I looked out for that at the last one of these affairs; made all my arrangements and engagements then. Ah, you bet, I don't get left on any dance. That's the way you want to rustle.

Ah," he went on, "had a bully sleep last night. I knew I was going to be out late to-night, so I went to bed at nine; didn't wake up till seven. Had a fine cutlet for breakfast."

It was precisely at this moment that Geary got his first advancement in life. Mr. Beale, Jr., head clerk in the great firm of Beale & Story, came up to him as he was drawing off his overcoat:

"How is Fischer?" asked Geary.

Beale, Jr. pulled him over into a corner, talking in a low voice. "He's even worse than yesterday," he answered. "I think we shall have to give him a vacation, and that's what I want to speak to you about. If you can, Geary, I should like to have you take his place for a while, at least until we get through with this contract case. I don't know about Fischer. He's sick so often, I'm afraid we may have to let him go altogether."

Suddenly the orchestra downstairs broke out into a clash of harmony and then swung off with the beat and cadence of a waltz. The dance was beginning; a great bustle and hurrying commenced about the dressing-rooms and at the head of the stairs; everybody went down. In the front parlour by the mantel Henrietta Vance and Turner stood on either side of Mrs. Vance, receiving, shaking hands, and laughing and talking with the different guests who came up singly, in couples, or in noisy groups.

No one was dancing yet. The orchestra stopped with a flourish of the cornet, and at once a great crowding and pushing began amidst a vast hum of talk. The cards were being filled up, a swarm of men gathered about each of the more popular girls, passing her card from hand to hand while she smiled upon them all helplessly and good-naturedly. The dance-cards had run short and some of the men were obliged to use their visiting cards; with these in one hand and the stump of a pencil in the other, they ran about from group to group, pushing, elbowing, and calling over one another's heads like brokers in a stock exchange.

Geary, however, walked about calmly, smiling content-edly, very good-humoured. From time to time he stopped such a one of the hurrying, excited men as he knew and showed him his card made out weeks before, saying, "Ah, how's that? *I* am all fixed; made all my engagements at the last one of these affairs, even up to six extras. That's the way you want to rustle."

Young Haight was very popular; everywhere the girls nodded and smiled at him, many even saving a place on their cards for him before he had asked.

Ellis took advantage of the confusion to disappear. He went up into the deserted dressing-room, chose a cigar, unbuttoned his vest and sat down in one chair, putting his feet upon another. The hum of the dance came to him in a prolonged and soothing murmur and he enjoyed it in some strange way of his own, listening and smoking, stretched out at ease in the deserted dressing-room.

Vandover went up to Turner Ravis smiling and holding out his hand. She seemed to be curiously embarrassed when she saw him, and did not smile back at him. He asked to see her card, but she drew her hand quickly from his, telling him that she was going home early and was not dancing at all, that in fact she had to "receive" instead of dance. It was evident to Vandover that he had done something to displease her, and he quickly concluded that it was because he had not asked her to go with him that evening.

He turned from her to Henrietta Vance as though nothing unusual had happened, resolving to see her later in the evening and in the meanwhile invent some suitable excuse. Henrietta Vance did not even see his hand; she was a very jolly girl, ordinarily, and laughed all the time. Now she looked him squarely in the face without so much as a smile, at once angry and surprised; never had anything seemed so hateful and disagreeable. Vandover put his hand back into his pocket, trying to carry it all off with a laugh, saying in order to make her laugh with him as he used to do, "Hello! how do you do this evening? It's a pleasant morning this afternoon." "How do you do?" she answered nervously, refusing to laugh. Then she turned from him abruptly to talk to young Haight's little cousin Hetty.

Mrs. Vance was neither embarrassed nor nervous as the girls had been. She stared calmly at Vandover and said with a peculiar smile, "I am surprised to see you here, Mr. Vandover."

An hour later the dance was in full swing. Almost every number was a waltz or a two-step, the music being the topical songs and popular airs of the day set to dance music.

About half-past ten o'clock, between two dances, the cornet sounded a trumpet call; the conversation ceased in a moment, and Henrietta Vance's brother, standing by the piano, called out, "The next dance will be the *first extra*," adding immediately, "a *waltz*." The dance recommenced; in the pauses of the music one heard the rhythmic movement of the feet shuffling regularly in one-two-three time.

Some of the couples waltzed fast, whirling about the rooms, bearing around corners with a swirl and swing of silk skirts, the girls' faces flushed and perspiring, their eyes half-closed, their bare, white throats warm, moist, and alternately swelling and contracting with their quick breathing. On certain of these girls the dancing produced a peculiar effect. The continued motion, the whirl of the lights, the heat of the room, the heavy perfume of the flowers, the cadence of the music, even the physical fatigue, reacted in some strange way upon their oversensitive feminine nerves, the monotony of repeated sensation producing some sort of mildly hypnotic effect, a morbid hysterical pleasure the more exquisite because mixed with pain. These were the girls whom one heard declaring that they could dance all night, the girls who could dance until they dropped.

Other of the couples danced with the greatest languor and gravity, their arms held out rigid and at right angles with their bodies.

About the doors and hallways stood the unhappy gentlemen who knew no one, watching the others dance, feigning to be amused. Some of them, however, had ascended to the dressing-room and began to strike up an acquaintance with each other and with Ellis, smoking incessantly, discussing business, politics, and even religion.

In the ladies' dressing-room two of the maids were holding a long conversation in low tones, their heads together;

evidently it was concerning something dreadful.   They
continually exclaimed "Oh!" and "Ah!" suddenly sitting
back from each other, shaking their heads, and biting their
nether lips.   On the top floor in the hall the servants in
their best clothes leaned over the balustrade, nudging each
other, talking in hoarse whispers or pointing with thick
fingers swollen with dish-water.   All up and down the
stairs were the couples who were sitting out the dance,
some of them even upon the circular sofa in the hall
over the first landing.

The music stopped, leaving a babel of talk in the air, the
couples fell apart for an instant, but a great clapping of
hands broke out and the tired musicians heroically recommenced.

As soon as the short *encore* was done there was a rush
for the lemonade and punch bowls.   The guests thronged
around them joking each other.   "Hello! are you here
again?"   "Oh, this is dreadful!"   "This makes *six*
times I've seen you here."

A smell of coffee rose into the air from the basement.
It was about half-past eleven; the next dance was the supper dance and the gentlemen hurried about anxiously
searching the stairs, the parlours, and the conservatory
for the girls who had promised them this dance weeks before.
The musicians were playing a march, and the couples
crowded down the narrow stairs in single file, the ladies
drawing off their gloves.   The tired musicians stretched
themselves, rubbed their eyes, and began to talk aloud
in the deserted parlours.

Supper was served in the huge billiard-room in the basement and was eaten in a storm of gayety.   The same

parties and "sets" tried to get together at the same table; Henrietta Vance's party was particularly noisy: at her table there was an incessant clamour of screams and shouts of laughter.   One ate oysters *à la poulette*, terrapin-salads, and croquettes; the wines were Sauternes and champagnes.   With the nuts and dessert the caps came on, and in a few minutes were cracking and snapping all over the room.

Six of the unfortunates who knew no one, but who had managed through a common affliction to become acquainted with each other, gathered at a separate table. Ellis was one of their number; he levied a twenty-five assessment, and tipped the waiter a dollar and a half. This one accordingly brought them extra bottles of champagne in which they found consolation for all the *ennui* of the evening.

After supper the dancing began again.   The little stiffness and constraint of the earlier part of the evening was gone; by this time nearly everybody, except the unfortunates, knew everybody else.   The good dinner and the champagne had put them all into an excellent humour, and they all commenced to be very jolly.   They began a Virginia Reel still wearing the magician's caps and Phrygian bonnets of tissue paper.

Young Haight was with Turner Ravis as much as possible during the evening, very happy and excited.   Something had happened; it was impossible for him to say precisely what, for on the face of things Turner was the same as ever.   Nothing in her speech or actions was different, but there was in her manner, in the very air that surrounded her, something elusive and subtle that set him all in a tremor. There was a change in his favour; he felt that she liked to have him with her and that she was trying to have him feel as much in some mysterious way of her own. He could see, however, that she was hardly conscious of doing this and that the change was more apparent to his eyes than it was to hers.

"Must you really go home now?" he said, as Turner began to talk of leaving, soon after supper. They had been sitting out the dance under a palm at the angle of the stairs.

"Yes," answered Turner; "Howard has the measles and I promised to be home early. Delphine was to come for me and she ought to be here now."

"Delphine?" exclaimed young Haight. "Didn't you come with Van?"

"No," answered Turner quietly. Only by her manner, and by something in the way she said the word, Haight knew at once that she had broken definitely with Vandover. The talk he had had with her at her house came back to him on the instant. He hesitated a moment and then asked:

"There is something wrong? Has Van done anything — never mind, I don't mean that; it's no business of mine, I suppose. But I know you care for him. I'm sorry if —— "

But he was not sorry. Try as he would, his heart was leaping in him for joy. With Vandover out of the way, he knew that all would be different; Turner herself had said so.

"Oh, everything is wrong," said Turner, with tears in her eyes. "I have been so disappointed in Van; oh, terribly disappointed."

"I know; yes, I think I know what you mean," answered young Haight in a low voice.

"Oh, please don't let's talk about it at all," cried Turner. But young Haight could not stop now.

"Is Van really out of the question, then?" he asked.

"Oh, yes," she exclaimed, not seeing what he was coming to. "Oh, yes; how could I — how *could* I care for him after — after what has happened?"

Very much embarrassed, young Haight went on: "I know it's unfair to take advantage of you now, but do you remember what you said once? That if Vandover were out of the question, that '*perhaps*' you might — that it would be — that there might be a chance for me?"

Turner was silent for a long time, and then she said: "Yes, I remember."

"Well, how about that *now?*" asked young Haight with a nervous laugh.

"Ah," answered Turner, "how do I know — so soon!"

"But what do you *think*, Turner?" he persisted.

"But I haven't thought at all," she returned.

"Well, think now!" he went on. "Tell me — how about that?"

"About *what?*"

"Ah, you know what I mean," young Haight replied, feeling like a little boy, "about what you said at your house that Sunday night. Please tell me; you don't know how much it means to me."

"Oh, there's Delphine at the door!" suddenly exclaimed Turner. "Now, really, I *must* go down. She doesn't know where to go; she's so stupid!"

"No," he answered, "not until you tell me!" He caught her hand, refusing to let it go.

"Ah, how mean you are to corner me so!" she cried laughing and embarrassed. "Must I — well —— I know I shouldn't. *O-oh*, I just *detest* you!" Young Haight turned her hand palm upward and kissed the little circle of crumpled flesh that showed where her glove buttoned. Then she tore her hand away and ran downstairs, while he followed more slowly.

On her way back to the dressing-room she met him again, crossing the hall.

"Don't you want to see me home?" she said.

"Do I *want* to?" shouted young Haight.

"Oh, but I forgot," she cried. "You can't. I won't let you. You have your other dances engaged!"

"Oh, damn the other dances!" he exclaimed, but instead of being offended, Turner only smiled.

Toward one o'clock there was a general movement to go. Henrietta Vance and Mrs. Vance were inquired for, and the blue and white opera cloaks reappeared, descending the stairs, disturbing the couples who were seated there. The banging of carriage doors and the rumble of wheels recommenced in the street. The musicians played a little longer. As the party thinned out, there was greater dance room and a consequent greater pleasure in dancing. These last dances at the end of the evening were enjoyed more than all the others. But the party was breaking up fast: Turner had already gone home; Mrs. Vance and Henrietta were back at their places in front of the mantel, surrounded by a group of gentlemen in cape-coats and ladies in opera wraps. Every one was crying "Good-bye"

or "Good night!" and assuring Mrs. Vance and Henrietta
of the enjoyableness of the occasion. Suddenly the musicians played "Home Sweet Home." Those still dancing
uttered an exclamation of regret, but continued waltzing
to this air the same as ever. Some began to dance again
in their overcoats and opera wraps. Then at last the tired
musicians stopped and reached for the cases of their instruments, and the remaining guests, seized with a sudden
panic lest they should be the last to leave, fled to the dressing-rooms. These were in the greatest confusion, every
one was in a hurry; in the gentlemen's dressing-room there
was a great putting on of coats and mufflers and a searching for misplaced gloves, hats and canes A base hum of
talk rose in the air, bits and ends of conversation being
tossed back and forth across the room. "*You* haven't
seen my hat, have you, Jimmy?" ' Did you meet that
girl I was telling you about?" "Hello, old man! have a
good time to-night?" "Lost your hat? No, I haven't
seen it." "Yes, about half-past ten!" "Well, I told him
that myself!" "Ah, you bet it's the man that rustles
that gets there." "Come round about four, then."
"What's the matter with coming home in *our* carriage?"

At the doors of the dressing-rooms the ladies joined
their escorts, and a great crowd formed in the halls, worm-
ing down the stairs and out upon the front steps. As the
first groups reached the open air there was a great cry:
"Why, it's pouring rain!" This was taken up and
repeated and carried all the way back into the house.
There were exclamations of dismay and annoyance:
"Why, it's raining right *down*!" "What *shall* we do!"
Tempers were lost, brothers and sisters quarrelling with

each other over the question of umbrellas. "Ah," said
Geary, delighted, peeling the cover from his umbrella in
the vestibule, "I *thought* it was going to rain before I
left and brought mine along with me. Ah, you bet I
always look out for rain!" On the horse-block stood the
caller, chanting up the carriages at the top of his voice.
The street was full of coupés, carriages, and hacks, the
raindrops showing in a golden blur as they fell across the
streaming light of their lamps. The horses were smoking
and restless, and the drivers in oilskins and rubber blankets were wrangling and shouting. At every instant there
was a long roll of wheels interrupted by the banging of the
doors. Near the caller stood a useless policeman, his
shield pinned on the outside of his wet rubber coat, on
which the carriage lamps were momentarily reflected in
long vertical streaks.

In a short time all the guests were gone except the one
young lady whose maid and carriage had somehow not
been sent. Henrietta Vance's brother took this one home
in a hired hack. Mrs. Vance and Henrietta sat down to
rest for a moment in the empty parlours. The canvas-
covered floors were littered with leaves of smilax and La
France roses, with bits of ribbon, ends of lace, and discarded Phrygian bonnets of tissue paper. The butler
and the second girl were already turning down the gas
in the other rooms.

Long before the party broke up Vandover had gone
home, stunned and dazed, as yet hardly able to realize
the meaning of what had happened. Some strange and
dreadful change had taken place; things were different,

people were different to him; not every one had been so outspoken as Turner, Henrietta Vance and her mother, but even amongst others who had talked to him politely and courteously enough, the change was no less apparent. It was in the air, a certain vague shrinking and turning of the shoulder, a general atmosphere of aversion and repulsion, an unseen frown, an unexpressed rebuff, intangible, illusive, but as unmistakable as his own existence. The world he had known knew him now no longer. It was ostracism at last.

But why? Why? Sitting over his tiled flamboyant stove, brooding into the winking coals, Vandover asked himself the question in vain. He knew what latitude young men were allowed by society; he was sure nothing short of discovered crime could affect them. True enough he had at one time allowed himself to drift into considerable dissipation, but he was done with that now, he had reformed, he had turned over a new leaf. Even at his worst he had only lived the life of the other young men around him, the other young men who were received as much as ever, even though people, the girls themselves, practically knew of what they did, knew that they were often drunk, and that they frequented the society of abandoned women. What had he done to merit this casting off? What *could* he have done? He even went so far as to wonder if there was anything wrong about his father or his sudden death.

A little after one o'clock he heard Geary's whistle in the street outside. "Hello, old man!" he cried as Vandover opened the window. "I was just on my way home from the hoe-down; saw a light in your window and

thought I'd call you up.   Say, have you got anything wet
up there?   I'm extra dry."

"Yes," said Vandover, "come on up!"

"Did you hear what Beale said to me this evening?"
said Geary, as he mixed himself a cocktail at the sideboard.
"Oh, I tell you, I'm getting right in, down at that office.
Beale wants me to take the place of one of the assistants
in the firm, a fellow who's got the consumption, coughing
up his lungs all the time.   It's an important place, hundred a month; that's right.   Yes, sir; you bet, I'm going
to get in and rustle now and make myself so indispensable
in that fellow's place that they can't get along without me.
I'll crowd him right out; I know it may be selfish, but,
damn it! that's what you have to do to get along.   It's
human nature.   I'll tell you right here to-night," he exclaimed with sudden energy, clenching his fist and slowly
rapping the knuckles on the table to emphasize each word,
"that I'll be the head of that firm some day, or I'll know
the reason why."

When Geary finally became silent, the two looked into
the fire for some time without speaking.   At last Geary
said:

"You came home early to-night, didn't you?"

"Yes," answered Vandover, stirring uneasily.   "Yes,
I did."

There was another silence.   Then Geary said abruptly:
"It's too bad.   They are kind of stinky-pinky to you."

"Yes," said Vandover with a grin.   "*I* don't know
what's the matter.   Everybody seems nasty!"

"It's that business with Ida Wade, you know," replied
Geary.   "It got around somehow that she killed herself

on your account. Everybody seems to be on to it. I
heard it — oh, nearly a month ago."

"Oh," said Vandover with a short laugh, "that's it, is
it? I was wondering."

"Yes, that's it," answered Geary. "You see they
don't know for sure; no one *knows*, but all at once every
one seemed to be talking about it, and they suspect an
awful lot. I guess they are pretty near right, aren't
·they?" He did not wait for an answer, but laughed
clumsily and went on: "You see, you always have to be
awfully careful in those things, or you'll get into a box.
Ah, you bet I don't let any girl *I* go with know *my* last
name or *my* address if I can help it. I'm clever enough
for that; you have to manage very carefully; ah, you bet!
You ought to have looked out for that, old man!" He
paused a moment and then went on: "Oh, I guess it will
be all right, all right, in a little while. They will forget
about it, you know. I wouldn't worry. I guess it will
be all right."

"Yes," answered Vandover absently, "I guess so — perhaps."

A few days later Vandover was in the reading-room of
the Mechanics Library, listlessly turning over the pages
of a volume of *l'Art*. It was Saturday morning and the
place was full of ladies who were downtown for their shopping and marketing, and who had come in either to change
their books or to keep appointments with each other. On
a sudden Vandover saw Turner just passing into the
Biography alcove. He got up and followed her. She
was standing at the end of the dim book-lined tunnel,
searching the upper shelves, her head and throat bent back,

and her gloved finger on her lip.   The faint odour of the
perfume she always affected came to him mingled with
the fragrance of the jonquils at her belt and the smell of
leather and of books that exhaled from the shelves on
either side.   He did not offer to take her hand, but came
up slowly, speaking in a low voice.

It was the last time that Vandover ever met Turner
Ravis.   They talked for upward of an hour, leaning
against the opposite book-shelves, Vandover with his
fists in his pockets, his head bent down, and the point of
his shoe tracing the pattern in the linoleum carpet; Turner,
her hands clasped in front of her, looking him squarely
in the face, speaking calmly and frankly.

"Now, I hope you see just how it is, Van," she said at
length.   "What has happened hasn't made me cease to
care for you, because if I had really cared for you the way
I thought I did, the way a girl ought to care for the man
she wants to marry, I would have stood by you through
everything, no matter what you did.   I don't do so now,
because I find I don't care for you as much as I thought
I did.   What has happened has only shown me that.   I'm
sorry, oh, so sorry to be disappointed in you, but it's because I only think of you as being once a very good friend
of mine, not because I love you as you think I did.   Once
— a long time ago — when we first knew each other, then,
perhaps — things were different then.   But somehow we
seem to have grown away from that.   Since then we have
both been mistaken; you thought I cared for you in that
way, and I thought so, too, and I thought you cared for
me; but it was only that we were keeping up appearances,
pretending to ourselves just for the sake of old times.

We don't love each other now; you know it.   But I have
never intentionally deceived you or tried to lead you on;
when I told you I cared for you I really thought I did.   I
meant to be sincere; I always thought so until this happened, and then when I saw how easily I could let you go,
it only proved to me that I did not care for you as I
thought I did.   It was wrong of me, I know, and I should
have known my own mind before, but I didn't, I didn't.
You talk about Dolly Haight; but it is not Dolly Haight
at all who has changed my affection for you.   I will be just
as frank as I can with you, Van.   I may learn really to
love Dolly Haight; I don't know, I think perhaps I will,
but it isn't that I care for him *just* because I don't care for
you.   Can't you see, it's just as if I had never met you.
You know it's very hard for me to say this to you, Van,
and I suppose it's all mixed up, but I can't help it.   You
don't know how sorry I am, because we have been such
old friends — because I really did care for you as a friend;
it's a proof of it, that there is no other man in the world
I could talk to like this.   I think, too, Van, that was the
only way you cared for me, just as a good friend — except
perhaps at first, when we first knew each other.   You
know yourself that is so.   We really haven't loved each
other at all for a long time, and now we have found it out
before it was too late.   And even if everything were different, Van, don't you know how it is with girls?   They
really love the man who loves them the most.   Half the
time they're just in love with being loved.   That's the
way most girls love nowadays, and you know yourself,
Van, that Dolly Haight really loves me more than you do."
She gathered up her books and went on after a pause,

straightening up, ready to go: "If I should let myself think of what you have done, I feel — as if — as if — why, dreadful—I — that I should hate you, loathe you; but I try not to do that. I have been thinking it all over since the other night. I shall always try to think of you at your best; I have tried to forget everything else, and in forgetting it I forgive you. I can honestly say that," she said, holding out her hand, "I forgive you, and you must forgive me because once, by deceiving myself, I deceived you, and made you think that I cared for you in that way when I didn't." As their hands fell apart Turner faced him and added, with tears in her eyes: "You know this must be good-bye for good. You don't know how it hurts me to tell you. I know it looks as if I were deserting you when you were alone in the world and had most need of some one to influence you for the good. But, Van, won't you be better now? Won't you break from it all and be your own self again? I have faith in you. I believe it's in you to become a great man and a good man. It isn't too late to begin all over again. Just be your better self; live up to the best that's in you; if not for your own sake, then for the sake of that other girl that's coming into your life some time; that other girl who is good and sweet and pure, whom you will really, really love and who will really, really love you."

All the rest of that month Vandover was wretched. So great was his shame and humiliation over this fresh disaster that he hardly dared to show himself out of doors. His grief was genuine and it was profound. Yet he took his punishment in the right spirit. He did not blame any

one but himself; it was only a just retribution for the
thing he had done. Only what made it hard to bear was
the fact that the chastisement had fallen upon him long
after he had repented of the crime, long after he had
resolved to lead a new and upright life; but with shut
teeth he determined still to carry out that resolve; he would
devote all his future life to living down the past. It might
be hard; it might be one long struggle through many,
many years, but he would do it. Ah, yes, he would show
them; they had cast him off, but he would go away to
Paris now as he had always intended. As invariably
happened when he was deeply moved, he turned to his
art, blindly and instinctively. He would go to Paris now
and study his paintings, five, ten years, and come back at
last a great artist, when these same people who had cast
him off would be proud to receive him. Turner was right
in saying that he had in him the making of a great man.
He *knew* that she was right; knew that if he only gave the
better part of him, the other Vandover, the chance, that
he would become a great artist. Well, he would do so, and
then when he came back again, when all the world was at
his feet, and there were long articles in the paper announcing his arrival, these people would throng around him; he
would show them what a great and noble nature he really
had; he would forgive them; he would ignore what they
had done. He even dramatized a little scene between
himself and Turner, then Mrs. Haight. They would
both be pretty old then and he would take her children
on his lap and look at her over their heads — he could
almost see those heads, white, silky and very soft — and
he would nod at her thoughtfully, and say, "Well, I have

taken your advice, do you remember?" and she was to answer, "Yes, I remember." There were actually tears in his eyes as he saw the scene.

At the very first he thought that he could not live without Turner; that he loved her too much to be able to give her up. But in a little while he saw that this was not so. She was right, too, in saying that he had long since outlived his first sincere affection for her. He had felt for a long time that he did not love her well enough to marry her; that he did not love her as young Haight did, and he acknowledged to himself that this affair at least had ended rightly. The two loved each other, he could see that; at last he even told himself that he would be glad to see Turner married to Dolly Haight, who was his best friend. But for all that, it came very hard at first to give up Turner altogether; never to see her or speak to her again.

As the first impressions of the whole affair grew dull and blunt by the lapse of time, this humble penitential mood of Vandover's passed away and was succeeded by a feeling of gloomy revolt, a sullen rage at the world that had cast him off *only* because he had been found out. He thought it a matter of self-respect to resent the insult they had put upon him. But little by little he ceased to regret his exile; the new life was not so bad as he had at first anticipated, and his relations with the men whom he knew best, Ellis, Geary, and young Haight, were in nowise changed. He was no longer invited anywhere, and the girls he had known never saw him when he passed them on the street. It was humiliating enough at first, but he got used to it after a while, and by dint of thrusting the disagreeable subject from his thoughts, by refusing to let

the disgrace sink deep in his mind, by forgetting the whole
business as much as he could, he arrived after a time to be
passably contented.   His pliable character had again rearranged itself to suit the new environment.

Along with this, however, came a sense of freedom.
Now he no longer had anything to fear from society; it
had shot its bolt, it had done its worst, there was no longer
anything to restrain him, now he could do anything.

He was in precisely this state of mind when he received
the cards for the opening of the roadhouse, the "resort"
out on the Almshouse drive, about which Toby, the waiter
at the Imperial, had spoken to him.

Vandover attended it.   It was a debauch of forty-eight
hours, the longest and the worst he had ever indulged in.
For a long time the brute had been numb and dormant;
now at last when he woke he was raging, more insatiable,
more irresistible than ever.

The affair at the roadhouse was but the beginning.
All at once Vandover rushed into a career of dissipation,
consumed with the desire of vice, the perverse, blind, and
reckless desire of the male.   Drunkenness, sensuality, gambling, debauchery, he knew them all.   He rubbed elbows
with street walkers, with bookmakers, with saloonkeepers,
with the exploiters of lost women.   The bartenders
of the city called him by his first name, the policemen, the night detail, were familiar with his face, the
drivers of the nighthawks recognized his figure by the
street lamps, paling in the light of many an early dawn.
At one time and another he was associated with all the
different types of people in the low "sporting set," acquaintances of an evening, whose names grew faint to

his recollection amidst the jingle of glasses and the popping of corks, whose faces faded from his memory in the
haze of tobacco smoke and the fumes of whisky; young
men of the city, rich without apparent means of livelihood,
women and girls "recently from the East" with rooms
over the fast restaurants; owners of trotting horses,
actresses without engagements, billiard-markers, pool-
sellers and the sons of the proprietors of halfway houses
and "resorts." With all these Vandover kept the pace at
the Imperial, at the race-track, at the gambling tables in
the saloons and bars along Kearney and Market streets,
and in the disreputable houses amid the strong odours of
musk and the rustle of heavy silk dresses. It lasted for a
year; by the end of that time he had about forgotten his
determination to go to Paris and had grown out of touch
with his three old friends, Ellis, Geary, and Haight. He
seldom saw them now; occasionally he met them in one
of the little rooms of the Imperial over their beer and
Welsh rabbits, but now he always went on to the larger
rooms where one had champagne and terrapin. He felt
that he no longer was one of them.

That year the opera came to San Francisco, and Vandover hired a messenger boy to stand in line all night at
the door of the music store where the tickets were to be
sold. Vandover could still love music. In the wreckage
of all that was good that had been going on in him his love
for all art was yet intact. It was the strongest side of his
nature and it would be the last to go.

CHAPTER FOURTEEN

THE house was crowded to the doors; there was no longer any standing room and many were even sitting on the steps of the aisles. In the boxes the gentlemen were standing up behind the chairs of large plain ladies in showy toilets and diamonds. The atmosphere was heavy with the smell of gas, of plush upholstery, of wilting bouquets and of sachet. A fine vapour as of the visible exhalation of many breaths pervaded the house, blurring the lowered lights and dimming the splendour of the great glass chandelier.

It was warm to suffocation, a dry, irritating warmth that perspiration did not relieve, while the air itself was stale and close as though fouled by being breathed over and over again. In the topmost galleries, banked with tiers of watching faces, the heat must have been unbearable.

The only movement perceptible throughout the audience was the little swaying of gay-coloured fans like the balancing of butterflies about to light. Occasionally there would be a vast rustling like the sound of wind in a forest, as the holders of librettos turned the leaves simultaneously.

The orchestra thundered; the French horns snarling, the first violins wailing in unison, while all the bows went up and down together like parts of a well-regulated machine; the kettle-drums rolled sonorously at exact intervals, and now and then one heard the tinkling of the harp like the pattering of raindrops between peals of thunder. The leader swayed from side to side in his place, beating time with his baton, his hand, and his head.

On the stage itself the act was drawing to a close. There had just been a duel. The baritone lay stretched upon the floor at left centre, his sword fallen at some paces from him. On the left of the scene, front, stood the tenor who had killed him, singing in his highest register, very red in the face, continually striking his hand upon his breast and pointing with his sword toward his fallen enemy. Next him on the extreme left was his friend the basso, in high leather boots, growling from time to time during a sustained chord, "*Mon honneur et ma foi.*" In the centre of the stage, the soprano, the star, the prima donna chanted a fervid but ineffectual appeal to the tenor who cried, "*Jamais, jamais!*" striking his breast and pointing with his sword. The prima donna cried, "*Ah, mon Dieu, ayez pitié de moi.*" Her confidante, the mezzo-soprano, came to her support, repeating her words with an impersonal meaning, "*Ayez pitié d'elle.*" "*Mon honneur et ma foi,*" growled the basso. The contralto, dressed as a man, turned toward the audience on the extreme right, bringing out her notes with a wrench and a twist of her body and neck, and intoning, "*Ah, malheureuse!   Mon Dieu, ayez pitié d'elle.*"

The leader of the chorus, costumed as the captain of the watch, leaned over the dead baritone and sang, "*Il est mort, il est mort.   Mon Dieu, ayez pitié de lui.*" The soldiers of the watch were huddled together immediately back of him. They wore tin helmets, much too large, and green peplums, and repeated his words continually.

The chorus itself was made up of citizens of the town; it was in a semicircle at the back of the stage — the men on one side, the women on the other. They made all their gestures together and chanted without ceasing: "*O horreur, O mystére! Il est mort. Mon Dieu, ayez pitié de nous!*"

"*De Grace!*" cried the prima donna.

"*Jamais, jamais!*" echoed the tenor, striking his breast and pointing with his sword.

"*O mystére!*" chanted the chorus, while the basso struck his hand upon his sword hilt, growling "*Mon honneur et ma foi.*"

The orchestra redoubled. The finale began; all the pieces of the orchestra, all the voices on the stage, commenced over again very loud. They all took a step forward, and the rhythm became more rapid, till it reached a climax where the prima donna's voice jumped to a C in alt, holding it long enough for the basso to thunder, "*Mon honneur et ma foi*" twice. Then they all struck the attitudes for the closing tableau and in one last burst of music sang all together, "*Mon Dieu, ayez pitié de moi*" and "*de lui*" and "*d'elle*" and "*de nous.*" Then the orchestra closed with a long roll of the kettle-drums, and the prima donna fainted into the arms of her confidante. The curtain fell.

There was a roar of applause. The gallery whistled and stamped. Every one relaxed his or her position, drawing a long breath, looking about. There was a general stir; the lights in the great glass chandelier clicked and blazed up, and a murmur of conversation arose.   The footlights were lowered and the orchestra left their places and disappeared underneath the stage, leaving the audience with the conviction that they had gone out after beer.   All over the house one heard the shrill voices of boys crying out, "Op'ra books — books for the op'ra — words and music for the op'ra."

Throughout the boxes a great coming and going took place and an interchange of visits.   The gentlemen out in the foyer stood about conversing in groups or walked up and down smoking cigarettes, often pausing in front of the big floral piece that was to be given to the prima donna at the end of the great scene in the fourth act.

There was a little titter of an electric bell.   The curtain was about to go up, and a great rush for seats began.   The orchestra were coming back and tuning up.   They sent up a prolonged medley of sounds, little minor chirps and cries from the violins, liquid runs and mellow gurgles from the oboes, flutes, and wood-wind instruments, and an occasional deep-toned purring from the bass viols.   A bell rang faintly from behind the wings, the house lights sank, and the footlights blazed up.   The leader tapped with his baton; a great silence fell upon the house, while here and there one heard an energetic "Ssh! ssh!"   The fourth act was about to begin.

When the curtain rose on the fourth act one saw the prima donna standing in a very dejected pose in the midst of a vast apartment that might have been a bedchamber, a council hall, or a hall of audience.   She was alone.   She wore a loose cream-coloured gown knotted about the waist; her arms were bare, and her hair unbound and flow-

ing loose over her shoulders to her girdle.   She was to die
in this act; it promised to be harrowing; and the first few
notes she uttered recurred again later on as the motif for
the famous quartet in the "great scene."

But for all this, the music had little by little taken possession of Vandover, and little by little he had forgotten his
surroundings, the stifling air of the house, the blinding
glitter of the stage and the discomfort of his limbs cramped
into the narrow orchestra chair.   All music was music to
him; he loved it with an unreasoned, uncritical love, enjoying even the barrel organs and hand pianos of the
streets.   For the present the slow beat and cadence of the
melodies of the opera had cradled all his senses, carrying
him away into a kind of exalted dream.   The quartet
began; for him it was wonderfully sweet, the long-sus-
tained chords breathing over the subdued orchestral
accompaniment, like some sweet south wind passing in
long sighs over the pulse of a great ocean.   It seemed to
him infinitely beautiful, infinitely sad, subdued minor
plaints recurring persistently again and again like sighs
of parting, but could not be restrained, like voices of regret
for the things that were never to be again.   Or it was a
pathos, a joy in all things good, a vast tenderness, so
sweet, so divinely pure that it could not be framed in
words, so great and so deep that it found its only expression in tears.   There came over him a vague sense of
those things which are too beautiful to be comprehended,
of a nobility, a self-oblivion, an immortal eternal love and
kindness, all goodness, all benignity, all pity for sin, all
sorrow for grief, all joy for the true, the right, and the pure.

To be better, to be true and right and pure, these were

the only things that were worth while, these were the things that he seemed to feel in the music. It was as if for the moment he had become a little child again, not ashamed to be innocent, ignorant of vice, still believing in all his illusions, still near to the great white gates of life.

The appeal had been made directly to what was best and strongest in Vandover, and the answer was quick and overpowering. All the good that still survived in him leaped to life again in an instant, clamouring for recognition, pleading for existence. The other Vandover, the better Vandover, wrestled with the brute in him once more, never before so strong, never so persistent. He had not yet destroyed all that was good in him; now it had turned in one more revolt, crying out against him, protesting for the last time against its own perversion and destruction. Vandover felt that he was at the great crisis of his life.

After all was over he walked home through the silent streets, proceeding slowly, his hands in his pockets, his head bent down, his mind very busy. Once in his rooms he threw off his things and, having stirred up the drowsing fire in the tiled stove, sat down before it in his shirt-sleeves, the bosom of his full dress shirt bulging from his vest and faintly creaking as from time to time he drew a long breath. He had been lured into a mood where he was himself at his very best, where the other Vandover, the better Vandover, drew apart with eyes turned askance, looking inward and downward into the depths of his own character, shuddering, terrified. Far down there in the darkest, lowest places he had seen the brute, squat, deformed, hideous; he had seen it crawling to and fro dimly, through a dark shadow he had heard it growling, chafing at the least restraint, restless to be free. For now at last it was huge, strong, insatiable, swollen and distorted out of all size, grown to be a monster, glutted yet still ravenous, some fearful bestial satyr, grovelling, perverse, horrible beyond words.

And with the eyes of this better self he saw again, little by little, the course of his whole life, and witnessed again the eternal struggle between good and evil that had been going on within him since his very earliest years. He was sure that at the first the good had been the strongest. Little by little the brute had grown, and he, pleasure-loving, adapting himself to every change of environment, luxurious, self-indulgent, shrinking with the shrinking of a sensuous artist-nature from all that was irksome and disagreeable, had shut his ears to the voices that shouted warnings of the danger, and had allowed the brute to thrive and to grow, its abominable famine gorged from the store of that in him which he felt to be the purest, the cleanest, and the best, its bulk fattened upon the rot and the decay of all that was good, growing larger day by day, noisome, swollen, poddy, a filthy inordinate ghoul, gorged and bloated by feeding on the good things that were dead.

Besides this he saw how one by one he had wrenched himself free from all those influences that had tended to foster and to cultivate all the better part of him.

First of all, long ago it seemed now, he had allowed to be destroyed that first instinctive purity, that fragile, delicate innocence which dies young in almost every human being, and that one sees evaporating under the earliest taint of vice with a smile partly of contempt, partly of pity, partly of genuine regret.

Next it had been his father. The Old Gentleman had exerted a great influence over Vandover; he had never forgotten that scene the morning after he had told him of his measure of responsibility in Ida Wade's suicide, the recovery from the first shock of dazed bewilderment and then the forgiveness, the solicitude and the encouragement to begin over again, to live it down and to do that which was right and good and true. Not only had he stopped his ears to this voice, but also, something told him, he had done much to silence it forever. Despite the Old Gentleman's apparent fortitude the blow must have carried home. What must he not have suffered during those long weeks while Vandover was away, what lonely broodings in the empty house; and then the news of the wreck, the days of suspense!

It all must have told; the Old Gentleman was not strong; Vandover could not but feel that he had hastened his death, and that in so doing he had destroyed another influence which would have cultivated and fostered his better self, would have made it strong against the attacks of the brute.

The other person who had helped to bring out all that was best in Vandover had been Turner Ravis. There was no denying that when he had first known her he had loved her sincerely. Things were vastly different with him when Turner had been his companion; things that were unworthy, that were low, that were impure and vicious, did not seem worth while then; not only did they have no attraction for him, but he even shunned and avoided them.

He knew he was a better man for loving her; invariably she made him wish to be better.   But little by little as he frequented the society of such girls as Ida Wade, Grace Irving, and Flossie, his affection for Turner faded.   As the habits of passionate and unhealthy excitement grew upon him he lost first the taste and then the very capacity for a calm, pure feeling.   His affection for her he frittered away with fast girls and abandoned women, strangled it in the foul musk-laden air of disreputable houses, dragged and defiled it in the wine-lees of the Imperial.   In the end he had quite destroyed it, wilfully, wantonly killed it. As Turner herself had said, she could only be in love with being loved; her affection for him had dwindled as well; at last they had come to be indifferent to each other, she no longer inspired him to be better, and thus he had shaken off this good influence as well.

Public opinion had been a great check upon him, the fear of scandal, the desire to stand well with the world he knew.   Trivial though he felt it to be, the dread of what people would say had to a great extent held Vandover back.   He had a position to maintain, a reputation to keep up in the parlours and at the dinner tables where he was received.   It could not be denied that society had influenced Vandover for good.   But this, too, like all the others, he had cast from him.   Now he was ostracized, society cared no longer what he did, his position was gone, his reputation was destroyed.   There was no one now to stand in his way.

Vandover could not fall back on any religious influence. Religion had never affected him very deeply.   It was true that he had been baptized, confirmed, and had gone

to church with considerable regularity. If he had been
asked if he was a Christian and believed in God he would
have answered "Certainly, certainly." Until the time
of his father's death he had even said his prayers every
night, the last thing before turning out the gas, sitting
upon the edge of his bed in his night-gown, his head in
both his hands. He added to the Lord's Prayer certain
other petitions as to those who were in trouble, sorrow,
poverty, or any other privations; he asked for blessings
upon his father and upon himself, praying for the former's
health and prosperity, and for himself, that he might become a great artist, that the "Last Enemy" might be
admitted to the Salon when he had painted it, and that
it might make him famous. But, as a rule, Vandover
thought very little about religious matters and when he
did, told himself that he was too intelligent to believe in a
literal heaven, a literal hell, and a personal God personally
interfering in human affairs like any Jove or Odin. But
the moment he rejected a concrete religion Vandover was
almost helpless. He was not mystic enough to find any
meaning in signs or symbols, nor philosophic enough to
grasp vague and immense abstractions. Infinities, Pres-
ences, Forces, could not help him withstand temptation,
could not strengthen him against the brute. He felt that
somewhere, some time, there was punishment for evildo-
ing, but, as happened in the case of Ida Wade's death, to
dwell on such thoughts disturbed and terrified him. He
did not dare to look long in that direction. Conscience,
remorse, repentance, all these had been keen enough at
first, but he had so persistently kicked against the pricks
that little by little he had ceased to feel them at all.

Then an immense and overwhelming terror seized upon him. Was there nothing, then — nothing left which he could lay hold of to save him? He knew that he could not deliver himself by his own exertions. Religion could not help him, he had killed his father, estranged the girl he might have loved, outraged the world, and at a single breath blighted the fine innate purity of his early years. It was as if he had entered into his life in the world as into some vast labyrinth, wandering on aimlessly, flinging from him one by one the threads, the clues, that might have led him again to a safe exit, going down deeper and deeper until, when near the centre, he had suddenly felt the presence of the brute, had heard its loathsome muttering growl, had at last seen it far down at the end of a passage, dimly and in a dark shadow; terrified, he had started back, looking wildly about for any avenue of escape, searching with frantic haste and eagerness for any one of those clues he had so carelessly cast from him, realizing that without such guidance he would inevitably tend down again to that fatal central place where the brute had its lair.

There was nothing, nothing. He clearly saw the fate toward which he was hurrying; it was not too late to save himself if he only could find help, but he could find *no* help. His terror increased almost to hysteria. It was one of those dreadful moments that men sometimes undergo that must be met alone, and that when past, remain in the memory for all time; a glimpse far down into the springs and wheels of life; a glimpse that does not come often lest the reason brought to the edge of the fearful gulf should grow dizzy at the sight, and reeling, topple headlong.

But suddenly Vandover rose to his feet, the tears came to his eyes, and with a long breath he exclaimed: "Thank God for it!"   He grew calmer in a moment, the crisis had passed, he had found a clue beneath his groping fingers.

He had remembered his art, turning to it instinctively as he always did when greatly moved.   This was the one good thing that yet survived.   It was the strongest side of him; it would be the last to go; he felt it there yet.   It was the one thing that could save him.

The thought had come to him so suddenly and with such marvellous clearness that in his present exalted state of mind it filled him with a vague sense of awe, it seemed like a manifestation, a writing on the wall.   Might it not be some sort of miracle?   He had heard of men reforming their lives, transformed almost in an instant, and had scoffed at the idea.   But might it not be true, after all?   What was this wonderful thing that had happened to him?   Was this less strange than a miracle?   Less divine?

The following day Vandover rented a studio.   It was the lofty room with hardwood floors and the immense north light in that suite which he had rejected when looking for rooms on the former occasion.   He gave notice to the clerk in the apartment house where his quarters were situated that he intended to vacate after the first of the month.   Charming as he had found these rooms, he gave up, with scarcely a regret, the idea of living in them any longer.   In a month it would be summer and he would be on his way to Paris.

But so great was his desire for work now, so eager was he to start the "Last Enemy," so strong was the new energy that shook him, that Vandover could not wait until summer to begin work again.   He grudged everything now that kept him away from his easel.

He disappeared from the sight of his ordinary companions; he did not even seek the society of Geary or of young Haight.   All the sketches he had made for the "Last Enemy," together with his easel and his disused palette, his colour-box, tubes, brushes and all the other materials and tools for his work, he caused to be transferred to the new studio.   Besides this he had the stretcher made, best twill canvas on a frame four feet long, two and a half feet high.   This was for the large sketch of the picture.   But the finished work he calculated would demand an eight by five stretcher.

He did not think of decorating the room, of putting any ornaments about the wall.   He was too serious, too much in earnest now to think of that.   The studio was not to be his lounging place, but his workshop.   His art was work with him now, hard, serious work.   It was above all *work* that he needed to set him right again, regular work, steady, earnest work, not the dilettante fancy of an amateur content with making pretty things.

Never in his life had Vandover been so happy.   He came and went continually between his rooms, his studio, and his art dealers, tramping grandly about the city, whistling to himself, strong, elated, filled with energy, vigour, ambition.   At times his mind was full of thankfulness at this deliverance at the eleventh hour; at times it was busy with the details of the picture, its composition, its colour scheme.   The main effects he wanted to produce were isolation and intense heat, the shadows on the sand would be blue, the horizon line high on the canvas, the sky would be light in tone, almost white near the earth.

The morning when he first began to work was charming. His new studio was in the top floor of a five-story building, and on arriving there, breathless from his long climb up the stairs, Vandover threw open the window and gazed out and down upon the city spread out below him, enjoying the view a moment before settling to his work.

A little later the trades would be blowing strong and brisk from the ocean, driving steadily through the Golden Gate, filling the city with a taint of salt; but at present the air was calm, touched with a certain nimbleness, a sparkling effervescence, invigourating, exhilarating.

It was early in the forenoon, not yet past nine o'clock, and the mist that gathers over the city just before dawn was steaming off under the sun, very thin and delicate, turning all distant objects a flat tone of pale blue. Over the roofs of the houses he could catch a glimpse of the distant mountains, faint purple masses against the pale edge of the sky, rimming the horizon round with a fillet of delicate colour. But any larger view was barred by a huge frame house with a slated mansard roof, directly opposite him across the street, a residence house, one of the few in the neighbourhood. It had been newly painted white and showed brave and gay against the dark blue of the sky and the ruddy greens of the great garden in which it stood. Vandover from his window could from time to time catch the smell of eucalyptus trees coming to him in long aromatic breaths mingled with the odour of wet grass and fresh paint. Somewhere he heard a humming-bird singing, a tiny tweedling thread of song, while farther off two roosters were crowing back and forth at each other with strained and raucous trumpet calls.

Vandover turned back to his work. Under the huge north light was the easel, and clamped upon it the stretcher, blank, and untouched. The very sight of the heavy cream-white twill was an inspiration. Already Vandover saw a great picture upon it; a great wave of emotion suddenly welled up within him and he cried with enthusiasm:

"By God! it is in moods like this that *chef d'oeuvres* are made."

Around the baseboard of the room were a row of *esquisses* for the picture, on small landscape-stretchers, mere blotches of colour laid on with the palette knife and large brushes, almost unintelligible to any one but Vandover. He selected two or three of these and fastened them to the easel above the big stretcher where he could have them continually in his eye. He lit his pipe, rolled up his shirt-sleeves, and standing before the easel, began to sharpen a stick of charcoal with an old razor, drawing the blade toward him so as to keep the point of the stick from breaking. Then at last with a deep breath of satisfaction he began blocking in the first large construction lines of his picture.

It was one o'clock before he knew it. He went downtown and had a hasty lunch, jealous of every moment that was not spent on his picture. The sight of it as he reentered the room sent a thrill all over him; he was succeeding better than he could have expected, doing better than he thought he would. He felt sure that now he should do good work; every stage of the picture's progress was an inspiration for the next one.   At this time the figures had only been "placed," broadly sketched in large lines, "blocked in" as he called it.   The next step was the second drawing, much more finished.

He rapped the stretcher sharply with his knuckles; it responded sonorously like a drumhead, the vibration shaking the charcoal from the tracings, filling the air with a fine dust.   The outlines grew faint, just perceptible enough to guide him in the second more detailed drawing.

He brought his stick of charcoal to a very fine edge and set to work carefully.   In a moment he stopped and, with his chamois cloth, dusted out what he had drawn.   He had made a false start, he began but could not recall how the lines should run, his fingers were willing enough; in his imagination he saw just how the outlines should be, but somehow he could not make his hand interpret what was in his head.   Some third medium through which the one used to act upon the other was sluggish, dull; worse than that, it seemed to be absent.   *"Well,"* he muttered, "can't I make this come out right?"   Then he tried more carefully.   His imagination saw the picture clearer, his hand moved with more assurance, but the two seemed to act independently of each other.   The forms he made on the canvas were no adequate reflection of those in his brain; some third delicate and subtle faculty that coördinated the other two and that called forth a sure and instant response to the dictates of his mind, was lacking.   The lines on his canvas were those of a child just learning to draw; one saw for what they were intended, but they were crude, they had no life, no meaning.   The very thing that would have made them intelligible, interpretive,

that would have made them art, was absent. A third,
a fourth, and a fifth time Vandover made the attempt.
It was useless. He knew that it was not because his
hand lacked cunning on account of long disuse; such a
thing, in spite of popular belief, never happened to artists
— a good artist might abandon his work for five years,
ten years — and take it up again precisely where he had
laid it down with no loss of technical skill. No, this thing
seemed more subtle, so subtle that at first he could hardly
grasp it. But suddenly a great fear came upon him, a
momentary return of that wild hysterical terror from
which he believed he had forever escaped.

"Is it gone?" he cried out. "Is it gone from me?
My art? Steady," he went on, passing his hand over his
face with a reassuring smile; "steady, old man, this won't
do, again — and so soon! It won't do for you to get
scared twice like that. This is just nervousness, you are
overexcited. Pshaw! What's the matter with me?
Let's get to work."

Still another time he dusted out what he had done and
recommenced, concentrating all his attention with a
tremendous effort of the will. Grotesque and meaningless
shapes, the mocking caricatures of those he saw in his
fancy, grew under his charcoal, while slowly, slowly, a
queer, numb feeling came in his head, like a rising fog,
and the touch of that unreasoning terror returned, this
time stronger, more persistent, more tenacious than before.

Vandover nerved himself against it, not daring to give
in, fearing to allow himself to see what this really meant.
He passed one hand over his cheek and along the side of
his head, the fingers dancing. "Hum!" he muttered,

looking vaguely about him, "this is bad. I mustn't let
this get the better of me now. I'll knock off for to-day,
take a little rest, begin again to-morrow."

In ten minutes he was back at his easel again. His
charcoal wandered, tracing empty lines on his canvas, the
strange numbness grew again in his head. All the objects
in the range of his eyes seemed to move back and stand
on the same plane. He became a little dizzy.

"It's the *tobacco*," he exclaimed. "That pipe always
was too strong." He turned away to the open window,
feeling an irresistible need of distraction, of amusement,
and he remained there resting on his elbows, listening and
looking, trying to be interested.

It was toward the middle of the afternoon. The morning mist was long since evaporated and the first faint puffs
of the inevitable trade wind were just stirring the leaves
of the eucalyptus across the street. In the music-room of
the white house the young lady of the family had opened
the piano and was practising finger-exercises. The scales
and arpeggios following one another without interruption,
came to his ears in a pleasant monotone. A Chinese
"boy" in a stiff blouse of white linen, made a great splashing as he washed down the front steps with a bucket of
water and the garden hose. Grocery and delivery wagons
came and went, rattling over the cobbles and car-tracks,
while occasionally a whistle blew very far off. At the
corner of the street by a livery-stable a little boy in a flat-
topped leather cap was calling incessantly for some unseen
dog, whistling and slapping his knees. An express-wagon
stopped a few doors below the white house and the driver
pulled down the back-board with a strident rattle of

chains; the cable in its slot kept up an unceasing burr and
clack while the cars themselves trundled up and down the
street, starting and stopping with a jangling of bells, the
jostled glass windows whirring in a prolonged vibrant
note. All these sounds played lightly over the steady
muffled roar that seemed to come from all quarters at
once; it was that deep murmur, that great minor diapason
that always disengages itself from vast bodies, from mountains, from oceans, from forests, from sleeping armies.

The desire for movement, for diversion, for anything
that would keep him from thinking was not to be resisted.
Vandover caught up his hat and fled from the room, not
daring to look again at the easel.   Once outside, he began
to walk, anywhere, straight before him, going on with
great strides, his head in the air.

He found Charlie Geary and took him to supper.   Vandover talked continually on all sorts of subjects, speaking
very rapidly.   In the evening he insisted on Geary going
to the theatre with him.   He paid the closest attention
to the play, letting it occupy his mind entirely.   When the
play was over and the two were about to say good night,
Vandover began to urge Geary to sleep up at his rooms
that night.   He overrode his objections, interrupting him,
taking hold of his arm, and starting off.   But Geary,
a little surprised at his manner, refused.   There were certain law papers he had taken home with him from the
office that afternoon and that it was necessary he should
return in the morning.   Ah, you bet, he would get it
right in the neck if old Beale didn't have those depositions
the first thing when the office was open.   Ah, he was getting to be indispensable down there.   He had had Fischer's

place now for a year. Fischer had never come back, and
he had the promise of being taken on as head clerk as
soon as Beale Jr. went into the partnership with old
Beale. "I'll make my way in this town yet," he declared.
"I'll be in that partnership myself some day.   You see;
yes, sir; ah, you bet!"

The idea of passing the night alone terrified Vandover.
He started toward home, walking up Sutter Street, proceeding slowly, his hands in his pockets. All at once he
stopped, without knowing why; he roused himself and
looked about him. There was a smell of eucalyptus in
the air. Across the street was the huge white house, and
he found that he had stopped just before the door of the
building on the top floor of which his studio was situated.
All day Vandover's mind had been in the greatest agitation, his ideas leaping and darting hither and thither like
terrified birds in a cage. Just now he underwent a sudden
reaction. It had all been a matter of fancy, nothing but
nervousness; he had not drawn for some time, his hand
lacked cunning from long disuse. The desire for work
came upon him again overpoweringly. He wanted to
see again if he could not draw just as truly and freely as
in the old days. No, he could not wait till morning; he
must put himself to the test again at once, at the very
instant. It was a sudden feminine caprice, induced, no
doubt, by the exalted, strained, and unnatural condition
of his nerves, a caprice that could not be reasoned with,
that could not be withstood. He had his keys with him,
he opened the outside door and groped his way up the four
long flights of stairs to his studio.

The studio was full of a sombre half-light, like a fog,

spreading downward from the great north light in the sloping roof. The window was still wide open, the stretcher showed a pale gray blur. Vandover was about to light the gas when he checked himself, his arm still raised above his head. Ah, no; he did not dare to look at the result of his day's work. It would be better to start in afresh from the beginning. He found the chamois skin on the tray of the easel and rubbed out all the drawing on the canvas. Then he lit the gas.

As he turned to his work once more a little thrill of joy and of relief passed over him. This time his hand was sure, steady, his head was clear. It had been nervousness after all. As he picked up his charcoal he even exclaimed to himself, "Just the same, that *was* a curious experience this afternoon."

But the curious experience repeated itself again that night as soon as he tried to work. Once more certain shapes and figures were born upon his canvas, but they were no longer the true children of his imagination, they were no longer his own; they were changelings, grotesque abortions. It was as if the brute in him, like some malicious witch, had stolen away the true offspring of his mind, putting in their place these deformed dwarfs, its own hideous spawn.

Through the numbness and giddiness that gradually came into his head like a poisonous murk he saw one thing clearly: It was gone — his art was gone, the one thing that could save him. That, too, like all the other good things of his life, he had destroyed. At some time during those years of debauchery it had died, that subtle, elusive something, delicate as a flower; he had ruined it. Little

by little it had exhaled away, wilting in the air of unre-
strained debauches, perishing in the warm musk-laden
atmosphere of disreputable houses, defiled by the breath
of abandoned women, trampled into the spilt wine-lees of
the Imperial, dragged all fouled and polluted through the
lowest mire of the great city's vice.

For a moment Vandover felt as though he was losing
his hold upon his reason; the return of the hysteria shook
him like a dry, light leaf.   He suddenly had a sensation
that the room was too small to hold him; he ran, almost
reeled, to the open window, drawing his breath deep and
fast, inhaling the cool night air, rolling his eyes wildly.

It was night.   He looked out into a vast blue-gray space
sown with points of light, winking lamps, and steady slow-
burning stars.   Below him was the sleeping city.   All
the lesser staccato noises of the day had long since died to
silence; there only remained that prolonged and sullen
diapason, coming from all quarters at once.   It was like
the breathing of some infinitely great monster, alive and
palpitating, the sistole and diastole of some gigantic heart.
The whole existence of the great slumbering city passed
upward there before him through the still night air in one
long wave of sound.

It was Life, the murmur of the great, mysterious force
that spun the wheels of Nature and that sent it onward
like some enormous engine, resistless, relentless; an engine
that sped straight forward, driving before it the infinite
herd of humanity, driving it on at breathless speed through
all eternity, driving it no one knew whither, crushing out
inexorably all those who lagged behind the herd and who
fell from exhaustion, grinding them to dust beneath its

myriad iron wheels, riding over them, still driving on the herd that yet remained, driving it recklessly, blindly on and on toward some far-distant goal, some vague unknown end, some mysterious, fearful bourne forever hidden in thick darkness.

CHAPTER FIFTEEN

About a week later Hiram Wade, Ida's father, brought suit against Vandover to recover twenty-five thousand dollars, claiming that his daughter had killed herself because she had been ruined by him and that he alone was responsible for her suicide.

Vandover had passed this week in an agony of grief over the loss of his art, a grief that seemed even sharper than that which he had felt over the death of his father. For this last calamity was like the death of a child of his, some dear, sweet child, that might have been his companion throughout all his life. At times it seemed to him impossible that his art should fail him in this manner, and again and again he would put himself at his easel, only to experience afresh the return of the numbness in his brain, the impotency of his fingers.

He had begun little by little to pick up the course of his life once more, and on a certain Wednesday morning was looking listlessly through the morning paper as he sat in his window-seat. The room was delightful, flooded with the morning sun, the Assyrian *bas-reliefs* just touched with a ruddy light, the Renaissance portraits looking down at him through a fine golden haze; a little fire, just enough to blunt the keenness of the early morning air, snapping in the famous tiled and flamboyant stove. All about the room was a pleasant fragrance of coffee and good tobacco.

Vandover caught sight of the announcement of the suit with a sudden sharp intake of breath that was half gasp, half cry, starting up from the window-seat, reading it over again and again with staring eyes.

It was a very short paragraph, not more than a dozen lines, lost at the bottom of a column, among the cheap advertisements. It made no allusion to any former stage of the affair; from its tone Ida might have killed herself only the day before. It seemed hardly more than a notice that some enterprising reporter, burrowing in the records at the City Hall, had unearthed and brought to light with the idea that it might be of possible interest to a few readers of the paper. But there was his name staring back at him from out the gray blur of the type, like some reflection of himself seen in a mirror. Insignificant as the paragraph was, it seemed to Vandover as though it was the only item in the whole paper. One might as well have trumpeted his crime through the streets.

"But twenty-five thousand dollars!" exclaimed Vandover, terrified. "Where will *I* find twenty-five thousand dollars?" And at once he fell to wondering as to whether or no in default of payment he could be sent to the penitentiary. The idea of winning the suit did not enter his mind an instant; he did not even dream of fighting it.

For the moment it was like fire driving out fire. He forgot the loss of his art, his mind filled only with the sense of the last disaster. What could he do? Twenty-five thousand dollars! It would ruin him. A cry of exasperation, of rage at his own folly, escaped him. "Ah, what a fool I've been!"

For an hour he raged to and fro in the delightful sunlit

room, pacing back and forth in its longest dimension between the bamboo tea-table and the low bookcase, a
thousand different plans and projects coming and going
in his head. As his wits steadied themselves he began to
see that he must consult at once with some lawyer —
Field, of course — perhaps something could be done; a
clever lawyer might make out a case for him after all.
But all at once he became convinced that Field would not
undertake his defence; he knew he had no case; so what
could Field do for him? He would have to tell him the
truth, and he saw with absolute clearness that the lawyer
would refuse to try to defend him. The thing could not
honourably be done. But, then, what *should* he do? He
must have legal advice from some quarter.

He was still in this state of perplexity when Charlie
Geary arrived, pounding on the door and opening it immediately afterward as was his custom.

"Hello!" said Vandover, surprised. "Hello, Charlie!
is that you?"

"Say," exclaimed Geary without returning his greeting,
holding up his hand as if to interrupt him; "say, have you
seen your lawyer yet — seen *any* lawyer?"

"No," answered Vandover, shaking his head gravely;
"no, I've only this minute read about it in the paper."
He was glad that Geary had come; at once he felt a desire
to throw this burden upon his chum's shoulders, to let
him assume the management of the affair, just as in the
old college days he had willingly, weakly, submitted to the
dictatorship of the shrewder, stronger man who smoothed
out his difficulties for him, and extricated him from all his
scrapes. He knew Geary to be full of energy and resource,

and he had confidence in his ability as a lawyer, even though he was so young in years and experience. Besides this, he was his friend, his college chum; for all Geary's disagreeable qualities he knew he would do the right thing by him now.

"You're the one man of all others I wanted to see," he exclaimed as he gripped his hand. "By George! I'm glad you have come. Here, sit down and let's talk this over." Geary took the big leather chair behind the desk, and Vandover flung himself again upon the window-seat. It was as if the two were back in the room in Matthew's; hundreds of times in those days they had occupied precisely these positions, Geary bending over at the study table, intent, nervous, very keen, Vandover lounging idly upon the window-seat, resting easily on his elbow listening to the other man's advice.

"Now, what must I do, Charlie?" Vandover began. "See my lawyer, I suppose? But do you think a lawyer like Field would take my case? You know I haven't a leg to stand on."

"But you haven't seen him?" inquired Geary sharply. "Haven't seen anybody about it?" Vandover shook his head. "Sure?" insisted Geary anxiously.

"Why, I have only just heard about it twenty minutes ago," protested Vandover. "Why are you so particular about that?" he added. Then Geary exploded his mine.

"Because," he said, with a smile of triumph that he could not restrain, "because we are the counsel for the other side. I am on the case."

Vandover bounded from the window-seat speechless with astonishment, bitterly disappointed. "*You?*" he

shouted. Geary slowly nodded his head, enjoying Vandover's bewilderment. Vandover dropped back upon the
cushions again, staring at him wildly with growing sus-
picion and anger. He would not have thought it possible
that Geary could so sacrifice their old friendship to his
own personal interest. The two continued staring at each
other across the table for a moment. In the silence they
heard the long rumble of a cable-car passing the house,
and the persistent jangling of its bell as it approached the
street crossing. A grocery wagon went up the side street,
the horses' hoofs making a cadenced clapping sound upon
the asphalt.

"Well," exclaimed Vandover scornfully, "I suppose
that's business, but *I* would call it damned unkind!"

"Now, look here, old man," returned Geary consolingly.
"Don't you take the monkey-wrench off the safety valve
like that. What am I here for if it isn't to help you?
Maybe you don't know that this is a mighty unprofessional
thing to do. Ah, you bet, if old Beale knew this I would
get it right in the neck. Don't you suppose I can help you
more as Wade's lawyer than I could as yours? And now
that's the very first thing I've got to tell you — to keep
this dark, that I have seen you. I can't do anything for
you if you don't promise that."

"Oh, that's all right," returned Vandover, reassured.
"That's all right, you can ——"

"It's not considered the right thing to do," Geary continued, not heeding Vandover's answer, "but I just do it
because" — he began to make awkward gestures with
both his hands — "because we're old friends, like that.
That was the very first thing I thought of when Beale Jr.

told me that we two had the case — that I could get you out of this hole better as Wade's lawyer than as your own. Ah, you bet, I was clever enough to see that the first thing."

"I'm sure it was awfully good of you, old man," said Vandover sincerely. "I'm in a lot of trouble nowadays!"

"Well, now don't you bother, Van," answered Geary consolingly. "I guess we can pull you out of this all right." He drew up to the table, looking about from side to side. "Got any writing paper concealed about the premises?" he asked. Vandover pushed him over his writing pad, and Geary, taking the cap from his fountain pen, began asking a series of questions, taking down his answers in shorthand. After he had asked him as to his age, length of residence in the city, his property, and some few other technical matters, he leaned back in his chair and said:

"Now, let's hear your side of the story, Van. I don't suppose you like to go over the thing again, but you see I ought to know." Vandover told of the affair, Geary making notes as he went along. It was nearly noon before their interview was at an end. Then Geary gathered up the papers and reached for his hat and stick, saying:

"Well, now, that's all we can do to-day. I think I'll be up to see you again day after to-morrow, in the afternoon. Beale Jr. and I have a date with Mr. Wade again to-morrow, I think, and I can talk to you more definitely after that. You know this is the devil of a thing to do," he suddenly exclaimed apprehensively, "this playing back and forth between the two parties like this; regularly dishonourable, don't you know?"

"If you think it's dishonourable," said Vandover as he accompanied Geary to the door, "if you think it's dishonourable, Charlie, why, don't do it! I don't want to ask you to do anything dishonourable for me."

"Oh, that's all right," replied Geary uneasily; "I had just as soon do it for you, only listen to this: don't you say a word about the case to anybody, not to your lawyer, nor to anybody. If Field should write to you, you tell him you have counsel already. And, look here! you may have the reporters up here pretty soon, and don't you open your face to them; you mind that; don't you let them get a thing out of you. And there's another thing you must understand: I'm not your lawyer, of course; you see that. I could be disbarred if I was lawyer for both sides. It's like this, you see: I'm Wade's lawyer — at least the firm I am with are his lawyers — and of course I'm acting in Wade's interest. But you're an old chum of mine, and if I can I'm going to try and make it easier for you. You understand, don't you?"

"Yes, I understand, Charlie," answered Vandover, "and you are just a brick."

Vandover passed the rest of the day in his sitting-room, the suspense of the situation slowly screwing his nerves tenser and tenser. He walked for hours back and forth, his hands clasped behind his back, his head bent down, his forehead drawn into a frown of anxiety and exasperation, or he stood for a long time at the window looking out into the street with eyes that saw nothing. At supper that night he found that his appetite had left him; the very thought of food revolted him. He returned to his room between seven and eight o'clock, his body and mind completely fagged, feeling a crying need of some diversion, some escape from the thoughts that had been hounding him all day.

He made up his mind to read a little before going to bed, and all at once remembered a book that he had once begun a long time ago but had never finished: the story of two men who had bought a wrecked opium ship for fifty thousand dollars and had afterward discovered that she contained only a few tins of the drug. He had never read on to find how that story turned out. Suddenly he found himself repeating, "Twenty-five thousand dollars, twenty-five thousand dollars — where will *I* find twenty-five thousand dollars?" He wondered if he would go to jail if he failed to pay. His interest in the book was gone in a moment, and he took up another of his favourite novels, the story of a boy at the time of Christ, a Jewish boy unjustly condemned to the galleys, liberated afterward, and devoting his life to the overthrow of his enemy, whom at last he overcame and humbled, fouling him in a chariot race, all but killing him.

He sat down in the huge leather chair, and, drawing it up to the piano lamp and cocking his feet upon the table, began to read. In a few moments the same numbness stole into his head like a rising fog, a queer, tense feeling, growing at the back of his forehead and at the base of his skull, a dulness, a strange stupefying sensation as of some torpid, murky atmosphere. He looked about him quickly; all the objects in the range of his vision — the corner of the desk, the corduroy couch, the low bookcase with Flossie's yellow slipper and Barye's lioness upon it — seemed to move back and stand upon the same plane; the objects themselves appeared immovable enough, but the sensation of them in his brain somewhere behind his eyes began to move about in a slow, dizzy whirl. The old touch of unreasoning terror came back, together with a sudden terror of the spirit, a sickening sinking of the heart, a loathing of life, terrible beyond words.

Vandover started up, striving to keep himself in hand, fighting against a wild desire to rush about from wall to wall, shrieking and waving his arms. Over and over again he exclaimed, "Oh, *what* is the matter with me?" The strangeness of the thing was what unsettled and unnerved him. He had all the sensations of terror, but without any assignable reason, and this groundless fear became in the end the cause of a new fear: he was afraid of this fear that was afraid of nothing.

Very gradually, however, the crisis passed away. He became a little calmer, and as he was mixing himself a glass of whisky and water at the sideboard he decided that he would go to bed. He was sure that he would be better for a good night's rest; evidently his nerves were out of order; it would not do for him to read late at night. He realized all at once that his mind and body alike were exhausted.

He passed a miserable night, dozing and waking at alternate hours until three o'clock, when he found it impossible to get to sleep; hour after hour he lay flat on his back staring open-eyed into the darkness, listening to the ticking of the clock, the mysterious footsteps that creaked the floors overhead, and the persistent drip of a water faucet. Outside in the street he heard at long intervals the rattling of wheels as the early milk wagons came and went;

a dog began to bark, three gruff notes repeated monotonously at exact intervals; all at once there was a long
muffled roll and an abrupt clacking noise; it ceased, then
broke out again sharply, paused once more, then recommenced, settling to a prolonged minor hum; the cable was
starting up; it was almost morning, the window of his
room began to show a brighter blur in the darkness, while
very far off he could hear the steady puffing of a locomotive. As the first cable-car trundled by the house he
dropped off to sleep for the last time, being waked again
toward nine o'clock by the sound of some one shovelling
coal outside under his window, the shovel clinking and
rasping upon the stone sidewalk.

He felt a little refreshed, but as he entered the dining-
room for his late breakfast the smell of food repulsed him;
his appetite was gone; it was impossible for him to eat.
Toward eleven o'clock that same morning he was pottering
idly about his sitting-room, winding his clock and shaking
down the ashes in the tiled flamboyant stove; his mind
was still busy going over for the hundredth time all the
possibilities of Hiram Wade's suit, and he was just wondering whether something in the way of a compromise
might not be arranged, when with the suddenness of a
blow between the eyes the numbness in his head returned,
together with the same unreasoning fear, the same de-
pression of spirits, the same fearful sinking of the heart.
What! it was coming back again, this strange attack, coming back even when his attention was not concentrated,
even when there was no unusual exertion of his brain!

Then the torment began. This time the crisis did not
pass off; from now on it persisted continually. Vandover

began to feel strange. At first the room looked unfamiliar to him, then his own daily life no longer seemed recognizable, and, finally, all of a sudden, it was the whole world, all the existing order of things, that appeared to draw off like a refluent tide, leaving him alone, abandoned, cast upon some fearful, mysterious shore.

Nothing seemed worth while; all the thousand little trivial things that made up the course of his life and in which he found diversion and amusement palled upon him. A fearful melancholia settled over him, a despair, an abhorrence of living that could not be uttered. This only was during the day. It was that night that Vandover went down into the pit.

He went to bed early, his brain in a whirl, his frame worn out as if from long physical exertion. He was just dropping into a grateful sleep when his whole body twitched suddenly with a shock and a recoil of all his nerves; in an instant he was broad awake, panting and exhausted as if from a long run. Once more he settled himself upon the pillow, and once more the same leap, the same sharp spasm of his nerves caught him back to consciousness with the suddenness of a relaxed spring. At last sleep was out of the question; his drowsiness of the early part of the evening passed away, and he lay back, his hands clasped behind his head, staring up into the darkness, his thoughts galloping incessantly through his brain, suffering without pain as he had never imagined a human being could suffer though racked with torture from head to heel.

From time to time a slow torsion and crisping of all his nerves, beginning at his ankles, spread to every corner of his body till he had to shut his fists and teeth against the blind impulse to leap from his bed screaming. His hands felt light and, as he told himself, "jumpy." All at once he felt a peculiar sensation in them: they seemed to swell, the fingers puffing to an enormous size, the palms bulging, the whole member from the wrist to the nails distended like a glove when one has blown into it to straighten it out. Then he had a feeling that his head was swelling in the same way. He had to rub his hands together, to pass them again and again over his face to rid himself of the fancy.

But the strange numb feeling at the base of the skull did not keep him from thinking — he would have been glad if it had — and now at last when the terror overcame him it was no longer causeless; he knew now what he feared — he feared that he was going mad.

It was the punishment that he had brought upon himself, some fearful nervous disease, the result of his long indulgence of vice, his vile submission to the brute that was to destroy his reason; some collapse of all his faculties, beginning first with that which was highest, most sensitive — his art — spreading onward and downward till he should have reached the last stages of idiocy. It was Nature inexorably exacting. It was the vast fearful engine riding him down beneath its myriad spinning wheels, remorselessly, irresistibly.

The dreadful calamities that he had brought upon himself recoiled upon his head, crushing him to the dust with their weight of anguish and remorse: Ida Wade's suicide, his father's death, his social banishment, the loss of his art, Hiram Wade's lawsuit menacing him with beggary, and now this last, this approaching insanity. It was no longer

fire driving out fire; the sense of all these disasters seemed
to come back upon him at once, as keen, as bitter as when
they had first befallen.   He had told himself that he did
not believe in a hell.   Could there be a worse hell than
this?

But all at once, without knowing why, moved by an
impulse, a blind, resistless instinct, Vandover started up
in bed, raising his clasped hands above him, crying out,
"Oh, help me!   Why don't you *help* me?   You can if you
only will!"   Who was it to whom he had cried with such
unerring intuition?   He gave no name to this mysterious
"You," this strange supernatural being, this mighty super-
human power.   It was the cry of a soul in torment that
does not stop to reason, the wild last hope that feels its
own helplessness, that responds to an intuition of a force
outside of itself — the force that can save it in its time
of peril.

Trembling, his hands still clasped above him, Vandover
waited for an answer, waited for the miracle.   In the tortured exalted state of his nerves he seemed suddenly
possessed of a sixth sense; he fancied that he would know,
there in that room, in a few seconds, while yet his hands
remained clasped above his head.   It was his last hope:
if this failed him there was nothing left.   Still he waited;
he felt that he should know when the miracle came, that he
would suddenly be filled with a sense of peace, of quiet joy.
Still he waited — there was nothing, nothing but the vast
silence, the unbroken blackness of the night, a night that
was to last forever.   There was no answer, nothing but
the deaf silence, the blind darkness.   But in a moment
he felt that the very silence, the very lack of answer, was

answer in itself; there was nothing for him. Even that
vast mysterious power to which he had cried could not
help him now, *could* not help him, could not stay the in-
exorable law of nature, could not reverse that vast terrible
engine with its myriad spinning wheels that was riding
him down relentlessly, grinding him into the dust. And
afterward? After the engine had done its work, when
that strange other time should come, that other life, what
then? No, not even then, nothing but outer darkness
then and the gnashing of teeth, nothing but the deaf silence, nothing but the blind darkness, nothing but the
unbroken blackness of an eternal night.

It was the end of everything! With a muffled cry, "Oh,
I can't stand this!" Vandover threw himself from his bed,
groping his way out into the sitting-room. By this time
he was only conscious of a suffering too great to be borne,
everything else was blurred as in a thick mist. For nearly
an hour he stumbled about in the darkened room, bruising
himself against the furniture, dazed, numb, trying in vain
to find the drawer of the desk where he kept his father's
revolver. At last his hand closed upon it, gripping it so
tightly that the hundreds of little nicks and scratches made
by the contact of the tacks and nails which he had ham-
mered with it nipped and bit into his palm like the teeth
of tiny mice. A vague feeling of shame overcame him
at the last moment: he had no wish to be found sprawling
upon the floor, dressed only in his night-gown. He lit the
gas and put on his bathrobe, drawing the cords securely
about his waist and neck.

When he turned about to pick up the revolver again he
found that his determination had weakened considerably,

and he was obliged to reflect again upon the wreck of his
life and soul before he was back once more to the proper
pitch of resolution.   It was five minutes to two, and he
made up his mind to kill himself when the clock struck
the hour.   He spent the intervening moments in arrang-
ing the details of the matter.   At first he thought he would
do it standing, but he abandoned that idea, fearing to
strike his head against the furniture as he fell.   He was
about to decide upon the huge leather chair, when the
remembrance of his father's death made that impossible.
He finally concluded to sit upon the edge of his bed,
leaning a little backward so as not to fall upon the floor,
and he dragged the bed out into the sitting-room, preferring somehow to die there.   For a moment the idea of
lying at length upon the bed occurred to him, but in an
instant he recoiled from it, horrified at the thought of the
death that struck from above; no, it would be best to
sit upon the edge of the bed, falling backward with the
shot.   Then he wondered as to which it should be, his
heart or his head; evidently the head was the better; there
upon the right side in the little hollow of the temple,
and the next moment he found himself curiously touching
and pressing the spot with his fingers.   All at once he
heard the little clicking noise that the clock makes a
minute or so before the hour.   It was almost two; he sat
down upon the edge of the bed, cocking the revolver,
waiting for the clock to strike.   An idea came to him, and
he looked at the calendar that stood at the right of the
clock upon the top of the low bookcase.   It was the
twelfth of April, Thursday; that, then, was to be the date
of his death — Thursday, April twelfth, at two in the

morning, so it would read upon his gravestone.   For an instant the awfulness of the thing he was to do came upon him, and the next instant he found himself wondering if they still coursed jack-rabbits with greyhounds down at Coronado the way they used to do when he was there. All at once the clock struck two, and at the very last instant a strange impulse to seat himself before the mirror came upon him.   He drew up a chair before it, watching his reflection intently, but even as he raised the revolver he suddenly changed his purpose without knowing why, and all at once crammed the muzzle into his mouth.   He drew the trigger.

He heard no sound of a report; he felt no shock, but a great feebleness ran throughout his limbs, a relaxing and weakening of all his muscles; his eyes were open and he saw everything small and seemingly very far off as through the reversed end of an opera-glass.   Suddenly he fainted.

When Vandover came to himself again it was early morning.   The room was full of daylight, but the gas was still burning.   Little by little the fearful things of the night came back to him; he realized that he had shot himself, and he waited for the end, not daring to move, his eyes closed, his hand still gripping the scratched butt of the revolver in his lap.   For a long time he lay back in the chair, motionless, his consciousness slowly returning like an incoming tide.   At length he started to his feet with an expression of scorn and incredulity; he was as sound as ever, there was neither scratch nor scar upon him; he had not shot himself after all.

Curiously, he looked at the revolver, throwing open the breech — the cylinder was empty; he had forgotten to load it. "What a fool!" he exclaimed, laughing scornfully, and still laughing he walked to the centre of the room under the chandelier and turned out the gas.

But when he turned about, facing the day once more, facing that day and the next and the next throughout all the course of his life, the sense of his misery returned upon him in its full strength and he raised his clenched fist to his eyes, shutting out the light. Ah, no, he could not endure it — the horror of life overpassed the horror of death; he could not go on living. A new thought had come to him. Wretched as he was, he saw that in time his anguish of conscience, even his dread of losing his reason, would pass from him; he would become used to them; yes, even become used to the dread of insanity, and then he would return once more to vice, return once more into the power of the brute, the perverse and evil monster that was knitted to him now irrevocably, part for part, fibre for fibre. He saw clearly that nothing could save him, he had had his answer that night, there was to be no miracle. Was it not right, then, that he should destroy himself? Was it not even his duty? The better part of him seemed to demand the act; should he not comply while there yet was any better part left? In a little while the brute was to take all.

On the shelves above his washstand Vandover found the cartridges in a green pasteboard box, and loaded all the chambers of the revolver, carefully. He closed the breech; but as he was about to draw back the hammer all his courage, all his resolution, crumbled in an instant like a tower of sand. He did not dare to shoot himself — he was afraid. The night before he had been brave enough;

how was it now that he could not call up the same courage,
the same determination? When he thought over the
wreck, the wretched failure of his life, the dreadful prospect of the future years, his anguish and his terror were as
keen as ever. But now there was a shrinking of his every
nerve from the thought of suicide, the instinctive animal
fear of death, stronger than himself. His suffering had
to go on, had to run its course, even death would not help
him. Let it go on, it was only the better part of him that
was suffering; in a little while this better part would be
dead, leaving only the brute. It would die a natural death
without any intervention from him. Was there any need
of suicide? Suicide! Great God! his whole life had been
one long suicide.

That same morning Charlie Geary had eaten a very
thick underdone steak for breakfast after enjoying a fine
long sleep of eight hours. Toward eight o'clock he went
downtown. He did not take a car; he preferred to walk;
it helped his digestion and it gave him exercise. At
night he walked home as well; that gave him an appetite;
besides, with the ten cents that he saved in this way, he
bought himself a nice cigar that he smoked in the evening
to help digest his supper. He was very careful of his
health. Ah, you bet, one had to look out for one's health.

At the office that morning he had a long talk with
Beale, Jr., as to Hiram Wade's suit. The great firm of
Beale & Storey, into whose office Geary had been received,
made a specialty of damage suits, and especially those
suits that were brought against a certain great monopoly
which it was claimed was ruining the city and the state;

such a case involving nearly a quarter of a million of dollars was now occupying the attention of the heads of the firm and, indeed, of the whole office. Hiram Wade's suit was assigned to the assistants. Beale, Jr., was one of these, and Charlie Geary had managed to push himself into the position of his confidential clerk. But Beale, Jr., himself took little interest in the Wade suit; the suit against the great monopoly was coming to a head; it was a battle of giants; the whole office found itself embroiled, and little by little Beale, Jr., allowed himself to be drawn into the struggle. The management of the Wade case was given over to Geary's hands.

When he had first heard of his assignment to the case Geary had been unwilling to act against his old chum, but it was the first legal affair of any great importance with which he had been connected, and he was soon devoured with an inordinate ambition to distinguish himself in the eyes of the firm to get a "lift," to take a long step forward toward the end of his desires, which was to become one of the firm itself. He knew he could make a brilliant success of the case. Geary was at this time nearly twenty-eight, keen, energetic, immensely clever; and the case against Vandover was strong. No one knew better than he himself how intimate Vandover had been with Ida Wade; Vandover had told him much of the details of their acquaintance. Besides this, a letter which Ida had written to Vandover the day before her suicide had been found, torn in three pieces, thrust between the leaves of one of the books that she used to study at the normal school. It directly implicated Vandover — it was evidence that could not be gainsaid. Geary had resolved to

push the case against his old chum. Vandover ought to
see that with Geary it was a matter of business; he, Geary,
was only an instrument of the law; if Geary did not take
the case some other lawyer would. At any rate, whether
Van would see it in this light or not, Geary was determined
to take the case; it was too good an opportunity to let slip;
he was going to make his way in the law or he would know
the reason why. Every man for himself, that was what
he said. It might be damned selfish, but it was human
nature; if he had to sacrifice Van, so much the worse.
It was evident that his old college chum was going to the
dogs anyway, but come whatever would, *he*, Geary, was
going to be a *success*. Ah, you bet, he would make his
way and he would make his money.

Ever since he had come into his little patrimony Geary
had been making offers to Vandover for his block in the
Mission. Geary would offer only eight thousand dollars,
but Brunt steadily advised Vandover against listening
to such a figure, assuring him that the property was valued
at twelve thousand six hundred. Vandover had often
wondered at Geary's persistence in the matter, and had
often asked him what he could possibly want of the block.
But Geary was very vague in his replies, generally telling
Vandover that there was money in the investment if one
could and would give the proper attention to pushing it.
He told Vandover that he — Vandover — was no business
man, which was the lamentable truth, and would much
prefer to live upon the interest of his bonds rather than
to be continually annoyed by defective plumbing, complaints, and repairs. The truth of the matter was that
Geary knew that a certain immense boot and shoe concern

was after the same piece of property. The houses themselves were nothing to the boot and shoe people; they
wanted the land in order to build their manufactory upon
it. A siding of the railroad ran down the alley just back
of the property, a fact that hurt the lot for residence pur-
poses, but that was indispensable for the boot and shoe
people. Geary knew that the heads of the manufactory
were determined to buy the lot, and he was sure that if
properly handled by clever brokers they could be induced
to offer at least one third more than its appraised valuation. It was a chance for a fine speculation, and it was
torture to Geary to think that Vandover, or in fact any one
besides himself, was going to profit by it.

The afternoon of the day upon which Hiram Wade
had brought suit for twenty-five thousand dollars, while
Geary was pottering about his swivel office chair with an
oil can trying to find out where it creaked, a brilliant idea
had suddenly occurred to him, a stroke of genius, a veritable
inspiration. Why could he not make the Wade suit a
machine with which to force Vandover into the sale of the
property?

His first idea had been to push the case so vigorously
that Vandover would surely lose it. But on second
thought this course did not seem to promise any satisfactory results. Geary knew very well that though Hiram
Wade had sued for twenty-five thousand dollars he could
not recover more than five thousand, if as much as that.
Geary did not know the exact state of Vandover's affairs,
but he did not think that his chum would sell any property
in order to make the payment of damages. It was much
more likely that he would raise the five thousand, or what-

ever it might be, by placing a second mortgage on some of
his property. This, however, was presuming that Wade
would get judgment for about five thousand dollars. But
suppose that Vandover thought that Wade could actually
recover twenty-five thousand! Suppose that Geary himself
should see Vandover and induce him to believe such a
story, and to settle the affair out of court! Vandover
was as ignorant of law as he was of business. Geary
might frighten him into a sale. Yet this plan seemed
very impracticable. In the first place, it would be unprofessional for Geary to have an interview with Vandover
under such circumstances, the story was almost too mon-
strous even for Vandover's credibility, and besides, Geary
would not pay, could not pay twenty-five thousand for
the property. This last was a serious tangle. In order
to get Vandover to sell, Geary would have to represent the
damage suit as involving a larger sum of money than
Geary was willing to give for the block, even a far larger
sum than that which the boot and shoe manufacturers
could be induced to pay for it. It seemed to be a dead-
lock. Geary began to see that the whole idea was out of
the question. Yet the desire of it came back upon him
again and again. He dwelt upon it constantly, smelling
out the chance for a "deal" somewhere in the tangle with
the instinct of the keen man of business. At last he
seemed to have straightened it out. The idea of a compromise came into his mind. What if Vandover and
Hiram Wade could be made to compromise upon eight
thousand dollars! Geary would be willing to pay Vandover eight thousand for the block. That was his original
offer. Wade, though he had sued for twenty-five thousand,

could easily be made to see that eight thousand was as
much as he could reasonably expect, and Geary knew the
boot and shoe manufacturers would pay fifteen thousand
for the lot, perhaps more.

But in order to carry out the delicate and complicated
affair it was absolutely necessary to keep Vandover from
seeing a lawyer.   Geary knew that any lawyer would fight
the proposition of a compromise at eight thousand dollars:
five thousand was as much as Wade could possibly get in
court, and if judgment for such amount was rendered,
Vandover's counsel would advise him to raise the sum by
mortgaging some property instead of selling the block.

Yet as soon as Geary arrived at a solution of the problem, as soon as the "deal" began to seem feasible, he commenced to hesitate.   It was not so much that the affair
was crooked, that his rôle in it was, to say the least, unprofessional, as it was the fact that Vandover was his old
college chum and that, to put the matter into plain words,
Geary was swindling his best friend out of a piece of property valued at twelve thousand six hundred dollars, and
preventing him from reselling the same piece at a very
advanced figure.   Again and again he wished that it was
some other than Vandover; he told himself that in such
case he would put the screw on without the least compunction.   All through one night Geary was on the rack torn
between his friendship for his chum and his devouring,
inordinate ambition to make his way and to make his
pile.   In the end Vandover was sacrificed — the opportunity was too good — Geary could not resist the chance
for a "deal."   Ah, you bet, just think of it, after all, not
only would Vandover believe that Geary was doing him a

great service, but the office would be delighted with him
for winning his first case, they would get a heavy fee from
Wade, and he would nearly double his money invested in
the block in the Mission.   As soon as he had made up his
mind to put the "deal" through, he had seen Vandover at
his rooms early in the morning and had induced him to
promise not to engage any other counsel and in general
keep very quiet about the whole business.

The day after, he and Beale, Jr., had an appointment
with Hiram Wade, but toward noon Beale, Jr., disappeared,
leaving word for Geary that he had gone to court with his
father to hear the closing arguments in the great suit
against the monopoly, the last struggle in the tremendous
legal battle that had embroiled the whole office; Geary
was to use his own judgment in the Wade case.   Geary
laboured with Hiram Wade all that afternoon.   The old
fellow mistrusted him on account of his youth and his
inexperience, was unwilling to arrive at any definite
conclusion without the sanction of Geary's older associate,
and for a long time would listen to nothing less than ten
thousand dollars, crying out that his gray hairs had been
dishonoured, and striking his palm upon his forehead.
Nothing could move him.   He, also, had his ambitions;
it was his dream to own the carpet-cleaning establishment
in which he now had but a three-fourths interest.   Summer was coming, the time of year when people were going
into the country, leaving their carpets to be cleaned in
their absence.   If he could obtain complete ownership of
his business within the month he fancied that he saw an
opportunity to make more money than he had done before
at any previous season.

"Why, I tell you, Mister Geary," he exclaimed indignantly, wagging his head, "it would seem like selling my daughter's honour if we should compromise at any less figure. I am a father. I — I have my feelings, haven't I?"

"Well, now, it isn't like that at all, Mr. Wade," answered Geary, making awkward gestures with both his hands. "It isn't what we *ought* to get out of him. Could any sum of money, could millions compensate you for Miss Ida's death? I guess not. It's what we *can* get. If this thing comes into court we won't get but five thousand out of him; I'll tell you that right now. He could raise that by a mortgage, easy; but if we compromise we can squeeze him for eight thousand. You see, the fact that we can act directly with him instead of through counsel makes it easier for us. Of course, as I tell you, it isn't just the legal thing to do, but I'm willing to do it for you because I think you've been wronged and outraged."

Wade struck his hand to his head. "I tell you, he's brought dishonour upon my gray hairs," he exclaimed.

"Exactly, of course, I understand how you feel," replied Geary, "but now about this eight thousand? I tell you what I'll do." He had resolved to stake everything upon one last hazard. "See here, Mr. Wade, there's a difference, of course, between eight thousand dollars and ten thousand, but the use of money is worth something, isn't it? And money down, cold hard cash, is worth something, isn't it? Well, now, suppose you got that eight thousand dollars money down within three days?"

Hiram Wade still demurred a little longer for the sake

of his own self-respect and his dishonoured hairs, but in the end it was agreed that if the money was paid over to him in full before the end of the following week he would be content and would agree to the compromise. Eight thousand dollars would still be enough to buy out his partner's interest, and even then he would have a little left over with which to improve a certain steaming apparatus. If the amount was paid in full within a week he could get control of the cleaning-works in time to catch all of the summer trade.

Geary had calculated that this last argument would have its weight; the great difficulty now was to get Vandover to sell at such a low figure and upon such short notice. He almost despaired of his success in this quarter; however, it all depended upon Vandover now.

Early in the forenoon of the next day Geary pounded on the door of Vandover's sitting-room, pushing it open without waiting for an answer. Vandover was lying in his shirt-sleeves on the corduroy divan under the huge rug of sombre colours that hung against the wall, and he did not get up as Geary came in; in fact, he hardly stirred.

"Hello!" cried Geary, closing the door with his heel. "Didn't expect to find *you* up so early. *I*'ve been up since half-past six; had breakfast at seven, fine cutlet, and then got down to the office at twenty minutes of eight. How's that for rustling, hey?"

"Yes?" said Vandover, dully.

"But, say," exclaimed Geary, "what's all the matter with *you*? You look all frazzled out, all pale around the wattles. Ah, you've been hitting up a pace again. You're

a bird, Van, there's no use talking!   All night racket this
trip?"

"I suppose so," answered Vandover, never moving.

"But you *do* look gone-in this morning, sure," continued
Geary, seating himself on the edge of the table and pushing back his hat.   "Never saw you looking so bad; you
ought to be more careful, Van; there'll be a smash some
time.   Ah, you bet a man ought to look out for his health.
I walk downtown every morning, and three times a week
I take a cold shower as soon as I get up.   Ah, I tell
you, that braces a fellow up; you ought to try it; it's better
than a dozen cocktails.   You keep on getting thin like
you have for the past few days and I'll have to be calling
you Skinny Seldom-fed again, like we used to.   Now, tell
the truth, what time did you get to bed last night?   Did
you go to bed at all?"

"No," replied Vandover with a long breath, looking
vaguely at the pipe-rack on the opposite wall.

"I thought as much," answered Geary.   "Well, that's
like you."   He paused a moment, and then went on, nervously gesturing with both his hands simultaneously.
"Well, I've had a long talk with Wade.   I tell you, Van,
that old boy is as stubborn as a mule.   You see, he knows
he's got a case.   I couldn't talk him out of that.   I'll
tell you how it is," continued Geary, preparing to spring
another mine; "he's found a letter Ida wrote you the
day before she killed herself."   He paused to watch
the effect upon Vandover.   Vandover waited for him to
go on, but seeing that he did not and that he expected him
to say something, nodded his head once and answered:

"I see."

"Don't you know, that letter that she wrote to you telling you how it was, how she was fixed?" repeated Geary, puzzled and irritated at Vandover's indifference.

"I know."

"Well, he's got it, anyhow," pursued Geary, "and of course that tells against you. Well, I had a long talk with him yesterday afternoon and I got him to compromise. Of course, you know in suits like this one a party sues for a great deal more than he expects to get. At first you know he said twenty-five thousand; that figure was decided upon at the first interview he had with us. Of course, he could never get judgment for that much. But he hung out at ten thousand; said it would be selling his daughter if he took any less. Now I knew you couldn't raise that much on any property you have, especially in these hard times —— " Geary paused for the fraction of an instant; he had thrown out the last remark as a feeler, to see what Vandover would say; but his chum said nothing, staring vaguely at the opposite wall, merely making a faint sign to show that he understood, closing his eyes and bending his head. "And so," continued the other, "I jewed him down, and what do you suppose? Well, sir, from twenty-five thousand I brought him right down to, say, eight thousand. I could see that he had some scheme that he wants to go into right away, and that he wants ready money, right on the nail, you know, to carry it through. Ah, you bet, I was clever enough to see that. I waltzed him right over when I began to speak of ready money, cash down. As soon as he'd squeal I'd spring cold cash on him, money down, and he's hit gravel like an ostrich. Well," he went on deliberately after a pause, getting up from the table and standing before Vandover, his hands in his pockets, "well, I think that's the best I can do for you, Van. It's a good deal better than I expected, but I've done the best I could for you, and I would advise you to see him on the proposition."

"All right," said Vandover. "Go ahead."

Geary was perplexed. "Well, you think that's a good thing, don't you? You think I've done my best for you? You see it as I do, don't you?"

Vandover withdrew his eyes from the other wall, glancing under heavy eyelids at Geary, and with a slight movement of his head and shoulders replied:

"Of course."

"Have you got the money?" asked Geary eagerly; then, irritated at his indiscretion, hastened to interrupt himself. "You see, he hasn't put his proposition into writing yet, but it's like this: if you can pay him eight thousand dollars in cash before the end of next week he'll sign a document to the effect that he is satisfied."

"I've got no money," said Vandover quietly.

"I was afraid you wouldn't have," said Geary, "but you can raise it somewhere. You had better close with the old man as soon as you can, Van, while he's in the mood for it; you'll make a clear two thousand by it. You can see that as well as I can. Now, where can you — how is your property fixed? Let's see! Here's the statement you made to me the other day," continued Geary, drawing his shorthand notes from his portfolio. "How about this piece on California Street, the one that you have rented, the homestead, you know?"

"Yes, there's that," answered Vandover, changing the position of his head upon his clasped hands.

"But that's pretty well papered up already," returned Geary, consulting his notes. "You couldn't very well raise another mortgage on *that*."

"I'd forgotten," answered Vandover. "There's the block in the Mission. He can have that."

Geary began to tremble with excitement. It looked as though he might be able to make the deal after all. But the next instant he grew suspicious. Vandover's indifference puzzled him. Might he not have some game of his own? The idea of playing off his cleverness against that of an opponent strung his nerves in an instant; the notion of an impending struggle was almost an inspiration, and his innate desire of getting the better of a competitor, even though it was his closest friend, aroused his wits and sharpened his faculties like a stimulant. He had no hesitancy in sacrificing his chum. It was business now; friendship ceased to be a factor in the affair. Ah, Van was going to be foxy; he'd show him that *he* could be foxy, too.

"He can have it?" echoed Geary. "You don't mean to sign it over to him bodily?"

"Oh, I suppose it could be mortgaged," answered Vandover.

"Yes, that's the idea," returned Geary. "You want me to figure that out for you? I can just as well as not. Well, now, let's see," he went on, settling himself at the desk, and figuring upon a sheet of Vandover's stamped letter-paper. "The banks will never give you more than two thirds of the appraised value; that's as much as we can expect; that would come to — well, let's see — that would

come to six thousand on that piece; then you could mortgage something else to make up the difference."

"Wouldn't it be more than six thousand?" asked Vandover with a little show of interest. "I think that block
has been appraised at something over twelve thousand."

"Ah, yes," returned Geary, putting his chin in the air,
"that was your agent's valuation five years ago; but you
know property out there, in fact, property all over the
city, what they call inside property, has been going right
down for the last ten years. That's what I've always been
telling you. You couldn't possibly get more than nine
thousand for that block to-day. You see the railroad
there hurts it."

"I suppose so," replied Vandover. "I've heard the
governor say as much in his time."

"Of course," exclaimed Geary, delighted at this unexpected turn.

"Well, then, he can have my bonds," said Vandover.
"I've got eighty-nine hundred in bonds; he can have those.
Let him have anything he wants."

"Oh, don't touch your bonds," answered Geary.
"Hang on to those. Bonds are always good—U. S. bonds.
You don't want to sell those, Van. You see, the
homestead is already mortgaged. And, besides, you
know, too, that the banks are asking an awful big per cent.
for mortgages on real estate; it's seven and a half nowadays. Don't sell your bonds. I'll tell you why: U. S.
bonds are always good; they never depreciate, but it's
different with realty, especially in this city just now.
It's been depreciating ever since your father's time, and
it's going to go right on depreciating. If you want to

sell anything, sell your realty before it gets any lower. Now you don't want to sell your home, do you? You don't like that idea. You've lived there so long, and then what would you do with the furniture; besides, the rent of that," he glanced again at his notes, "is bringing you in a good hundred and twenty-five a month. If you've got to sell at all, why not sell your Mission block?"

"All right," said Vandover, as if wearied by Geary's clamour, "I'll sign it over to him."

"No, that's not the idea at all," Geary insisted. "He wants the ready money; he don't want depreciated real estate. You'll have to find a purchaser in the next week if you possibly can in such a short time, and make over the money to Wade. But if you can't sell in that time you will have to dig up ten thousand instead of eight. It's a hard position for you, Van; it's just a chance, you know, but I thought I would give you the benefit of that chance. If you want to give me a power of attorney I'll try and sell it for you."

"I guess Brunt would do that," replied Vandover.

"Yes," retorted Geary, watchful as a lynx, "but they would charge you a big commission. Of course I wouldn't think of asking you anything more than the actual costs. I am afraid that they would try to sell it at auction, too, if they knew you had to realize on it in so short a time, and it would go for a mere song then; you know how it is."

"I thought," inquired Vandover, "that you wanted that property."

"Yes," replied Geary, hesitating, "I — I did want to buy it of you once; well, for that matter I do now. But you know how it is with me."

"I might as well sell it to you as to any one else," returned Vandover.

"Well, now, it's like this, Van," said Geary. "I know that block is worth nine thousand dollars; I won't deceive you. But I can only give you eight thousand for it. That's all the money I've got. But I'm not going to take advantage of your position to jew you down. I want the block, I'll admit that, but I'm not going to have you sacrifice it for me, or for any one else. I think you can get nine thousand for it. I know you could if we had a little more time, and I'm not sure but what I could find a purchaser for you within the next week that would give you nine thousand."

"Oh, I don't care, Charlie; I'm sick of everything; eight thousand, nine thousand, anything you like; take it at your own figure."

Geary began to tremble once more, and this time his excitement was so great that he hardly dared to trust himself to speak; his breath grew short, his hands in his pockets twitched nervously, and curled themselves into fists, his heart seemed to him to beat high in his throat; he hesitated long, pretending to deliberate as he steadied himself.

Vandover remained silent, his hands still clasped back of his head, staring at the opposite wall with eyes that saw nothing. The little clock began to strike ten.

"I don't know, Van," said Geary; "I don't like to do this, and yet I would like to help you out of this muss. You see, if I should ever benefit by the property you would feel as though I had taken advantage of you at this time and worked a flim-flam on you!"

"Oh, I'll look out for that," returned Vandover.

"No, no, I don't feel quite right about it," answered Geary, wagging his head and shutting his eyes. "Better see what we can do at a forced sale."

"Why, don't you see you would be doing me a favour?" said Vandover wearily. "I *ask* you to buy the block. I don't care what your figure is!"

Once more Geary hesitated, for the last time going over the whole deal in his mind from beginning to end, testing it, looking for weak points. It was almost perfect. Suppose the boot and shoe people did not buy the lot? He could resell it elsewhere, even below its appraised value and yet make money by the transaction; the lot was cheap at ten thousand; it might bring twelve; even as an ordinary, legitimate speculation it was to be desired at such a figure. Suppose the boot and shoe people backed out entirely, suppose even he could not find another purchaser for the property, why, then, he could hold on to it; the income from the rents was fully 10 per cent. of the price he would have paid for it.

"Well, Van," he said at last, making a slow, awkward gesture with his left hand, all the fingers extended, "well, I'll take you up — but I don't feel as though I should ——" He suddenly interrupted himself with a burst of sincerity, exclaiming: "Sure, old man, if I had nine thousand I'd give it to you for the block, that's straight goods." He felt that he was conscientious in saying this. It was true he would have given nine thousand if he had had it. For that matter he might have given ten or twelve.

"Can't we settle the whole matter to-day?" said Vandover. "Right here — now. I'm sick of it, sick of everything. Let's get it done with."

Geary nearly bounded from his seat. He had been wondering how he might accomplish this very thing. "All right," he said briskly, "no reason in waiting." He had seen to it that he should be prepared to close the sale the moment that Vandover was willing. Long ago, when he had first had the idea of buying the block, he had spent a day in the offices of the county recorder, the tax collector, and the assessor, assuring himself of the validity of the title, and only two days ago he had gone over the matter again in order to be sure that no encumbrances had been added to the block in the meanwhile. He found nothing; the title was clear.

"Isn't this rather rushing the thing through?" he asked. "Maybe you might regret it afterward. Don't you want to take two or three days to think it over?"

"No."

"Sure now?" persisted Geary.

"But I've *got* to sell before three days," answered Vandover. "Otherwise he'll want ten thousand."

"That's a fact," admitted the other. "Well," he went on, "if your mind's made up, why — we can go right ahead. As I say, there's no reason for waiting; better take up Wade while he's in the mood for it. You see, he hasn't signed any proposition as yet, and he might go back on us." Vandover drew a long breath and got up slowly, heavily, from the couch, saying:

"What's the odds to me what I sell for? *I* don't get the money."

"Well, what do you say if we go right down to a notary's office and put this thing right through," Geary suggested.

"Come on, then."

"Have you got your abstract here, the abstract of the block?" Vandover nodded. "Better bring it along, then," said Geary.

The office of the notary adjoined those of the firm of Beale & Storey; in fact, he was in a sense an attaché of the great firm and transacted a great deal of legal business for them. Vandover and Geary fell upon him in an idle moment. A man had come to regulate the water filter, which took the place of an ice cooler in a corner of one of the anterooms, and while he was engaged at his work the notary stood at his back, abusing him and exclaiming at the ineffectiveness of the contrivance. The notary was a middle-aged man with a swollen, purple face; he had a toothpick behind each ear and wore an office coat of gray linen, ripped at the shoulders.

Then the transfer was made. It was all settled in less than half an hour, unceremoniously, almost hastily. For the sake of form Geary signed a check for eight thousand dollars which Vandover in his turn made over to Hiram Wade. The notary filled out a deed of grant, bargain, and sale, pasting on his certificate of acknowledgment as soon as Vandover and Geary had signed. Geary took the abstract, thrusting it into his breast-pocket. As far as Vandover was concerned, the sale was complete, but he had neither his property nor its equivalent in money.

"Well," declared Geary at length, "I guess that's all there is to be done. I'll get a release from old man Wade and send it to you to-morrow or next day. Now, let's go down to the Imperial and have a drink on it." They went out, but the notary returned to the anteroom, turning the spigot of the filter to right and left, frowning at it suspiciously, refusing to be satisfied.

CHAPTER SIXTEEN

That particular room in the Lick House was well toward the rear of the building, on one of the upper floors, and from its window, one looked out upon a vast reach of roofs that rose little by little to meet the abrupt rise of Telegraph Hill. It was a sordid and grimy wilderness, topped with a gray maze of wires and pierced with thousands of chimney stacks. Many of the roofs were covered with tin long since blackened by rust and soot. Here and there could be seen clothes hung out to dry. Occasionally upon the flanking walls of some of the larger buildings was displayed an enormous painted sign, a violent contrast of intense black and staring white amidst the sooty brown and gray, advertising some tobacco, some newspaper, or some department store. Not far in the distance two tall smokestacks of blackened tin rose high in the air, above the roof of a steam laundry, one very large like the stack of a Cunarder, the other slender, graceful, with a funnel-shaped top. All day and all night these stacks were smoking; from the first, the larger one, rolled a heavy black smoke, very gloomy, waving with a slow and continued movement like the plume of some sullen warrior. But the other one, the tall and slender pipe, threw off a series of little white puffs, three at a time, that rose buoyant and joyous into the air like so many white doves, vanishing at last, melting away in the higher sunshine, only to be followed by another flight. They came three at a time, the pipe tossing them out with a sharp gay sound like a note of laughter interrupted by a cough.

But the interior of the room presented the usual dreary aspect of the hotel bedroom — cheerless, lamentable.

The walls were whitewashed and bare of pictures or ornaments, and the floor was covered with a dull red carpet. The furniture was a "set," all the pieces having a family resemblance. On entering, one saw the bed standing against the right-hand wall, a huge double bed with the name of the hotel in the corners of its spread and pillowcases. In the exact middle of the room underneath the gas fixture was the centre-table, and upon it a pitcher of ice-water. The blank, white monotony of one side of the room was jarred upon by the grate and mantelpiece, iron, painted black, while on the mantelpiece itself stood a little porcelain matchsafe with ribbed sides in the form of a truncated cone. Precisely opposite the chimney was the bureau, flanked on one side by the door of the closet, and on the other in the corner of the room by the stationary washstand with its new cake of soap and its three clean, glossy towels. On the wall to the left of the door was the electric bell and the directions for using it, and tacked upon the door itself a card as to the hours for meals, the rules of the hotel, and the extract of the code defining the liabilities of innkeepers, all printed in bright red. Everything was clean, defiantly, aggressively clean, and there was a clean smell of new soap in the air.

But the room was bare of any personality. Of the hundreds who had lived there, perhaps suffered and died there, not a trace, not a suggestion remained; their differ-

ent characters had not left the least impress upon its air or
appearance.   Only a few hairpins were scattered on the bottom of one of the bureau drawers, and two forgotten medicine bottles still remained upon the top shelf of the closet.

This had been the appearance of Vandover's new home
when he had first come to it, after leaving his suite of
rooms in the huge apartment house on Sutter Street.   He
had lived here now for something over a year.

It had all commenced with the seizure of his furniture
by the proprietors of the apartment house.   Almost before he knew it he owed for six months' room and board;
when the extras were added to this bill it swelled to nearly
a thousand dollars.   At first he would not believe it; it
was not possible that so large a bill could accumulate without his knowledge.   He declared there was a mistake,
tossing back the bill to the clerk who had presented it,
and shaking his head incredulously.   This other became
angry, offered to show the books of the house.   The
manager was called in and attempted to prove the clerk's
statement by figures, dates, and extracts from the entries.
Vandover was confused by their noise, and grew angry in
his turn; vociferating that he did not propose to be
cheated, the others retorted in a rage, the interview
ended in a scene.

But in the end they gained their point; they were right,
and at length Vandover was brought around to see that he
was in the wrong, but he had no ready money, and while
he hesitated, unwilling to part with any of his bonds or to
put an additional mortgage upon the homestead, the
hotel, after two warnings, suddenly seized upon his furniture.   What a misery!

In a moment of time it was all taken from him, all the lovely bric-à-brac, all the heavy pieces, all the little articles of *vertu* which he had bought with such intense delight and amongst which he had lived with such happiness, such contentment, such never-failing pleasure. Everything went — the Renaissance portraits, the pipe-rack, the chair in which the Old Gentleman had died, the Assyrian *bas-reliefs* and, worst of all, the stove, the famous tiled stove, the delightful cheery iron stove with the beautiful flamboyant ornaments. For the first few months after the seizure Vandover was furious with rage and disappointment, persuaded that he could never live anywhere but in just such a room; it was as if he had been uprooted and cast away upon some barren, uncongenial soil. His new room in the hotel filled him with horror, and for a long time he used it only as a place where he could sleep and wash. For a long time even his pliable character refused to fit itself to such surroundings, refused to be content between four enormous white walls, a stuccoed ceiling, and a dark red carpet. He passed most of his time elsewhere, reading the papers at the Mechanics Library in the morning, and in the afternoon sitting about the hotel office and parlours until it was time to take his usual little four o'clock stroll on Kearney and Market streets. He had long since become a familiar figure on this promenade. Even the women and girls of Flossie's type had ceased to be interested in this tall, thin young man with the tired, heavy eyes and blue-white face. One day, however, a curious incident did for a moment invest Vandover with a sudden dramatic interest. It was just after he had moved down to the Lick House, about a

month after he had sold the block in the Mission.   Vandover was standing at Lotta's fountain at the corner of
Kearney and Market streets, interested in watching a
policeman and two boys reharnessing a horse after its
tumble.   All at once he fell over flat into the street,
jostling one of the flower venders and nearly upsetting
him.   He struck the ground with a sodden shock, his arms
doubled under him, his hat rolling away into the mud.
Bewildered, he picked himself up; very few had seen him
fall, but a little crowd gathered for all that.   One asked
if the man was drunk, and Vandover, terrified lest the
policeman should call the patrol wagon, hurried off to a
basement barber shop near by, where he brushed his
clothes, still bewildered, confused, wondering how it had
happened.

The fearful nervous crisis which Vandover had under-
gone had passed off slowly.   Little by little, bit by bit,
he had got himself in hand again.   However, the queer
numbness in his head remained, and as soon as he concentrated his attention on any certain line of thought, as
soon as he had read for any length of time, especially if
late at night, the numbness increased.   Somewhere back
of his eyes a strange blurring mist would seem to rise;
he would find it impossible to keep his mind fixed upon
any subject; the words of a printed page would little by
little lose their meaning.   At first this had been a source
of infinite terror to him.   He fancied it to be the symptoms of some approaching mental collapse, but, as the
weeks went by and nothing unusual occurred, he became
used to it, and refused to let it worry him.   If it made his
head feel queer to read, the remedy was easy enough —

he simply would not read; and though he had been a great reader, and at one time had been used to spend many delightful afternoons lost in the pages of a novel, he now gave it all up with an easy indifference.

But, besides all this, the attack had left him with nerves all unstrung; even his little afternoon walk on Kearney and Market streets exhausted him; any trifling and sudden noise, the closing of a door, the striking of a clock, would cause him to start from his place with a gasp and a quick catch at the heart.   Toward evening this little spasm of nerves would sometimes come upon him even when there was nothing to cause it, and now he could no longer drop off to sleep without first undergoing a whole series of these recoils and starts, that would sometimes bring him violently up to a sitting posture, his breath coming short and quick, his heart galloping, startled at he knew not what.

At first he had intended to see a doctor, but he had put off carrying his intention into effect until he had grown accustomed to the whole matter; otherwise, he was well enough, his appetite was good, and when he finally did get to sleep he would not wake up for a good eight hours.

One evening, however, about three months after the first crisis and just as Vandover was becoming well accustomed to the condition of body and mind in which it had left him, the second attack came on.   It was fearful, much worse than on the first occasion, and this time there was no room for doubt.   Vandover knew that for the moment he was actually insane.

Ellis had been with Vandover most of that afternoon, the two had been playing cards in Vandover's room until nearly

six o'clock. All the afternoon they had been drinking
whisky while they played, and by supper-time neither of
them had any appetite. Ellis refused to go down, declaring that if he should eat now it would make him sick.
Vandover went down alone, but once in the dining-room
he found that *he* could not eat either. However, he knew
that it was not the whisky. For two days his appetite
had been failing him. The smell of food revolted him,
and he left the supper-table, going up to his bare and
lamentable room with the feeling that he was about to
undergo a long spell of sickness. In the deserted hall,
between the elevator and the door of his room, the second
crisis came upon him all at once. It was so sudden that
it was as if some enemy had leaped upon his back, springing out of the shadow, gripping him from behind, holding
him close. Once more the hysteria shook him like a dry
leaf. The little nervous starts came so fast that they ran
together, mingling to form one long thrill of terror, the
blind, unreasoning terror of something unknown; the
numbness weighed down upon his brain until consciousness dwindled to a mere point and mercifully dulled the
torture of his crisping nerves. It seemed to him that his
hands and head were rapidly swelling to enormous size.

All this he had felt before; it was his old enemy, but now
with this second attack began a new and even stranger
sensation. In his distorted wits he fancied that he was
in some manner changing, that he was becoming another
man; worse than that, it seemed to him that he was no
longer human, that he was sinking, all in a moment, to the
level of some dreadful beast.

Later on in that same evening Ellis met young Haight

coming out of one of the theatres, and told him a story that Haight did not believe. Ellis was very pale, and he seemed to young Haight to be trying to keep down some tremendous excitement.

"If he was drunk," said Ellis, "it was the strangest drunk I ever saw. He came back into the room on all fours — not on his hands and knees, you understand, but running along the floor upon the palms of his hands and his toes — and he pushed the door of the room open with his head, nuzzling at the crack like any dog. Oh, it was horrible. *I* don't know what's the matter with Van. You should have seen him; his head was hanging way down, and swinging from side to side as he came along; it shook all his hair over his eyes. He kept rattling his teeth together, and every now and then he would say, way down in his throat so it sounded like growls, 'Wolf — wolf — wolf.' I got hold of him and pulled him up to his feet. It was just as though he was asleep, and when I shook him he came to all at once and began to laugh. 'What's the matter, Van?' says I. 'What are you crawling on the floor that way for?' 'I'm damned if I know,' says he, rubbing his eyes. 'I guess I must have been out of my head. Too much whisky!' Then he says: 'Put me to bed, will you, Bandy? I feel all gone in.' Well, I put him to bed and went out to get some bromide of potassium; he said that made him sleep and kept his nerves steady. Coming back, I met a bell-boy just outside of Van's door, and told him to ask the hotel doctor to come up. You see, I had not opened the door of the room yet, and while I was talking to the bell-boy I could hear the sound of something four-footed going back and forth inside the room.   When I got inside there was Van, perfectly naked, going back and forth along the wall, swinging his head very low, grumbling to himself.   But he came to again as soon as I shook him, and seemed dreadfully ashamed, and went to bed all right.   He got to sleep finally, and I left the doctor with him, to come out and get something for my own nerves."

"What did the doctor say was the matter?" asked young Haight, in horror.

"*Lycanthropy-Mathesis*.   I never heard the name before — some kind of nervous disease.   I guess Van had been hitting up a pretty rapid gait, and then I suppose he's had a good deal to worry him, too."

Once more the attack passed off, leaving Vandover exhausted, his nerves all jangling, his health impaired. Every day he seemed to grow thinner, great brown hollows grew under his eyes, and the skin of his forehead looked blue and tightly drawn.   By degrees a deep gloom overcame him permanently, nothing could interest him, nothing seemed worth while.   Not only were his nerves out of tune, but they were jaded, deadened, slack; they were like harpstrings that had been played upon so long and so violently that now they could no longer vibrate unless swept with a very whirlwind.

As he had foreseen, Vandover had returned again to vice, to the vice that was knitted into him now, fibre for fibre, to the ways of the brute that by degrees was taking entire possession of him.   But he no longer found pleasure even in vice; once it had been his amusement, now it was his occupation.   It was the only thing that seemed to ease the horrible nervousness that of late had begun to prey upon him constantly.

But though nothing could amuse him, on the other hand nothing could worry him; in the end the very riot of his nerves ceased even to annoy him. He had arrived at a state of absolute indifference. He had so often rearranged his pliable nature to suit his changing environment that at last he found that he could be content in almost any circumstances. He had no pleasures, no cares, no ambitions, no regrets, no hopes. It was mere passive existence, an inert, plantlike vegetation, the moment's pause before the final decay, the last inevitable rot.

One day after he had been living nearly a year at the Lick House, Adams & Brunt, the real estate agents, sent him word that they had an offer for his property on California Street. It was the homestead. The English gentleman, the president of the fruit syndicate who had rented the house of Vandover, was now willing to buy it. His business was by this time on a firm and paying basis and he had decided to make his home in San Francisco. He offered twenty-five thousand dollars for the house, including the furniture.

Brunt had several talks with Vandover and easily induced him to sell. "You can figure it out for yourself, Mr. Vandover," he said, as he pointed out his own calculations to him; "property has been going down in the city for the last ten years, and it will continue to do so until we can get a competing railroad through. Better sell when you can, and twenty-five thousand is a fair price. Of course, you will have to pay off the mortgage; you won't get but about fifteen thousand out of it, but at the same time you won't have to pay the interest on that mortgage to the banks; that will be so much saved a month; add that to what you could get for your fifteen thousand at, say, 6 per cent., and you would have a monthly income nearly equal to the present rent of the house, and much more certain, too.   Suppose your tenant should go out, then where would you be?"

"All right, all right," answered Vandover, nodding his head vaguely.   "Go ahead, *I* don't care."   He parted from his old home with as much indifference as he had parted from his block in the Mission.

Vandover signed the deed that made him homeless, and at about the same time the first payment was made. Ten thousand dollars was deposited in one of the banks to his credit, and a check sent to him for the amount.   The very next day Vandover drew against it for five hundred dollars.

At one time he had had an ambition to buy back his furniture from the huge apartment house in which he had formerly lived, and with it to make his cheerless bedroom in the Lick House seem more like a home.   He felt it almost as a dishonour to have strangers using this furniture, sitting in the great leather chair in which the Old Gentleman had died, staring stupidly at his Renaissance portraits and copies of Assyrian *bas-reliefs*.   Above all, it was torture to think that other hands than his own would tend the famous tiled and flamboyant stove, a stove that had its moods, its caprices, like any living person, a stove that had to be coaxed and humoured, a stove that he alone could understand.   He had told himself that if ever again he should have money enough he would bring back this furniture to him. At first its absence had been a matter for the keenest regret and grief. He had been so used to pleasant surroundings that he languished in his new quarters as in a prison. His indulgent, luxurious character continually hungered after subdued, harmonious colours, pictures, ornaments, and soft rugs. His imagination was forever covering the white walls with rough stone-blue paper, and placing screens, divans, and window-seats in different parts of the cold bare room. One morning he had even gone so far as to pin about the walls little placards which he had painted with a twisted roll of the hotel letter-paper dipped into the ink-stand. "Pipe-rack Here." "Mona Lisa Here." "Stove Here." "Window-seat Here." He had left them up there ever since, in spite of the chambermaid's protests and Ellis' clumsy satire.

Now, however, he had plenty of money. He would have his furniture back within the week. He came back from the bank, the money in his pocket, and went up to the room directly, with some vague intention of writing to the proprietors of the apartment house at once. But as he shut the door behind him, leaning his back against it and looking about, he suddenly realized that his old-time desire was passed; he had become so used to these surroundings that it now no longer made any difference to him whether or not they were cheerless, lamentable, barren. It was like all his other little ambitions — he had lost the taste for them, nothing made much difference after all. His money had come too late.

Why should he spend his five hundred dollars on something that could no longer amuse him? It would be much

wiser to spend it all in having a good time somewhere —
champagne dinners with Flossie, or betting on the races
— he did not know exactly what. It was true that even
these alternatives would not amuse him very much — he
would fall back upon them as things of habit. For that
matter everything was an *ennui*, and Vandover began to
long for some new pleasure, some violent untried excitement.

Since the sale of the block in the Mission he had seen
but little of Geary; young Haight had not been his companion since the time when Turner Ravis had broken with
him, but little by little he had begun to associate with
Ellis and his friend the Dummy. Almost every evening
the three were together, sometimes at the theatre, sometimes in the back rooms of the Imperial, sometimes even
in the parlours of certain houses, amid the murmur of
heavy silks and the rustle of stiffly starched skirts. At
times they would be drunk four nights of the week, and
on these occasions it was tacitly understood between
Ellis and Vandover that they should try to get the Dummy
so full that he could talk.

However, Ellis' vice was gambling; he and the Dummy
often passed the whole night over their cards, and as
Vandover came more and more under Ellis' influence —
succumbing to it as weakly as he had succumbed to the
influence of Charlie Geary — he began to join these parties. They played Van John at five dollars a corner.
Vandover won as often as he lost, but the habit of cards
grew upon him steadily.

Toward eleven o'clock the evening of the day upon
which he had drawn his five hundred, Vandover went

around to the Imperial looking for his two friends.   He
found Ellis drinking whisky all alone in one of the little
rooms, as was his custom; fifteen minutes later the Dummy
and Flossie joined them.   Flossie had grown stouter since
Vandover had first known her, nearly ten years ago.   She
had a double chin, and puffy, discoloured pockets had
come under her eyes.   Now her hair was dyed, her cheeks
and lips rouged, and her former air of health and good
spirits gone.   She never laughed.   She had smoked so
many cigarettes that now her voice hardly rose above a
whisper.   At one time she had been accustomed to boast
that she never drank, and it had been one of her peculiarities for which she was well known.   But on this occasion she joined Ellis in his whisky.   She had long since
departed from her old-time rule of temperance, and nowadays drank nothing else but whisky.   She had even become well known for the quantity of whisky she could drink.

For half an hour the four sat around the little table,
talking about the new, enormous Sutro Baths that were
building at that time.   After a while Flossie left them, and
the Dummy began to imitate the motions of some one
dealing cards, looking at the same time inquiringly into
their faces.

"How about that, Bandy?" asked Vandover.   "Shall
we have a game to-night?"

The man of few words merely nodded his head and
drank off the rest of his whisky at a swallow.   They all
went up to Vandover's room.   Vandover got out the cards,
the celluloid chips, and a fresh box of cigars.   The Dummy
held up two fingers of his left hand, shutting them together afterward with his right and making a hissing

noise between his teeth. He raised his eyebrows at Vandover. Vandover understood, and, ringing for a bell-boy, ordered up three bottles of soda in siphon bottles.

The game was *vingt et un*, or, as they called it, Van John. They cut for banker. Ellis turned the first ace, and Vandover bought the bank from him. For the first hour they were very jolly, laughing and talking back and forth at each other; the Dummy especially communicative, continually scribbling upon his writing-pad, holding it toward the others. But it was not necessary for them to put their replies in writing — he understood from watching the movement of their lips. The luck had not declared itself as yet; none of them had lost or won very much. The bell-boy brought up the siphons. The Dummy took off his coat, and the other two followed his example. They were all smoking, and an acrid blue haze filled the room, making a golden blur about each gas globe.

But little by little the passion of the gambling seized upon them. The luck had begun to declare itself, alternating between Ellis and the Dummy. Vandover lost steadily; twice already his bank had been broken, and he had been forced to buy in. The play resolved itself into two parts, Vandover struggling to keep up with the game on one side, and on the other a great battle going on between Ellis and the Dummy. Long since they had ceased to laugh, and not a word was spoken; each one was absorbed in the game, intently watching the cards as they were turned. The four gas-jets of the chandelier flared steadily, filling the room with a crude raw light that was reflected with a blinding glare from the four staring white walls, the room grew hot, the layer of foul warm air just beneath the ceiling, slowly descending. The acrid tobacco smoke no longer rose, but hung in long, slow-waving threads just above their heads. They played on steadily; a great stillness grew in the room, a stillness broken only by the little rattle of chips and subdued rustle of the shuffled cards. Once Vandover stopped, just time enough to throw off his vest, his collar, and his scarf. For a moment the luck seemed about to settle on him. He was still banking, and twice in succession he drew Van John, both times winning heavily from the Dummy, and a little later tied Ellis at twenty when the latter had staked on nearly a third of his chips. But in the next half-dozen hands Ellis got back the lead again, winning from both the others. From this time on it was settled. The luck suddenly declared openly for Ellis, the Dummy and Vandover merely fighting for second place. Ellis held his lead; at one o'clock he was nearly fifty dollars ahead of the game. The profound silence of the room seemed to widen about them. After midnight the noises in the hotel, the ringing of distant call bells, the rattle of dishes from the kitchens, the clash of closing elevator doors, gradually ceased; only at long intervals one heard the hurried step of a bell-boy in the hall outside and the clink of the ice in the water pitcher that he was carrying. Outside a great quiet seemed in a sense to rise from the sleeping city, the noises in the streets died away. The last electric car went down Kearney Street, getting under way with a long minor wail. Occasionally a belated coupé, a nighthawk, rattled over the cobbles, while close by, from over the roofs, the tall slender stack upon the steam laundry puffed incessantly, three puffs at a time, like some kind of halting clock. The room became more and more close, none of them would take the time to open the window, from ceiling to floor the air was fouled by their breathing, by the tobacco smoke and by the four flaring gas-jets. By this time a sombre excitement burnt in their eyes and quivered in their fingers. Never for an instant did their glances leave the cards. Ellis was drinking whisky again, mixed with soda, his hand continually groping for the glass with a mechanical gesture; the Dummy was so excited he could not keep his cigar alight, and contented himself with chewing the end with an hysterical motion of his jaws. The perspiration stood in beads on the back of Vandover's hands, running down in tiny rivulets between his fingers, his teeth were shut close together and he was breathing short through his nose, a fine trembling had seized upon his hands so that the chips in his palm rattled like castanets. In the stale and murky atmosphere of the overheated room in the midst of the vast silence of the sleeping city they played on steadily.

Then they began to "plunge," agreeing to play a no limit game and raising the value of a red chip to ten dollars; at times they even played with the coins themselves when their chips were exhausted. Vandover had lost all his ready money, and now for a long time had been gambling with the five hundred dollars he had that day drawn from the bank. Ellis had practically put the Dummy out of the play, and now the game was between him and Vandover. Ellis was banking, and at length offered to sell the bank to either one of them. For the first time since the real gambling began they commenced to talk a little, but in short, brief sentences, answering by monosyllables and by signs.

"How much for the bank?" inquired Ellis, holding up the deck and looking from one to the other. Instantly the Dummy wrote ten dollars, in figures, on his pad, and showed it to him. Vandover looked at what the Dummy had written, and said:

"Fifteen.

"Twenty," scribbled the Dummy, as he watched Vandover's lips form the word.

"Twenty-five," returned Vandover. The Dummy hesitated a moment and then wrote "thirty." Ellis shook his head saying, "I'll keep the bank myself at that."

"Forty dollars!" cried Vandover. The Dummy shook his head, leaning back in his chair. Ellis shoved the pack across the table to Vandover, and Vandover gave him a twenty-dollar bill and two red chips.

On Vandover's very first deal around, the Dummy "stood" on the second card, for twelve chips; Ellis bet twenty-five on his first card, and, as he got the second, turned both of them face up. He had two jacks. "Twenty-five on each of these," he said. "I'll draw to each one." Vandover looked at his own card; it was a ten-spot. All at once he grew reckless, and seized with a sudden folly, resolved to attempt a great *coup*. "Double up!" he ordered. The Dummy set out twelve more chips, and Ellis another fifty, making his bet an even hundred. Vandover began to deal to Ellis. On the first jack Ellis drew eighteen and stood at that; the first card that fell to the second jack was an ace. "Van John," he remarked quietly. The Dummy drew three cards and stood on nineteen. Vandover turned up his own card and began to deal for himself. He already had a ten; now he drew a seven-spot and king in succession.

"The bank pays," he exclaimed. He paid the Dummy twenty-four chips. He gave Ellis fifty for the eighteen he had drawn on his first jack, and one hundred for the Van John upon the second, since the latter combination called for double the amount wagered; besides this, the bank was lost to him. Including the forty that he had paid for the bank, he had lost in all two hundred and fourteen dollars.

Never in his life had Vandover played so high a game, never before had he won or lost more than fifty dollars at a sitting. But he was content to have it thus. Here at last was the new pleasure for which he had longed, the fresh violent excitement that alone could rouse his jaded nerves, the one thing that could amuse him. However, the failure of his *coup* had left him without chips; he was out of the game. He decided that he would stop; more than half of his five hundred dollars was gone already. He drank off a glass of soda, the dregs of one of the siphon bottles, and got up yawning, shivering a little and stretching his arms high above. The other two played on steadily. The Dummy began to gain slowly upon Ellis, playing very cautiously, betting only upon face cards, aces, and ten-spots. Twice Ellis offered to sell him the bank, but he refused, fearful lest it should change his luck.

Vandover sat behind the Dummy's chair, watching his game, but at length, worn out, he began to drop off to sleep, waking every now and then with a sudden leap and recoil of all his nerves. An hour later the persistent scratching of a match awoke him. Ellis and the Dummy were still playing, and the Dummy was once more re-lighting the stump of his cigar. Ellis continued to deal, winning at almost every play; a great pile of chips and money lay at his elbow. For a few minutes Vandover watched the Dummy's game, leaning forward in his chair, his elbows on his knees. But it was evident that the Dummy had lost his nerve. Ellis' continued winnings had at length demoralized him. At one time he would bet heavily on worthless cards, and at another would throw back nines and tens for no apparent reason. Finally Ellis dealt him a queen, which he kept, betting ten chips. His next card was a seven-spot. He signed to Ellis that he would stand. Ellis drew twenty in three cards. Van-dover could not restrain an exclamation of impatience at the Dummy's stupidity. What a fool a man must be to stand on seventeen with only two in the game. All at once he tossed twenty dollars across the table to Ellis, saying, "Give me that in chips. I'm coming in again." Once more he resumed his seat at the table, and Ellis dealt him a hand.

But Vandover's interruption had for an instant taken Ellis' mind from the game. He stirred in his chair and looked about the room, puffing out his cheeks and blowing between his lips.

"Say, this room is close enough to strangle you. Open the window behind you, Van, you're nearest to it." As Vandover raised the curtain he uttered a cry: "Look here! will you?"

It was morning; the city was flooded by the light of the sun already an hour high. The sky was without a cloud. Over the roofs and amongst the gray maze of telegraph wires swarms of sparrows were chittering hoarsely, and as Vandover raised the window he could hear the newsboys far below in the streets chanting the morning's papers.

"Come on, Van!" exclaimed Ellis impatiently; "we're waiting for you."

That night decided it. From that time on, Vandover's only pleasure was gambling. Night and day he sat over the cards, the passion growing upon him as he continued to lose, for his ill luck was extraordinary. It was a veritable mania, a wild blind frenzy that knew no limit. At first he had contented himself with a game in which twenty or thirty dollars was as much as he could win or lose at a sitting, but soon this palled upon him; he was obliged to raise the stakes continually in order to arouse in him the interest, the keen tense excitement, that his jaded nerves craved.

The five hundred dollars that he had drawn from the ten thousand, the first payment on his old home, melted away within a week. Only a few years ago Vandover would have stopped to reflect upon the meaning of this, would have resisted the temptation that drew him constantly to the gambling-table, but the idea of resistance never so much as occurred to him. He did not invest his fifteen thousand, but drew upon it continually to satisfy his last new craze. It was not with any hope of winning that he gambled — the desire of money was never strong in him — it was only the love of the excitement of the moment.

Little by little the fifteen thousand in the bank dwindled. It did not all go in cards. Certain habits of extravagance grew upon Vandover, the natural outcome of his persistent gambling, the desire of winning easily being balanced by the impulses to spend quickly. He took a certain hysterical delight in flinging away money with both hands. Now it was the chartering of a yacht for a ten-days' cruise about the bay, or it was a bicycle bought one week and thrown away the next, a fresh suit of clothes each month, gloves worn but once, gold-pieces thrust into Flossie's pockets, suppers given to bouffe actresses — twenty-four-hour acquaintances — a race-horse bought for eight hundred dollars, resold for two hundred and fifty — rings and scarf-pins given away to the women and girls of the Imperial, and a whole world of follies that his poor distorted wits conceived from hour to hour. His judgment was gone, his mind unbalanced. All his life Vandover had been sinking slowly lower and lower; this, however, was the beginning of the last plunge. The process of degeneration, though inevitable, had been gradual as long as he indulged generally in all forms of evil; it was only now when a passion for one particular vice absorbed him that he commenced to rush headlong to his ruin.

The fifteen thousand dollars — the price of his old home — he gambled or flung away in a little less than a year. He never invested it, but ate into it day after day, sometimes to pay his gambling debts, sometimes to indulge an absurd and extravagant whim, sometimes to pay his bill at the Lick House, and sometimes for no reason at all, moved simply by a reckless desire for spending.

On the evening of a certain Thanksgiving day, nine months after he had sold the house, Vandover came in through the ladies' entrance of the Imperial, going slowly down the passageway, looking into the little rooms on his right for Ellis or the Dummy. There had been a great intercollegiate football game that day, and Vandover, remembering that he had once found an interest in such things, had at first determined to see it. But toward eleven o'clock in the morning the rain had begun to fall, and Ellis, who was to have gone with him, declared that he did not care enough about the game to go out to it in the rain. Vandover was disappointed; he fancied that he could have enjoyed the game — as much as he could enjoy anything of late — but he hated to go to places alone. In the end, however, he resolved to go whether Ellis went or not. It was a holiday. Vandover had Ellis and the Dummy to lunch with him at the hotel, where they arranged the menu of a famous Thanksgiving dinner for that evening: they would meet in one of the little rooms of the Imperial and go from there to the restaurant. As they were finishing their lunch Vandover said:

"I got a new kind of liqueur yesterday — has a colour like violets and smells like cologne. You fellows better come up to my room and try it. I've got to go up and change anyway, if I go out to that game." They all went up to Vandover's cheerless room, and Ellis began to argue with Vandover against the folly of going anywhere in the rain.

"*You* don't want to go to that game, Van. Just look how it's raining. I'll bet there won't be a thousand people there. They'll probably postpone the game anyway. Say, this *is* queer looking stuff. What do you call it?"

"*Crème violette.*"

The Dummy set down his emptied liqueur glass on the

mantelshelf, and nodded approvingly at Vandover; then he scribbled, "Out of sight," on his tablet.

"Tastes like cough syrup and alcohol," growled Ellis, scowling and sipping. "I think a pint of this would make the Dummy talk Dutch. Keep it up, Dummy," he continued, articulating distinctly so that the other could catch the movement of his lips. "Drink some more — make you talk." Vandover was cutting the string around a pasteboard box that had just come from his tailor's; it was a new suit of clothes, rough cheviot, brown with small checks. He dressed slowly and tipped forward the swinging mirror of the bureau to see how the trousers set. Meanwhile Ellis and the Dummy had got out the cards and chips from the drawer of the centre-table and had begun a game.

"Better change your mind, Van," said Ellis without raising his eyes from the cards.

"No, sir," answered Van. "You don't know how it is — you never were a college man. Why, I wouldn't miss a football game for anything. Talk about your horse-racing, talk about your baseball — I tell you there's nothing in the world so exciting as a hot football game." He swung into his long high-coloured waterproof and stood behind Ellis, watching his game for a moment while he tied a couple of long silk streamers to his umbrella handle.

"It's one of the college colours," he explained. "Seems like old times back at Harvard." Ellis snorted with contempt.

"Such kids!" he growled.

"I saw one of the coaches go down the street a little while ago," continued Vandover, still watching Ellis shuffle and deal. "There were about twenty college men on top, and they had a big bulldog all harnessed out in their colours, and they were blowing fish-horns, and I tell you it made me wish I was one of them again." Ellis did not answer; it was probable he did not hear. Both he and the Dummy were settling down for a game that no doubt would last all the afternoon. Vandover made them free of his room, and they often gambled there when he was away. But it invariably made Ellis nervous to have any one stand behind his chair while he was playing; he began to move about uneasily. By and by he looked at his watch. "Better get a move on," he said, "you'll be late."

"Just a minute," answered Vandover, more and more interested in the game. "Go on playing; don't bother about me. Oh, I saw Charlie Geary, too," he continued, "on another coach; there was a party of them. Charlie was with Turner Ravis on the box seat. You remember Turner Ravis, don't you, Bandy? The girl I used to go with."

"There's a girl I never liked," observed Ellis. "She always struck me as being one of these regular snobs."

"Ah, snob is no name for it," assented Vandover. "She thought she was too damned high-toned for me. As soon as I got into that mess about Ida Wade, she threw me over. No, she didn't want to be associated with me any longer. Well, she can go to the devil. Geary's welcome to her."

"I thought Dolly Haight was going to marry her," said Ellis. "What was the matter *there?*"

"*I* don't know," returned Vandover; "probably Dolly

Haight didn't have enough money to suit her. Guess
she wants a man that will make his pile in this town and
make his way, too. Ah, you bet!"

Half an hour later he was still behind Ellis' chair.
Ellis had become so fidgety that he was losing steadily.
Once more he turned to Vandover, speaking over his
shoulder, "Come on, come on, Van, go along to your football; you make me nervous standing there." Vandover
pushed a ten-dollar gold-piece across the table to the
Dummy, who was banking, and said:

"Give me that in chips. I'm coming in."

"I thought you were going to the game?" inquired
Ellis.

"Ah, the devil!" answered Vandover. "Too much
rain."

They had played without interruption all that afternoon, and for once Vandover had all the luck. When they
broke up about five o'clock with the understanding to
meet again in the Imperial at seven, he had won nearly a
hundred dollars.

When Vandover went out to keep this appointment he
found the streets — especially Kearney and Market
streets — crowded. It was about half-past six. The football game was over and the college men had returned.
They were everywhere, marching about in long files,
chain-gang fashion, each file headed by a man beating
upon a gong, or parading the sidewalks ten abreast,
singing college songs or shouting their slogan. At every
moment one heard the college yells answering each other
from street corner to street corner, "Rah, rah, rah —
Rah, rah, rah!" Vandover found the Imperial crowded

with students. The barroom was packed to the doors, every one of the little rooms in the front hall was full, while Flossie and Nannie had a great party of the young fellows in one of the larger rooms in the rear. Among the crowd in the barroom, three members of the winning team — heroes, with bandages about their heads — were breaking training, smoking and drinking for the first time in many long weeks.

Vandover found Ellis and the Dummy leaning against the wall in the crowded front passage. They were both in bad humour, the Dummy sulking because Flossie had left him for one of the football men, the full-back, a young blond giant with two dislocated fingers; Ellis in a rage because he could get no cocktails at the bar, only straight drinks that night — too much of a crowd. These damn college sports thought they owned the town. "Ah, let's get out of here, Van!" he called over the heads of the throng as soon as Vandover came in sight.

They went out into the street and started in the direction of the restaurant where they had decided to eat their Thanksgiving dinner. After leaving Vandover that afternoon Ellis had seen the head waiter of this restaurant and had explained to him the bill of fare that Vandover, the Dummy, and himself had arranged during their lunch at the Lick House. The streets had relapsed into a momentary quiet — it was between half-past six and seven — and most of the college men were gathered into the hotels and cafés eating dinner. About an hour later they would reappear again for a moment on their way to the theatre, which they were to attend in a body.

But Vandover suddenly discovered that he could not

eat a mouthful, the smell of food revolted him, and little by little an irregular twitching had overcome his hands and forearms.

He had received a great shock. That same evening, as he was leaving the hotel, the clerk at the office had handed him some letters that had accumulated in his box. Vandover could never think to ask for his mail in the morning as he went in to breakfast. Something was surely wrong with his head of late. Every day he found it harder and harder to remember things. There were three letters altogether: one was the tailor's bill mailed the same day that his last suit had been finished; a second was an advertisement announcing the near opening of the Sutro Baths that were building at that time; and the third a notice from the bank calling his attention to the fact that his account was overdrawn by some sixty dollars.

At first Vandover did not see the meaning of this notice, and thrust it back in his pocket together with the tailor's bill; then slowly an idea struggled into his mind. Was it possible that he no longer had any money at the bank? Was his fifteen thousand gone? From time to time his bank-book had been balanced, and invariably during the first days of each month his checks had come back to him, used and crumpled, covered with strange signatures and stamped in blue ink; but after the first few months he had never paid the least attention to these; he never kept accounts, having a veritable feminine horror of figures. But it was absurd to think that his money was gone. Pshaw! one could not spend fifteen thousand in nine months! It was preposterous! This notice was some technicality that he could not understand. He would

look into it the next day.   And so he dismissed the weari-
some matter from his mind with a shrug of his shoulders
as though ridding himself of some troublesome burden.
However, the idea persisted.   Somehow, between the
lines of the printed form he smelt out a fresh disaster.   He
read it over again and again.   All at once as he stood in
the doorway of the hotel, turning up the collar of his
waterproof and watching the little pools in the hollows of
the asphalt pavement to see if it were still raining, the
conviction came upon him.   In a second he knew that
he was ruined.   The true meaning of the notice became
apparent with the swiftness of a great flash of light.   He
had spent his fifteen thousand dollars!

The blow was strong enough, sudden enough to pene-
trate even Vandover's clouded and distorted wits.   His
nerves were gone in a minute, a sudden stupefying numbness fell upon his brain, and the fear of something unknown,
the immense unreasoning terror that had gripped him for
the first time the morning after Ida Wade's suicide came
back upon him, horrible, crushing, so that he had to shut
his teeth against a wild hysterical desire to rush through
the streets screaming and waving his arms.

By the time the three friends had reached the restaurant where they were to eat their Thanksgiving dinner,
Vandover's appetite had given place to a loathing of the
very smell of food, his nervousness was fast approaching
hysteria, the little nerve clusters all over his body seemed
to be crisping and writhing like balls of tiny serpents,
at intervals he would twitch sharply as though startled
at some sudden noise, his breath coming short, his heart
beating quick.

They had their dinner in one of the private rooms of the restaurant on the second floor. All through the meal Vandover struggled to keep himself in hand, fighting with all his strength against this reappearance of his old enemy, this sudden return of the dreadful crisis, determined not to make an exhibition of himself before the others.   He pretended to eat, and forced himself to talk, joining in with Ellis, who was badgering the Dummy about Flossie. The proper thing to do was to fill the Dummy's glass while his attention was otherwise absorbed, and in the end to get him so drunk that he could talk.   Toward the end of the dinner Ellis was successful.   All at once the Dummy got upon his feet, his eyes were glazed with drunkenness, he swayed about in an irregular circle, holding up, now by the table, now by the chair-back, and now by the wall behind him. He was very angry, exasperated beyond control by Ellis' raillery and abuse. He forgot himself and uttered a series of peculiar cries very faint and shrill, like the sounds of a voice heard through a telephone when some imperfection of transmission prevents one from distinguishing the words. His mouth was wide open and his tongue rolled about in an absurd way between his teeth.   Now and then one could catch a word or two. Ellis went into spasms of laughter, holding his sides, gasping for breath.   Vandover could not help being amused, and the two laughed at the Dummy's stammering rage until their breath was spent.   Throughout the rest of the evening the Dummy recommenced from time to time, rising unsteadily to his feet, shaking his fists, pouring out a stream of little ineffectual birdlike twitterings, trying to give Ellis abuse for abuse, trying to talk long after it had ceased to amuse the other two. Ellis had been drinking for nearly six hours, without the liquor producing the slightest effect upon him; long since, the Dummy was hopelessly drunk; and now Vandover, who had been drinking upon an empty stomach, began to grow very noisy and boisterous. Little by little Ellis himself commenced to lose his self-control. By and by he and Vandover began to sing, each independent of the other, very hoarse and loud. The Dummy joined them, making a hideous and lamentable noise which so affected Ellis that he pretended to howl at it like a little dog overcome by mournful music. But suddenly Ellis had an idea, crying out thickly, between two hiccoughs:

"Hey, there, Van, do your dog-act for us! Go on! Bark for us!"

By this time Vandover was very nearly out of his head, his drunkenness finishing what his nervousness had begun. The attack was fast approaching culmination; strange and unnatural fancies began to come and go in his brain.

"Go on, Van!" urged Ellis, his eyes heavy with alcohol. "Go on, do your dog-act!"

All at once it was as though an angry dog were snarling and barking over a bone there under the table about their feet. Ellis roared with laughter, but suddenly he himself was drunk. All the afternoon he had kept himself in hand; now his intoxication came upon him in a moment. The skin around his eyes was purple and swollen, the pupils themselves were contracted; they grew darker, taking on the colour of bitumen. Suddenly he swept glasses, plates, castor, knives, forks, and all from off the table with a single movement of his arm. Then the alcohol overcame him all in an instant like a poisonous gas. He swayed forward in his chair and fell across the stripped table, his head rolling inertly between his outstretched arms. He did not move again.

In a neighbouring room young Haight had been dining with some college fellows, fraternity men, all friends of his, upon whose coach he had ridden to and from the game. He had heard Vandover and Ellis in the room across the hall and had recognized their voices. Haight had never been a friend of Ellis, but no one, not even Turner, had grieved more over Vandover's ruin than had his old-time college chum.

Young Haight heard the noise of the falling crockery as Ellis swept the table clear, and turned his head sharply, listening. There was a moment's silence after this, and Haight, fearing some accident had happened, stepped out into the hall and stood there a moment listening again, his head inclined toward the closed door. He heard no groaning, no exclamations of pain, not even any noise of conversation; only through the closed door came a steady sound of barking.

Puzzled, he tried the door and, finding it locked, as he had expected, put one foot upon the knob and, catching hold of the top jamb, raised himself up and looked down through the open space that answered for a transom.

The room was very warm, the air thick with the smell of cooked food, the fumes of whisky, and the acrid odour of cigar smoke. Ellis had rolled from his chair and lay upon the floor sprawling on his face in the wreck of the table. Near to him, likewise upon the floor, but sitting up, his back against the wall, was the Dummy. He was muttering incessantly to himself, as if delighted at having found his tongue, his head swaying on his shoulders, and a strange murmur, soft, birdlike, meaningless, like sounds heard from a vast distance, coming from his wide-open mouth.

Vandover was sitting bolt upright in his chair, his hands gripping the table, his eyes staring straight before him. He was barking incessantly. It was evident that now he could not stop himself; it was like hysterical laughter, a thing beyond his control. Twice young Haight called him by name, kicking the door as his leg hung against it. At last Vandover heard him. Then as he caught sight of his face over the door he raised his upper lip above his teeth and snarled at him, long and viciously.

As Haight dropped down into the hall a waiter came running up; he, too, had heard the noise of the breaking dishes. As he thrust his key into the lock he paused a moment, listening and looking in a puzzled way at young Haight. "They have a dog in here, then? They had no dog when they came. That's funny!"

"Open the door," said young Haight quietly. Once inside Haight went directly to Vandover, crying out: "Come! come on, Van! come home with me." Vandover started suddenly, looking about him bewildered, drawing his hand across his face.

"Home," he repeated vaguely; "yes, that's the idea. Let's go home. I want to go to bed. Hello, Dolly! where did *you* come from? Say, Dolly, let me tell you — listen here — come down here close; you mustn't mind me; you know I'm a wolf mostly!"

They went down toward the Lick House. Vandover

grew steadier after a few minutes in the open air. Young
Haight locked arms with him; they went on together in
silence. By this time the streets were crowded again, the
theatres were over, and the college men were once more at
large. Now they were all gathered together into one immense procession, headed by a brass band in a brewer's
wagon, and they tramped aimlessly to and fro about
Kearney and Market streets, making a hideous noise. At
the head the band was playing a popular quick-step with
a great banging of a bass drum. The college men in the
front ranks were singing one song, those in the rear another, while the middle of the column was given over to
an abominable medley of fish-horns, policemen's rattles
and great Chinese gongs. At stated intervals the throng
would halt and give the college yell.

"Dolly, you and I used to do that," said Vandover,
looking after the procession. He had himself well in
hand by this time. "What was the matter with me back
there at the restaurant, Dolly?" he asked after a while.

"Oh, you'd been drinking a good deal, I guess," answered young Haight. "You — you had some queer idea
about yourself!"

"Yes, I know," answered Vandover quickly. "Fancied I was some kind of a beast, didn't I — some kind of
wolf? I have that notion sometimes and I can't get it
out of my head. It's curious just the same."

They went up to Vandover's room. Vandover lit the
gas, but he could hardly keep back an exclamation as the
glare suddenly struck young Haight's face. What in
heaven's name was the matter with his old-time chum?
He seemed to be blighted, shattered, struck down by some

terrible, overwhelming calamity. A dreadful anguish looked
through his eyes. The sense of a hopeless misery had drawn
and twisted his face.   There could be no doubt that something had made shipwreck of his life.   Vandover was looking at a ruined man.

"My God, Dolly!" exclaimed Vandover, "what's happened to you? You look like a death's-head, man!
What's gone wrong?   Aren't you well?"

Haight caught his friend's searching gaze, and for a
moment they looked at each other without speaking.
There was no mistaking the fearful grief that smouldered
behind Haight's dull, listless eyes.   For a moment Vandover thought of Turner Ravis. But even if she had
turned him off, that alone would not account for his friend's
fearful condition of mind and body.

"What is it, Dolly?" persisted Vandover. "We used to
be pretty good chums, not so long ago."

They sat down on the edge of the bed, and for a moment their positions seemed reversed: Haight the one to
be protected and consoled, Vandover the shielding and
self-reliant one.

Young Haight passed his hand over his face before he
answered, and Vandover noticed that his fingers trembled
like an old man's.

"Do you remember that night, Van, when you and
Charlie and I all went out to Turner's house, and we had
tamales and beer, and a glass broke in that peculiar way,
and I cut my lip?"

Vandover nodded, forcing his attention against the
alcoholic fumes, to follow his friend's words.

"We went down to the Imperial afterward," Haight

continued, "and ran into Ellis, and we had something more to eat. Do you remember that as we sat there, Toby, the waiter, brought Flossie in, and she sat there with us a while?"

He paused, choosing his words. Vandover listened closely, trying to recall the incident.

"She kissed me," said young Haight slowly, "and the court-plaster came off. You know I never had anything to do with women, Van. I always tried to keep away from them. But that's where my life practically came to an end."

"You mean ——" began Vandover. "You mean — that you — that Flossie ——?"

Haight nodded.

"Good God! I can't believe it. It's not possible! I *know* Flossie!"

Haight shook his head, smiling grimly.

"I can't help that, Van," said he. "There's no denying facts, there's no other possible explanation! As soon as I knew, I went to the doctors here, and then I went to New York for treatment, but there's no hope. I didn't know, you see. I didn't believe it possible. Turner Ravis and I were engaged. I waited too long! There's only one escape for me now." His voice dropped, he stared for a moment at the floor. Then he straightened up, and said in a different tone, "But, damn it, Van, let's not talk about it! I'm haunted with the thing day and night. I want to talk to you! I want to talk to you seriously. You know you are ruining yourself, old man!"

But Vandover interrupted him with a gesture, saying, "Don't go on, Dolly; it isn't the least use. There *was* a time for that, but that was long ago. I used to care, I used to be sorry and all that, but I'm not now. Ruining myself? Why, I *have* ruined myself long ago. We're both ruined — only in your case it wasn't your fault. It's too late for me now, and I'm even not sorry that it *is* too late. Dolly, I don't *want* to pull up. You can't imagine a man fallen as low as that, can you? I couldn't imagine it myself a few years ago. I'm going right straight to the devil now, and you might as well stand aside and give me a free course, for I'm bound to get there sooner or later. I suppose you would think that a man who could see this as plainly as I do would be afraid, would have remorse and all that sort of thing. Well, I did at first. I'll never forget the night when I first saw it; came near shooting myself, but I got over it, and now I'm used to the idea. Dolly, *I can get used to almost anything.*" Nothing makes much difference to me nowadays — only I like to play cards. Look here!" he went on, laying out the notice from the bank upon the table, "this came to-day. You see what it is! I sold the old house on California Street. Well, I've gambled away that money in less than a year. It seems that I'm a financial ruin now, but" — and he began to laugh — "I live through it somehow. The news didn't prevent me from getting drunk to-night."

After young Haight was gone, Vandover went to bed, turning out the gas and drawing down the window halfway from the top. The wine had made him sleepy; he was dropping away into a very grateful doze when a sudden shock, a violent leap of every nerve in his body, brought him up to a sitting posture, gasping for breath, his heart fluttering, his hands beating at the empty air. He settled down again, turning upon his pillow, closing his eyes, very weary, longing for a good night's sleep. Dolly Haight's terrible story, his unjustified fate, and the hopeless tragedy of it, came back to him. Vandover would gladly have changed places with him. Young Haight had the affection and respect of even those that knew. He, Vandover, had thrown away his friends' love and their esteem with the rest of the things he had once valued. His thoughts, released from all control of his will, began to come and go through his head with incredible rapidity, confused ideas, half-remembered scenes, incidents of the past few days, bits and ends of conversation recalled for no especial reason, all galloping across his brain like a long herd of terrified horses; an excitement grew upon him, a strange thrill of exhilaration. He was broad awake now, but suddenly his left leg, his left arm and wrist, all his left side jerked with the suddenness of a sprung trap; so violent was the shock that the entire bed shook and creaked with it. Then the inevitable reaction followed, the slow crisping and torsion of his nerves, twisting upon each other like a vast swarm of tiny serpents; it seemed to begin with his ankles, spreading slowly to every part of his body; it was a veritable torture, so poignant that Vandover groaned under it, shutting his eyes. He could not keep quiet a second — to lie in bed was an impossibility; he threw the bed-clothes from him and sprang up. He did not light the gas, but threw on his bathrobe and began to walk the floor. Even as he walked, his eyelids drooped lower and lower. The need of sleep overcame him like a narcotic, but as soon as he was about to lose himself he would **be** suddenly and violently awakened by the same shock, the same jangling recoil of his nerves.   Then his hands and head seemed to swell; next, it was as though the whole room was too small for him.   He threw open the window and, leaning upon his elbows, looked out.

The clouds had begun to break, the rain was gradually ceasing, leaving in the air a damp, fresh smell, the smell of wet asphalt and the odour of dripping woodwork.   It was warm; the atmosphere was dank, heavy, tepid.   One or two stars were out, and a faint gray light showed him the vast reach of roofs below stretching away to meet the abrupt rise of Telegraph Hill.   Not far off the slender, graceful smokestack puffed steadily, throwing off continually the little flock of white jets that rose into the air very brave and gay, but in the end dwindled irresolutely, discouraged, disheartened, fading sadly away, vanishing under the night, like illusions disappearing at the first touch of the outside world.   As Vandover leaned from his window, looking out into the night with eyes that saw nothing, the college slogan rose again from the great crowd of students who still continued to hold the streets.

"Rah, rah, rah!   Rah, rah, rah!"

He turned back into the room, groping among the bottles on his washstand for his bromide of potassium.   As he poured out the required dose into the teaspoon his hand twitched again sharply, flirting the medicine over his bared neck and chest, exposed by the bathrobe which he had left open at the throat.   It was cold, and he shivered a bit as he wiped it dry with the back of his hand.

He knew very well that his nervous attack was coming on again.   As he set down the bottle upon the washstand he muttered to himself, "Now I'm going to have a night of it." He began to walk the floor again with great strides, fighting with all his pitiful, shattered mind against the increasing hysteria, trying to keep out of his brain the strange hallucination that assailed it from time to time, the hallucination of a thing four-footed, a thing that sulked and snarled. The hotel grew quiet; a watchman went down the hall turning out each alternate gas jet. Just outside of the door was a burner in a red globe, fixed at a stair landing to show the exit in case of fire. This burned all night and it streamed through the transom of Vandover's room, splotching the ceiling with a great square of red light. Vandover was in torment, overcome now by that same fear with which he had at last become so familiar, the unreasoning terror of something unknown. He uttered an exclamation, a suppressed cry of despair, of misery, and then suddenly checked himself, astonished, seized with the fancy that his cry was not human, was not of himself, but of something four-footed, the snarl of some exasperated brute. He paused abruptly in his walk, listening, for what he did not know. The silence of the great city spread itself around him, like the still waters of some vast lagoon. Through the silence he heard the noise of the throng of college youths. They were returning, doubling upon their line of march. A long puff of tepid air breathing through the open window brought to his ears the distant joyous sound of their slogan:

"Rah, rah, rah! Rah, rah, rah!"

They passed by along the adjacent street, their sounds growing faint. Vandover took up his restless pacing

again. Little by little the hallucination gained upon
him; little by little his mind slipped from his grasp. The
wolf — the beast — whatever the creature was, seemed
in his diseased fancy to grow stronger in him from moment
to moment. But with all his strength he fought against
it, fought against this strange mania, that overcame him
at these periodical intervals — fought with his hands so
tightly clenched that the knuckles grew white, that the
nails bit into the palm. It seemed to him that in some
way his personality divided itself into three. There was
himself, the real Vandover of every day, the same familiar
Vandover that looked back at him from his mirror; then
there was the wolf, the beast, whatever the creature was
that lived in his flesh, and that struggled with him now,
striving to gain the ascendency, to absorb the real Vandover into its own hideous identity; and last of all, there
was a third self, formless, very vague, elusive, that stood
aside and watched the strife of the other two. But as he
fought against his madness, concentrating all his attention with a tremendous effort of the will, the queer numbness that came upon his mind whenever he exerted it
enwrapped his brain like a fog, and this third self grew
vaguer than ever, dwindled and disappeared. Somehow
it seemed to be associated with consciousness, for after
this the sense of the reality of things grew dim and blurred
to him. He ceased to know exactly what he was doing.
His intellectual parts dropped away one by one, leaving
only the instincts, the blind, unreasoning impulses of the
animal.

Still he continued his restless, lurching walk back and
forth in his room, his head hanging low and swinging from

side to side with the movement of his gait. He had become
so nervous that the restraint imposed upon his freedom of
movement by his bathrobe and his loose night-clothes
chafed and irritated him. At length he had stripped off
everything.

Suddenly and without the slightest warning Vandover's
hands came slowly above his head and he dropped forward, landing upon his palms. All in an instant he had
given way, yielding in a second to the strange hallucination of that four-footed thing that sulked and snarled.
Now without a moment's stop he ran back and forth along
the wall of the room, upon the palms of his hands and
his toes, a ludicrous figure, like that of certain clowns
one sees at the circus, contortionists walking about the
sawdust, imitating some kind of enormous dog. Still he
swung his head from side to side with the motion of his
shuffling gait, his eyes dull and fixed. At long intervals
he uttered a sound, half word, half cry, "Wolf — wolf!"
but it was muffled, indistinct, raucous, coming more from
his throat than from his lips. It might easily have been
the growl of an animal. A long time passed. Naked,
four-footed, Vandover ran back and forth the length of
the room.

By an hour after midnight the sky was clear, all the
stars were out, the moon a thin, low-swinging scimitar,
set behind the black mass of the roofs of the city, leaving
a pale bluish light that seemed to come from all quarters
of the horizon. As the great stillness grew more and more
complete, the persistent puffing of the slender tin stack,
the three gay and joyous little noises, each sounding like a
note of discreet laughter interrupted by a cough, became

clear and distinct.   Inside the room there was no sound
except the persistent patter of something four-footed going
up and down.   At length even this sound ceased abruptly.
Worn out, Vandover had just fallen, dropping forward
upon his face with a long breath.   He lay still, sleeping
at last.   The remnant of the great band of college men
went down an adjacent street, raising their cadenced
slogan for the last time.   It came through the open window, softened as it were by the warm air, thick with damp,
through which it travelled:

"Rah, rah, rah!   Rah, rah, rah!"

Naked, exhausted, Vandover slept profoundly, stretched
at full length at the foot of the bare, white wall of the room
beneath two of the little placards, scrawled with ink, that
read, "Stove here"; "Mona Lisa here."

CHAPTER SEVENTEEN

ON A certain Saturday morning two years later Vandover awoke in his room at the Reno House, the room he had now occupied for fifteen months.

One might almost say that he had been expelled from the Lick House. For a time he had tried to retain his room there with the idea of paying his bills by the money he should win at gambling. But his bad luck was now become a settled thing — almost invariably he lost. At last Ellis and the Dummy had refused to play with him, since he was never able to pay them when they won. They had had a great quarrel. Ellis broke with him sullenly, growling wrathfully under his heavy moustache, and the Dummy had written upon his pad — so hastily and angrily that the words could hardly be read — that he would not play with professional gamblers, men who supported themselves by their winnings. Damn it! one had to be a gentleman.

Next, Vandover had tried to borrow some money of Charlie Geary. Geary had told him that he could not afford as much as Vandover needed. Then Vandover became enraged. He had long since seen that Geary had practically swindled him out of his block in the Mission, and at that very moment the huge boot and shoe "concern" was completing the factory built upon the ground that Vandover had once owned. Geary had cleared seven thousand dollars on his "deal." His refusal to loan his old-time friend fifty dollars upon this occasion had exasperated Vandover out of all bounds. There was a scene. Vandover told Geary what he thought of his "deal" in very plain words. They shouted "swindler" and "gambler" into each other's faces; the whole office was aroused; Vandover was ejected by force. On a stair landing halfway to the street he sat down and cried into his arms folded upon his knees. When he returned to his room he had a sudden return of his dreadful nervous malady and barked and whined under the bed.

Then Vandover wrote a fifty-dollar check on the bank — the same bank that had just notified him that he was overdrawn — and passed it upon young Haight. How he came to do the thing he could not tell; it might have been the influence of Geary's successful robbery, or it might have been that he had at last lost all principle, all sense of honour and integrity. At any rate, he could not bring himself to feel very sorry. He knew that young Haight would not prosecute him for the dishonesty; he traded upon Haight's magnanimity; he only felt glad that he had the fifty dollars. But by this time Vandover did not even wonder at his own baseness and degradation. A few years ago this would have been the case; now his character was so changed that the theft seemed somehow consistent. He had destroyed young Haight's friendship for him. He had cast from him his college chum, his best friend, but neither did this affect him. Nothing made much difference to him now.

Nevertheless, Vandover was evicted from the Lick House three days after he had stolen young Haight's

money.   Instead of paying his bills with the amount, he
gambled it away in a back room of a new café on Market
Street with Toby, the red-eyed waiter from the Imperial,
and a certain German "professor," a billiard marker,
who wore a waistcoat figured with little designs of the
Eiffel Tower, and who was a third owner in a trotting mare
named Tomato Ketchup.

Vandover was now left with only his bonds, his U. S.
4 per cents.   These brought him in but sixty-nine dollars a quarter, or as he had had it arranged, twenty-three
dollars a month.   Just at this time, as if by a miracle, a
veritable God from the Machine, Vandover's lawyer, Mr.
Field, found him an opportunity to earn some money.
For the first and only time in his life Vandover knew what
it was to work for a living.   The work that Field secured
for him was the work of painting those little pictures on
the lacquered surface of iron safes, those little oval landscapes between the lines of red and gold lettering — landscapes, rugged gorges, ocean steamships under all sail,
mountain lakes with sailboats careening upon their surfaces, the boat indicated by two little triangular dabs of
Chinese white, one for the sail itself and the other for its
reflection in the water.   Sometimes even he was called
upon to paint other little pictures upon the sides of big
express wagons — two horses, one white and the other
bay, galloping very free in an open field, their manes and
tails flying, or a bulldog, very savage, sitting upon a green
and black safe, or the head of a mastiff with a spiked collar
about his neck.

What with the pay for this sort of work and the interest
of his bonds, Vandover managed to lead a haphazard sort

of life, living about in cheap lodging-houses and cheap
restaurants.   But he was never more than a second-class
workman, and he was so irregular that he could never be
depended upon.

The moment he began to paint again — even to paint
such pitiful little pictures as these — the same familiar
experience repeated itself, the unwillingness of his fingers,
their failure to rightly interpret his ideas, the resulting
crudity of his work, the sudden numbness in his brain,
the queer, tense sensation behind his eyes.   But Vandover
had long since become accustomed to these symptoms and
would not have minded them at this time had it not been
that they were occasionally followed by a nervous twitching and jerking of his whole arm, so that sometimes he
could not hold the brush steady a minute at a time.

For two years he had drifted about the city, living now
here and now there, a real hand-to-mouth existence, sinking a little lower each day.   Now, no one knew him.   He
had completely passed out of the lives of Haight, Geary,
and Ellis, just as before he had passed out of the life of
Turner Ravis.   At the end of the first year they had ceased
even to think about him.   For a long time they thought
that he was dead, until one day Ellis declared that he had
seen him far down on Kearney Street, near the Barbary
Coast, looking at the pictures in the illustrated weeklies
that were tacked upon the show-board on the sidewalk
in front of a stationer's.   Ellis had told the others that
on this occasion Vandover seemed to be more sickly than
ever; he described his appearance in detail, wagging his
head at his own story, pursing his lips, putting his chin
in the air.   Vandover had worn an old paint-stained pair

of blue trousers, fastened with a strap, so that his shirt showed below his vest; he had no collar, and he had allowed his beard to grow, a straggling thin beard, through which one could see the buttons of his shirt, a dirty beard full of the cracker crumbs from the free lunch-counters of cheap saloons; he had on a hat which he had worn when they had known him; but one should see that hat now!

It was all true: little by little Vandover had abandoned all interest in his personal appearance. Of course it was impossible for him to dress well at this time, but he had even lost regard for decency and cleanliness. He washed himself but rarely. He had even acquired the habit of sleeping with all his clothes on during the colder nights of the year.

Nothing made any difference. Gradually his mind grew more and more clouded; he became stupid, sluggish. He went about the city from dawn to dark, his feet dragging, his head hanging low and swinging from side to side with the motion of his gait. He rarely spoke; his eyes took on a dull, glazed appearance, filmy, like the eyes of a dead fish. At certain intervals his mania came upon him, the strange hallucination of something four-footed, the persistent fancy that the brute in him had now grown so large, so insatiable, that it had taken everything, even to his very self, his own identity — that he had literally *become the brute*. The attack passed off and left him wondering, perplexed.

The Reno House, where Vandover had lived for some fifteen months, was a sort of hotel on Sacramento Street below Kearney. The neighbourhood was low — just on the edge of the Barbary Coast, abounding in stores for second-hand clothing, saloons, pawnshops, gun-stores, bird-stores, and the shops of Chinese cobblers.   Around the corner on Kearney Street was a concert hall, a dive, to which the admission was free.   Near by was the old Plaza.

Underneath the hotel on the ground floor were two saloons, a barber shop, and a broom manufactory.   The lodgers themselves were for the most part "transients," sailors lounging about shore between two voyages, Swedes and Danes, farmhands, grape-pickers, and cow-punchers from distant parts of the state, a few lost women, and Japanese cooks and second-boys remaining there while they advertised for positions.

Vandover sank to the grade of these people at once with that fatal adaptability to environment which he had permitted himself to foster throughout his entire life, and which had led him to be contented in almost any circumstances.   It was as if the brute in him were forever seeking a lower level, wallowing itself lower and lower into the filth and into the mire, content to be foul, content to be prone, to be inert and supine.

It was Saturday morning about a quarter of nine.   The wet season had begun early that year.   Though this was but the middle of September, the rain had fallen steadily since the previous Wednesday.   Its steady murmur, prolonged and soothing like the purring of a great cat, filled Vandover's room with a pleasant sound.   The air of the room was thick and foul, heavy with the odour of cooking, onions, and stale bedding.   It was very warm; there was no ventilation.   Vandover lay upon the bed half awake, dozing under the thick coarse blankets and soiled counterpane.   With the exception of his shoes and coat he wore

all his clothes.   He was glad to be warm, to be stupefied
by the heat of the bedding and the bad air of the room.

In the next room a Portuguese fruit vender, very drunk,
was fighting with the tin pitcher and pasteboard bowl on
his wash-stand, trying to wet his head, swearing and making a hideous clatter.   At length he tipped them over upon
the floor and gave the pitcher a great kick.   The noise
roused Vandover; he sat up in bed, stretching, rubbing
his hands over his face.   About the same moment the
clock in the office downstairs struck nine.   Vandover let
his feet drop to the floor and sat on the edge of the bed,
looking vaguely about him.   His face, ordinarily very
pale, was oily from sleep and red upon one side from long
contact with the pillow, the marks of the creases still
showing upon his cheek.   His long straight hair fell about
his eyes and ears like a tangled mane.   A thin straggling
beard and moustache, of a brown much lighter than his
hair, covered the lower part of his face.   His nose was long
and pinched, while brown and puffed pockets hung beneath
his eyes.

He wore a white shirt very crumpled and dirty, a low
standing collar and a black four-in-hand necktie, very
greasy.   His trousers were striped and of a slate blue
colour — the "blue pants" of the ready-made clothing
stores.   Still sitting on the bed, Vandover continued his
stupid gaze about the room.

The room was small, and at some long-forgotten, almost
prehistoric period had been covered with a yellowish
paper, stamped with a huge pattern of flowers that looked
like the flora of a carboniferous strata, a pattern repeated
to infinity wherever the eye turned.   Newspapers were

pasted upon the ceiling and a great square of very dirty matting covered the floor. There were a few pieces of furniture, very old-fashioned, made of pine, with a black walnut veneer, two chairs, a washstand and the bed. A great pile of old newspapers tied up with bale rope was kicked into one corner. Two gas brackets without globes stretched forth their long arms over the empty space where the bureau should have been. Under the single window was Vandover's trunk, and upon it his colour box and pots of paint. His hat hung upon a hook screwed to the door. The hat had once been black, but it had long since turned to a greenish hue, and sweat stains were showing about the band.

Vandover dressed slowly. He straightened his hair a bit before the cheap mirror that hung over the washstand, putting on his hat immediately after to keep it in place. He washed his hands in the dirty water that had stood in his pasteboard bowl since the previous afternoon, but left his face as it was. He put on his coat, an old cutaway which had been his best years ago, but which was now absurdly small for him, the breast all spotted and streaked with old stains of soup and gravy. Last of all he drew on his shoes. They were new. Vandover had bought them two days before for a dollar and ninety cents. They were lined so as to make socks superfluous.

It had been a bad week with Vandover. The paint-shop had given him no work to do for ten days, and he had been forced to get along in some way upon the interest of his bonds — that is to say, upon five dollars and seventy-five cents a week. Two dollars and seventy-five cents of this went for his room rent, one dollar and ninety for his shoes, and Tuesday afternoon he had bought a package of cigarettes for ten cents. By Saturday morning he had spent seventy-five cents for food.

When the paint-shop gave him enough work it was Vandover's custom to buy a week's commutation ticket at a certain restaurant. He never ate at the hotel; it was too expensive. By the commutation system he could buy two dollars and twenty-five cents' worth of meals for two dollars, paying in tickets at each meal.

But such a thing had been impossible this week. He had been forced to fall back upon the free-lunch system. In two years Vandover had learned a great deal; even his dulled wits had been sharpened when it had come to a question of food. The brute in him might destroy all his finer qualities, but even the brute had to feed. When work failed him at the beginning of the week Vandover was not unprepared for the contingency; the thing had happened before and he knew how to meet it.

On Monday he beat up and down the Barbary Coast, picking out fifteen or twenty saloons which supported a free-lunch counter in connection with the bar. He took his breakfast Monday morning at the first of these. He paid five cents for a glass of beer and ate his morning's meal at the lunch counter: stew, bread, and cheese. At noon he made his dinner at the second saloon on his route. Here he had another glass of beer, a great plate of soup, potato salad, and pretzels. Thus he managed to feed himself throughout the week.

It was always his great desire to feed well at Sunday's dinner, to spend at least a quarter on that meal. It was something to be looked forward to throughout the entire week. But to get twenty-five cents ahead when he was out of work was bitter hard. That week he had started out with the determination to eat but two meals a day. He would thus save five cents daily and by Sunday morning would be thirty cents to the good. But each day his resolution broke down. At breakfast he would resolve to go without his lunch, at lunch he would make up his mind to go without supper, and at supper he would tell himself that now at least his determination was irrevocable — he would eat no breakfast the next morning. But on each and every occasion his hunger proved too strong, his feet carried him irresistibly to the saloon lunch counters, whether he would or no. At no time in his life had Vandover accustomed himself to self-denial; he could hardly begin now.

At length Saturday morning had come, and while he was dressing he realized that he could not look forward to any unusual dinner the next day at noon. The disappointment had all the force of an unexpected disaster and he began keenly to regret his weakness of the past week. Suddenly Vandover resolved that he would go without food all that day; it would be a saving of fifteen cents, which, added to the five cents that he would spend anyway for his dinner, would almost make a quarter. He knew where he could dine excellently well for twenty cents. However, he could not make up his mind to go without his Sunday morning's breakfast. That, he told himself, he must eat.

Once dressed, Vandover went out. Fortunately, the rain had stopped. He went on down through the reeking, steaming streets to one of the big fruit markets not far from the water front. The Portuguese fruit vender who roomed next to him at the Reno House was employed at a stall here. Vandover knew him a little, and it was not hard for him to get a thin slice of cocoanut out from the inside rind of one of those that were lying cracked open among his other wares.

All the morning Vandover chewed this slice of cocoanut, at the same time drinking a great deal of water; for hours he deadened the pang of hunger by this means. He passed the time for the most part sitting on the benches in the Plaza reading an old newspaper that he had found under a seat. The sun came out a little; Vandover found the warmth very grateful. He told himself that he could easily hold out until the next morning.

He had forgotten about the time and was surprised when the whistles all over the town began to blow for noon. In an instant Vandover was hungry again. It was all one that he chewed the little pulp of cocoanut rind more vigorously than ever, swallowed great draughts of water at the public fountains; the little gnawing just between his chest and his stomach began to persist. He got up and began to walk. He left the Plaza behind him, crossed Kearney Steet and went on down Clay Street till he reached the water front. For a time he found a certain diversion among the shipping and especially in watching a gang of caulkers knocking away at the seams of an immense coal steamer. He sat upon a great iron clamped pile, spitting into the yellow water below. The air was full of the smell of bilge and oakum and fish; the thousands of masts made a gray maze against the sky; occasionally an empty truck trundled over the hollow docks with a

sound of distant cannon.   A weakness, a little trembling
that seemed to come from the pit of his stomach, began
upon Vandover.   He was very hungry.   Evidently the
slice of cocoanut was no longer effective.   He swallowed
it and lit a cigarette, one of the half-dozen still left of the
pack he had bought the Tuesday before.

He smoked the cigarette slowly, inhaling as much of the
smoke as he could.   This quieted him for an hour, but he
had the folly to smoke again at the end of that time, and
at once — as he might have known — was hungry again.
Until dark he struggled along, drinking water continually,
chewing chips of wood, toothpicks, bits of straw, anything
so that the action of his jaws might cheat the demands of
his stomach.   Toward half-past seven in the evening he
returned to his room in the Reno House.   If he could get
to sleep that would be best of all.   On the stairs of the
hotel, while going up to his room, the strong smell of cooking
onions came suddenly to his nostrils.   It was delicious.   Vandover breathed in the warm savour with long sighs, closing his eyes; a great feebleness overcame him.   He asked
himself how he could get through the next twelve hours.

An hour later he went to bed, hiccoughing from the
water he had been drinking all day.   By this time he had
torn the paper from one of his cigarettes and was chewing
the tobacco.   This was his last resort, an expedient which
he fell back upon only in great extremity, as it invariably
made him sick to his stomach.   He slept a little, but in
half an hour was broad awake again, gagging and retching
dreadfully.   There was nothing on his stomach to throw
up, and now at length the hunger in him raged like a wolf.
Vandover was in veritable torment.

He could not keep his thoughts away from the money in his pocket, a nickel and two dimes. He could eat if he wanted to, could satisfy this incessant craving. At every moment the temptation grew stronger. Why should he wait until morning? He had the money; it was only a matter of a few minutes' walk to the nearest saloon. But he set his face against this desire; he had held out so long that it would be a pity to give in now; he was not so very hungry after all. No, no; he would not give in, he was strong enough; as long as he used his will he need not succumb. It was just a question of asserting his strength of mind, of calling up the better part of him. Even better than eating would be the satisfaction of knowing that he had shown himself stronger than his lower animal appetite. No; he would not give in.

Hardly a minute after he had arrived at this resolution Vandover found himself drawing on his coat and shoes making ready to go out — to go out and eat.

The gas in the room was lit, his money, the nickel and the two dimes, was shut in one of his fists. He was dressing himself with one hand, dressing with feverish, precipitate haste. What had happened? He marvelled at himself, but did not check his preparations an instant. He could not stop, whether he would or no; there was something in him stronger than himself, something that urged him on his feet, that drove him out into the street, something that clamoured for food and that would not be gainsaid. It was the animal in him, the brute, that would be fed, the evil, hideous brute grown now so strong that Vandover could not longer resist it — the brute that had long since destroyed all his finer qualities but that

still demanded to be fed, still demanded to live. All the
little money that Vandover had saved during the day he
spent that night among the coffee houses, the restaurants,
and the saloons of the Barbary Coast, continuing to eat
even after his hunger was satisfied. Toward daylight he
returned to his room, and all dressed as he was flung himself face downward among the coarse blankets and greasy
counterpane. For nearly eight hours he slept profoundly,
with long snores, prone, inert, crammed and gorged with
food.

It was the middle of Sunday afternoon when he awoke.
He roused himself and going over to the Plaza sat for a
long while upon one of the benches. It was a very bright
afternoon and Vandover sat motionless for a long time in
the sun while his heavy meal digested, very happy, content merely to be warm, to be well fed, to be comfortable.

CHAPTER EIGHTEEN

THAT winter passed, then the summer; September and October came and went, and by the middle of November the rains set in. One very wet afternoon toward the end of the month Charlie Geary sat at his desk in his own private office. He was unoccupied for the moment, leaning back in his swivel chair, his feet on the table, smoking a cigar. Geary had broken from his old-time habit of smoking only so many cigars as he could pay for by saving carfare. He was doing so well now that he could afford to smoke whenever he chose. He was still with the great firm of Beale & Storey, and while not in the partnership as yet, had worked up to the position of an assistant. He had cases of his own now, a great many of them, for the most part damage suits against that certain enormous corporation whom it was said was ruining the city and entire state. Geary posed as one of its bitterest enemies, pushing each suit brought against it with a tireless energy, with a zeal that was almost vindictive. He began to fit into his own niche, in the eyes of the public, and just in proportion as the corporation was hated, Geary was admired. Money came to him very fast. He was hardly thirty at this time, but could already be called a rich man.

His "deal" with Vandover had given him a taste for real estate, and now and then, with the greatest caution,

he made a few discreet investments. At present he had
just completed a row of small cottages across the street
from the boot and shoe factory. The cottages held two
rooms and a large kitchen. Geary had calculated that
the boot and shoe concern would employ nearly a thousand operatives, and he had built his row with the view of
accommodating a few of them who had families and who
desired to live near the factory. His agents were Adams
& Brunt.

It was toward half-past five, there was nothing more
that Geary could do that day, and for a moment he leaned
back in his swivel chair, before going home, smiling a
little, very well pleased with himself. He was still as
clever and shrewd as ever, still devoured with an incarnate
ambition, still delighted when he could get the better of
any one. He was yet a young man; with the start he
had secured for himself, and with the exceptional faculties,
the faculties of self-confidence and "push" that he knew
himself to possess, there was no telling to what position
he might attain. He knew that it was only a question of
time — of a short time even — when he would be the
practical head of the great firm. Everything he turned
his hand to was a success. His row of houses in the Mission might be enlarged to a veritable settlement for every
workman in the neighbourhood. His youth, his cleverness, and his ambition, supported by his money on the
one hand, and on the other by the vast machinery of the
great law firm, could raise him to a great place in the
world of men. Gazing through the little blue haze of
his cigar smoke, he began to have vague ideas, ideas of
advancement, of political successes. Politics fascinated

him — such a field of action seemed to be the domain
for which he was precisely suited — not the politics of the
city or of the state; not the nasty little squabbling of
boodlers, lobbyists, and supervisors, but something large,
something inspiring, something on a tremendous scale,
something to which one could give up one's whole life and
energy, something to which one could sacrifice everything
— friendships, fortunes, scruples, principles, life itself, no
matter what, anything to be a "success," to "arrive," to
"get there," to attain the desired object in spite of the
whole world, to ride on at it, trampling down or smashing
through everything that stood in the way, blind, deaf,
fists and teeth shut tight. Not the little squabbling politics of the city or state, but national politics, the sway
and government of a whole people, the House, the Senate,
the cabinet and the next — why not? — the highest, the
best of all, the Executive. Yes, Geary aspired even to the
Presidency.

For a moment he allowed himself the indulgence of the
delightful dream, then laughed a bit at his own absurdity.
But even the entertainment of so vast an idea had made
his mind, as it were, big; it was hard to come down to the
level again. In spite of himself he went on reasoning in
stupendous thoughts, in enormous ideas, figuring with
immense abstractions. And then after all, why not?
Other men had striven and attained; other men were even
now striving, other men would "arrive"; why should not
he? As well he as another. Every man for himself —
that was his maxim. It might be damned selfish, but it
was human nature: the weakest to the wall, the strongest
to the front. Why should not he be in the front? Why

not in the very front rank?   Why not be even before the
front rank itself — the leader?   Vast, vague ideas passed
slowly across the vision of his mind, ideas that could
hardly be formulated into thought, ideas of the infinite herd
of humanity, driven on as if by some enormous, relentless engine, driven on toward some fearful distant bourne, driven
on recklessly at headlong speed.   All life was but a struggle
to keep from under those myriad spinning wheels that
dashed so close behind.   Those were happiest who were
farthest to the front.   To lag behind was peril; to fall was
to perish, to be ridden down, to be beaten to the dust, to
be inexorably crushed and blotted out beneath that myriad
of spinning iron wheels.   Geary looked up quickly and
saw Vandover standing in the doorway.

For the moment Geary did not recognize the gaunt,
shambling figure with the long hair and dirty beard, the
greenish hat, and the streaked and spotted coat, but when
he did it was with a feeling of anger and exasperation.

"Look here!" he cried, "don't you think you'd better
knock before you come in?"

Vandover raised a hand slowly as if in deprecation, and
answered slowly and with a feeble, tremulous voice, the
voice of an old man: "I did knock, Mister Geary; I
didn't mean no offence."   He sat down on the edge of
the nearest chair, looking vaguely and stupidly about on
the floor, moving his head instead of his eyes, repeating
under his breath from time to time, "No offence — no,
sir — no offence!"

"Shut that door!" commanded Geary.   Vandover
obeyed.   He wore no vest, and the old cutaway coat,
fastened by the single remaining button, exposed his shirt

to view, abominably filthy, bulging at the waist like a blouse. The "blue pants," held up by a strap, were all foul with mud and grease and paint, and there hung about him a certain odour, that peculiar smell of poverty and of degradation, the smell of stale clothes and of unwashed bodies.

"Well?" said Geary abruptly.

Vandover put the tips of his fingers to his lips and rolled his eyes about the room, avoiding Geary's glance; then he dropped them to the floor again, looking at the pattern in the carpet.

"Well," repeated Geary, irritated, "you know I haven't got all the time in the world." All at once Vandover began to cry, very softly, snuffling with his nose, his chin twitching, the tears running through his thin, sparse beard.

"Ah, get on to yourself!" shouted Geary, now thoroughly disgusted. "Quit that! Be a man, will you? Stop that! do you hear?" Vandover obeyed, catching his breath and slowly wiping his eyes with the side of his hand.

"I'm no good!" he said at length, wagging his head and blinking through his tears. "I'm — I'm done for and I ain't got no money; yet, of course, you see I don't mean no offence. What I want, you see, is to be a man and not give in and not let the wolf get me, and then I'll go back to Paris. Everything goes round here, very slow, and seems far off; that's why I can't get along, and I'm that hungry that sometimes I twitch all over. I'm down. I ain't got another cent of money and I lost my job at the paint-shop. There's where I drew down twenty dollars a week painting landscapes on safes, you know, and then —— "

Geary interrupted him, crying out, "You haven't a cent? Why, what have you done with your bonds?"

"Bonds?" repeated Vandover, dazed and bewildered. "I ain't never had any bonds. What bonds? Oh, yes," he exclaimed, suddenly remembering, "yes, I know, *my* bonds, of course; yes, yes — well, I — those — those, I had to sell those bonds — had some debts, you see, my board and my tailor's bill. They got out some sort of paper after me. Yes, I had forgotten about my bonds. I lost every damned one of them playing cards — gambled 'em all away. Ain't I no good? But I was winner once — just in two nights I won ten thousand dollars. Then I must have lost it again. You see, I get so hungry sometimes that I twitch all over — so, just like that. Lend me a dollar."

For a few moments Geary was silent, watching Vandover curiously, as he sat in a heap on the edge of the chair, fumbling his greenish hat, looking about the floor. Presently he asked:

"When did you lose your job at the paint-shop?"

"Day before yesterday."

"And you are out of work now?"

"Yes," answered Vandover. "I'm broke; I haven't a cent. I'm blest if *I* know how I'm to get along. Lately I've been working for a paint-shop, painting landscapes on safes. I drew down fifty dollars a week there, but I've lost my job."

"Good Lord, Van!" Geary suddenly exclaimed, nodding his head toward him reflectively, "I'm sorry for you!"

The other laughed. "Yes; I suppose I'm a pitiable looking object, but I'm used to it. I don't mind much now as long as I can have a place to sleep and enough to eat. If you can put me in the way of some work, Charlie, I'd be much obliged. You see, that's what I want — work. I don't want to run any bunco game. I'm an honest man — I'm too honest. I gave away all my money to help another poor duck; gave him thousands; he was good to me when I was on my uppers and I meant to repay him. I was grateful. I signed a paper that gave him everything I had. It was in Paris. There's where my bonds went to. He was a struggling artist."

"Look here!" said Geary, willing to be interested, "you might as well be truthful with me. You can't lie to me. Have you gambled away all those bonds, or have you been victimized, or have you still got them? Come, now, spit it out."

"Charlie, I haven't a cent!" answered Vandover, looking him squarely in the face. "Would I be around here and trying to get work from you if I had? No; I gambled it all away. You know I had eighty-nine hundred in U. S. 4 per cents. Well, first I began to pawn things when my money got short — the Old Gentleman's watch that I said I never would part with, then my clothes. I couldn't keep away from the cards. Of course, you can't understand that; gambling was the only thing that could amuse me. Then I began to mortgage my bonds, very little at first. Oh, I went slow! Then I got to selling them. Well, somehow, they all went. For a time I got along by the work at the paint-shop. But they have let me out now; said I was so irregular. I owe for nearly a month at my lodging-place." His eyes sought the floor again, rolling about stupidly. "Nearly a month, and

that's what makes me jump and tremble so. You ought
to see me sometimes — *b-r-r-r-h!* — and I get to barking!
I'm a wolf mostly, you know, or some kind of an animal,
some kind of a brute. But I'd be all right if everything
didn't go round very slowly, and seem far off. But I'm
a wolf. You look out for me; best take care I don't bite
you! Wolf — wolf! Ah! It's up four flights at the
end of the hall, very dark, eight thousand dollars in a
green cloth sack, and lots of lights a-burning. See how
long my finger nails are — regular claws; that's the wolf,
the brute! Why can't I talk in my mouth instead of in
my throat? That's the devil of it. When you paint on
steel and iron your colours don't dry out true; all the
yellows turn green. But it would 'a' been all straight if
they hadn't fined me! I never talked to anybody — that
was *my* business, wasn't it? And when all those eight
thousand little lights begin to burn red, why, of course
that makes you nervous! So I have to drink a great deal
of water and chew butcher's paper. That fools him and
he thinks he's eating. Just so as I can lay quiet in the
Plaza when the sun is out. There's a hack-stand there,
you know, and every time that horse tosses his head so's
to get the oats in the bottom of the nose-bag he jingles
the chains on the poles and, by God! that's funny; makes
me laugh every time; sounds gay, and the chain sparkles
mighty pretty! Oh, I don't complain. Give me a dollar
and I'll bark for you!"

Geary leaned back in his chair listening to Vandover,
struck with wonder, marvelling at that which his old
chum had come to be. He was sorry for him, too, yet,
nevertheless, he felt a certain indefinite satisfaction, a

faint exultation over his misfortunes, glad that their positions were not reversed, pleased that he had been clever
enough to keep free from those habits, those modes of
life that ended in such fashion. He rapped sharply on
the table. Vandover straightened up, raising his eyes:

"You want some work?" he demanded.

"Yes; that's what I'm after," answered Vandover,
adding, "I must have it!"

"Well," said Geary, hesitatingly, "I can give you
something to do, but it will be pretty dirty."

Vandover smiled a little, saying, "I guess you can't
give me any work that would be too dirty for me!" With
the words he suddenly began to cry again. "I want to be
honest, Mister Geary," he exclaimed, drawing the backs
of his fingers across his lips; "I want to be honest; I'm
down and I don't mean no offence. Charlie, you and I
were old chums once at Harvard. My God! to think
I was a Harvard man once! Oh, I'm a goner now and I
ain't got a friend. When I was in the paint-shop they
paid me well. I've been in a paint-shop lately painting
the little pictures on the safes, little landscapes, you know,
and lakes with mountains around them. I pulled down
my twenty dollars and findings!"

"Oh, don't be a fool!" cried Geary, ashamed even to
see such an exhibition. "If you can't be a man, you can
get out. Now, see here, you came up here once and insulted me in my office, and called me a swindler. Ah,
you bet you had the swelled head then and insulted me,
attacked my honesty and charged me with shoving the
queer. Now I never forget those things generally, but
I am willing to let that pass this time. I could be nasty

now and tell you to rustle for yourself. If you want half a dollar now to get something to eat, why, I'll give it to you. But I don't propose to support you. Ah, no; I guess not! If you want to work I'll give you a chance, but I shall expect you to do good work if I give you my good money for it. You may be drunk now or — *I* don't know what's the matter with you. But you come up here to-morrow at noon, and if you come up here sober or straight or" — Geary began to make awkward gestures in the air with both hands — "come up here to talk *business*, I may have something for you, but I can't stop any longer this evening."

Vandover got upon his feet slowly, turning his greenish hat about by the brim, nodding his head. "All right, all right," he answered. "Thank you very much, Mister Geary. It's very good of you, I'm sure. I'll be around at noon sure."

When Geary was left alone, he walked slowly to his window, and stood there a moment looking aimlessly down into the street, shaking his head repeatedly, astonished at the degradation of his old-time chum. While he stood there he saw Vandover come out upon the sidewalk from the door of the great office building. Geary watched him, very interested.

Vandover paused a moment upon the sidewalk, turning up the collar of his old cutaway coat against the cold trade wind that was tearing through the streets; he thrust both his hands deep into his trousers pockets, gripping his sides with his elbows and drawing his shoulders together, shrinking into a small compass in order to be warm. The wind blew the tails of his cutaway about him like flapping wings. He went up the street, walking fast, keeping to the outside of the sidewalk, his shoulders bent, his head inclined against the wind, his feet dragging after him as he walked. For a moment Geary lost sight of him amid a group of men who were hoisting a piano upon a dray. The street was rather crowded with office boys, clerks, and typewriters going home to supper, and Geary did not catch sight of him again immediately; then all at once he saw him hesitating on a corner of Kearney Street, waiting for an electric car to pass; he crossed the street, running, his hands still in his pockets, and went on hurriedly, dodging in and out of the throng, his high shoulders, long neck, and greenish hat coming into sight at intervals. For a moment he paused to glance into the show window of a tobacconist and pipe-seller's store. A Chinese woman passed him, pattering along lamely, her green jade ear-rings twinkling in the light of a street lamp, newly lighted. Vandover looked after her a moment, gazing stupidly, then suddenly took up his walk again, zigzagging amid the groups on the asphalt, striding along at a great pace, his head low and swinging from side to side as he walked. He was already far down the street; it was dusk; Geary could only catch glimpses of his head and shoulders at long intervals. He disappeared.

About ten minutes before one the next day as Geary came back from lunch he was surprised to see Vandover peeping through the half-open door of his office. He had not thought that Vandover would come back.

Of the many different stories that Vandover had told about the disappearance of his bonds, the one that was

probably truest was the one that accounted for the thing
by his passion for gambling. For a long time after his
advent at the Reno House this passion had been dormant;
he knew no one with whom he could play, and every cent
of his income now went for food and lodging. But one
day, about six months before his visit to Geary's office,
Vandover saw that the proprietor of the Reno House had
set up a great bagatelle board in a corner of the reading-
room. A group of men, sailors, ranchmen, and fruit
venders were already playing. Vandover approached
and watched the game, very interested in watching the
uncertain course of the marble jog-jogging among the
pins. The clear little note of the bell or the dry rattle as
the marble settled quickly into one of the lucky pockets
thrilled him from head to foot; his hands trembled, all at
once his whole left side twitched sharply.

From that day the fate of the rest of Vandover's little
money was decided. In two weeks he had lost twenty
dollars at bagatelle, obtaining the money by selling a
portion of his bonds at a certain broker's on Montgomery
Street. As soon as he had begun to gamble again the
old habits of extravagance had come back upon him.
From the moment he knew that he could get all the money
he wanted by the mere signing of a paper, he ceased to be
economical, scorning the former niggardliness that had
led him to starve on one day that he might feast the next;
now, he feasted every day. He still kept his room at the
Reno House, but instead of taking his meals by any ticket
system, he began to affect the restaurants of the Spanish
quarter, gorging himself with the hot spiced meals three
and four times a day. He quickly abandoned the baga-

telle board for the card-table, gambling furiously with two
of the ranchmen. Almost invariably Vandover lost, and
the more he lost the more eager and reckless he became.

In a little time he had sold every one of his bonds and
had gambled away all but twenty dollars of the money
received from the last one sold. This sum, this twenty
dollars, Vandover decided to husband carefully. It was
all that was left between him and starvation. He made
up his mind that he must stop gambling and find something to do. He had long since abandoned his work at
the paint-shop, but at this time he returned there and asked
for his old occupation. They laughed in his face. Was
that the way he thought they did business? Not much;
another man had his job, a much better man and one who
was regular, who could be depended on. That same evening Vandover broke his twenty dollars and became very
drunk. A game of poker was started in a back room of
one of the saloons on the Barbary Coast. One of the
players was a rancher named Toedt, a fellow-boarder at
the Reno House, but the two other players were strangers;
and there in that narrow, dirty room, sawdust on the floor,
festoons of fly-specked red and blue tissue paper adorn-
ing the single swinging lamp, figures cut from bill-posters
of the Black Crook pasted on the walls, there in the still
hours after midnight, long after the barroom outside had
been closed for the night, the last penny of Vandover's
estate was gambled away.

The game ended in a quarrel, Vandover, very drunk,
and exasperated at his ill luck, accusing his friend Toedt,
the rancher, of cheating. Toedt kicked him in the stomach and made him abominably sick. Then they went

away and left Vandover alone in the little dirty room, racked with nausea, very drunk, fallen forward upon the table and crying into his folded arms. After a little he went to sleep, but the nausea continued, nevertheless, and in a few moments he gagged and vomited. He never moved. He was too drunk to wake. His hands and his coat-sleeves, the table all about him, were foul beyond words, but he slept on in the midst of it all, inert, stupefied, a great swarm of flies buzzing about his head and face. It was the day after this that he had come to see Geary.

"Ah," said Geary, as he came up, "it's you, is it? Well, I didn't expect to see you again. Sit down outside there in the hall and wait a few minutes. I'm not ready to go yet — or, wait; here, I tell you what to do." Geary wrote off a list of articles on a slip of paper and pushed it across the table toward Vandover, together with a little money. "You get those at the nearest grocery and by the time you are back I'll be ready to go."

That day Geary took Vandover out to the Mission. They went out in the cable-car, Geary sitting inside reading the morning's paper, Vandover standing on the front platform, carrying the things that Geary had told him to buy: a bar of soap, a scrubbing brush, some wiping cloths, a broom, and a pail.

Almost at the end of the car-line they got off and crossed over to where Geary's property stood. Vandover looked about him. The ground on which his own block had once stood was now occupied by an immense red brick building with white stone trimmings; in front on either side of the main entrance were white stone medal-

lions upon which were chiselled the head of a workman wearing the square paper cap that the workman never wears,
and a bent-up forearm, the biceps enormous, the fist gripping the short hammer that the workman never uses.
An enormous round chimney sprouted from one corner;
through the open windows came the vast purring of
machinery. It was a boot and shoe factory, built by the
great concern who had bought the piece of property from
Geary for fifteen thousand dollars, the same property
Geary had bought from Vandover for eight.

Across the street from the factory was a long row of
little cottages, very neat, each having a tiny garden in
front where nasturtiums grew. There were fifteen of
these cottages; three of them only were vacant.

"That was *my* idea," observed Geary, as they approached the row, willing to explain even though he
thought Vandover would not comprehend, "and it pays
like a nitrate bed. I was clever enough to see that cottages like these were just what's wanted by the workmen
in the factory that have families. I made some money
when I sold out my block to the boot and shoe people, and
I invested it again in these cottages. They are cheap
and serviceable and they meet the demand." Vandover
nodded his head in assent, looking vaguely about him,
now at the cottages, now at the great building across the
street. Geary got the keys to one of the vacant cottages
and the two went inside.

"Now here's what I want you to do," began Geary,
pointing about with his stick. "You see, when some
of these people go out they leave the rooms nasty, and
that tells against the house when parties come to look at

it. I want you to go all over it, top and bottom, end to end, and give it a good cleaning, sweep the floor, and wash the paint, you know. And now these windows, you see how dirty they are; wash those inside and out, but don't disturb the agents' signs; you understand?"

"Yes, I understand."

"Now come out here into the kitchen. Look at these laundry tubs and that sink. See all that grease! Clean that all out, and underneath the sink here. See that rubbish! Take that out, too. Now in here — look at that bathtub and toilet. You see how nasty they have left them. You want to make 'em look like new!"

"Yes."

"Now come downstairs. You see I give 'em a little floored basement, here; kind of a storeroom and coalroom. Here's where most of the dirt and rubbish is. Just look at it! See all that pile over there?"

"I see."

"Take it all out and pile it in the back yard. I'll have an ash-man come and remove it. Whew! there is a dead hen under here; sling that out the first thing."

They went back through the house again, and Geary pointed out the tiny garden to Vandover. "Straighten that up a bit, pick up those old newspapers and the tin cans. Make it look neat. Now you understand just what I want? You make a good job of it, and when you are through with this house, you begin on the next vacant one farther down the row. You can get the keys at the same place. You get to work right away. I should think you ought to finish this house this afternoon."

"All right," answered Vandover.

"I'm going to look around a little. I'll drop in again in about an hour and see how you're getting on."

With that Geary went away. It was Saturday afternoon, and as the law office closed at noon that day, Geary very often spent the time until evening looking about his property. He left Vandover and went slowly down the street, noting each particular house with immense satisfaction, even entering some of them, talking with the womenfolk, all the men being at the factory.

Vandover took off his coat, his old and greasy cutaway, and began work. He drew a pail of water from the garden faucet in a neighbour's yard, and commenced washing the windows. First he washed the panes from the inside, very careful not to disturb Adams & Brunt's signs, and then cleaned the outside, sitting upon the window ledge, his body half in and half out of the house.

Geary enjoyed himself immensely. The news of the landlord's visit had spread from cottage to cottage, awakening a mild excitement throughout the length of the row. The women showed themselves on the steps or on the sidewalks, very slatternly, without corsets, their hair coming down, dressed in faded calico wrappers just as they had come from the laundry tubs or the cook-stove. They bethought them of their various grievances, a leak here, a broken door-bell there, a certain bad smell that was supposed to have some connection with a rash upon the children's faces. They waited for Geary's appearance by ones and twos, timid, very respectful, but querulous for all that, filling the air with their lamentations.

Vandover had finished with the windows. Now he was cleaning out the sink and the laundry tubs. They smelt

very badly and were all foul with a greasy mixture of old
lard, soap, soot, and dust; a little mould was even beginning to form about the faucets of the tubs. The escape
pipe of the sink was clogged, and he had to run his finger
into it again and again to get it free. The kitchen was
very dirty; old bottles of sweet oil, mouldy vinegar and
flat beer cluttered the dusty shelves of the pantry.

Meanwhile Geary continued his rounds. He went about
among the groups of his tenants, very pleased and contented, smiling affably upon them. He enlarged himself, giving himself the airs of an English lord in the midst
of his tenantry, listening to their complaints with a good-
humoured smile of toleration. A few men were about,
some of whom were out of work for the moment; others
who were sick. To these Geary was particularly conde-
scending. He sat in their parlours, little, crowded rooms,
smelling of stale upholstery and of the last meal, where
knitted worsted tidies, very gaudy, covered the backs of
the larger chairs and where one inevitably discovered the
whatnot standing in one corner, its shelves filled with
shell-boxes, broken thermometers and little alabaster jars,
shaped like funeral urns, where one kept the matches.
The wife brought the children in, very dirty, looking sol-
emnly at Geary, their eyes enlarged in the direct unwink-
ing gaze of cows.

By this time Vandover had finished with the sinks and
tubs and was down upon his hands and knees scrubbing
the stains of grease upon the floor of the kitchen. It was
very hard work, as his water was cold. He was still working about this spot when Geary returned. By this time
Vandover was so tired that he trembled all over, his spine

seemed to be breaking in two, and every now and then he paused and passed his hand over the small of his back, closing his eyes and drawing a long breath.

"Well, how are you getting on?" asked Geary, as he came into the kitchen, drawing on his gloves, about ready to go home.

"Oh, I'm getting along," replied Vandover, rising up to his knees.

"You want to hurry up," answered Geary. "You must be done with this house by this evening.   You see, I want to advertise it in to-morrow's papers."

"All right; I'll have it done."

"Pretty dirty, wasn't it?"

"Yes, pretty dirty."

"You may have to work here a little later than usual this afternoon, but be sure you have everything cleaned up before you leave," Geary said.

"All right," answered Vandover, bending to his work again.

Just as Geary was leaving he had the admirable good fortune to meet on the steps of the cottage a little group who were house-hunting; two young women and a little boy. The mother of the little boy, so she explained to him, was married to one of the burnishers in the factory; the other woman was her sister.

Geary showed them about the little house, very eager to secure them as tenants then and there. He began to sing its praises, its nearness to the factory, its excellent plumbing, its bathroom and its one stationary wash-stand; its little garden and its location on the sunny side of the street. "I'm a good landlord," he said to them, as he ushered them into the kitchen. "Any one in the row will tell you that. I make it a point to keep my houses in good repair and to keep them clean. You see, I have a man here now cleaning out." Vandover glanced up at the women an instant. The two of them and the little boy looked down at him on all fours upon the floor. Then he went on with his work.

"This is the kitchen, you see," pursued Geary. "Notice how large it is; you see, here are your laundry tubs, your iron sink, your boiler, everything you need. Of course, it's a little grimy now, but by the time the man gets through, it will be as clean as your face. Now come downstairs here and I'll show the basement."

In a moment their voices sounded through the floor of the kitchen, an indistinct, continuous murmur. Then the party returned and passed by Vandover again and stood for a long time in the front room haggling. The cottage rented for fifteen dollars. The young woman was willing to take it at that, but with the understanding that Geary should pay the water rent. Geary refused, unwilling even to listen to such a thing. Every other tenant in the row paid for his own water. The young women went away shaking their heads sadly. Geary let them get halfway down the front steps and then called them back. He offered a compromise, the young women should pay for the water, but half of their first month's rent should be remitted. The burnisher's wife still hesitated, saying, "You know yourself this house is awfully dirty."

"Well, you see I'm having it cleaned!"

"It'll have to be cleaned pretty thoroughly. I can't stand *dirt*."

"It *will* be cleaned thoroughly," persisted Geary. "The man will work at it until it is. You can keep an eye on him and see that the work is done to suit you."

"You see," objected the burnisher's wife, "I would want to move in right away. I don't want to wait all week for the man to get through."

"But he is going to be through with this house to-night," exclaimed Geary delighted. "Come now, I know you want this cottage and I would like to have such nice-look-ing people have it. I know you would make good tenants. I can find lots of other tenants for this house, only you know how it is, a nasty, slovenly woman about the house and a raft of dirty children. And you don't like dirt, I can see that. Better call it a bargain, and let it go at that."

In the end the burnisher's wife took the house. Geary even induced her to deposit five dollars with him in order to secure it.

Vandover was down in the basement filling a barrel with the odds and ends of rubbish left by the previous tenants: broken bottles, old corsets, bones, rusty bed-springs. The dead hen he had taken out first of all, carry-ing it by one leg. It was a gruesome horror, partly eaten by rats, swollen, abnormally heavy, one side flattened from lying so long upon the floor. He could hardly stand; each time he bent over it seemed as though his backbone was disjointing. After cleaning out the débris he began to sweep. The dust was fearful, choking, blinding, so thick that he could hardly see what he was about. By and by he dimly made out Geary's figure in the doorway.

"Those people have taken the house," he called out,

"and I promised them you would be through with it by this evening. So you want to stay with it now till you're finished. I guess there's not much more to do. Don't forget the little garden in front."

"No; I won't forget!"

Geary went away, and for another hour Vandover kept at his work, stolidly, his mind empty of all thought, knowing only that he was very tired, that his back pained him. He finished with the basement, but as he was pottering about the little garden, picking up the discoloured newspapers with which it was littered, the burnisher's wife returned, together with her sister and the little boy; the little boy eating a slice of bread and butter. They re-entered the house; Vandover heard their voices, now in one room, now in another. They were looking over their future home again; evidently they lived close by.

Suddenly the burnisher's wife came out upon the front steps, looking down into the little garden, calling for Vandover. She was not pretty; she had a nose like a man and her chin was broad.

"Say, there," she called to Vandover, "do you mean to say that you've finished inside here?"

"Yes," answered Vandover, straightening up, nodding his head. "Yes, I've finished."

"Well, just come in here and look at this."

Vandover followed her into the little parlour. Her sister was there, very fat, smelling somehow of tallow candles and cooked cabbage; nearby stood the little boy still eating his bread and butter.

"Look at that baseboard," exclaimed the burnisher's wife. "You never touched that, I'll bet a hat." Vandover did not answer; he brought in the pail of water, and soaping his scrubbing brush, went down again on his hands and knees, washing the paint on the baseboard where the burnisher's wife indicated. The two women stood by, looking on and directing his movements. The little boy watched everything, never speaking a word, slowly eating his bread and butter. Streaks of butter and bread clung to his cheeks, stretching from the corners of his mouth to his ears.

"I don't see how you come to overlook that," said the burnisher's wife to Vandover. "That's the dirtiest base-board I ever saw. Oh, my! I just can't naturally stand *dirt!* There, you didn't get that stain off. That's tobacco juice, I guess. Go back and wash that over again." Vandover obeyed, holding the brush in one hand, crawling back along the floor upon one palm and his two knees, a pool of soapy, dirty water very cold gathered about him, soaking in through the old "blue pants" and wetting him to the skin, but he slovened through it indifferently. "Put a little more elbow grease to it," continued the burnisher's wife. "You have to rub them spots pretty hard to get 'em out. Now scrub all along here near the floor. You see that streak there — that's all gormed up with something or other. Bugs get in there mighty quick. There, that'll do, I guess. Now, is every-thing else all clean? Mister Geary said it was to be done to my satisfaction, and that you were to stay here until everything was all right."

All at once her voice was interrupted by the prolonged roar of the factory's whistle, blowing as though it would never stop. It was half-past five. In an instant the

faint purring of the machinery dwindled and ceased,
leaving an abrupt silence in the air. A moment later the
army of operatives began to pour out of the main entrance; men and girls and young boys, all in a great hurry,
the men settling their coat collars as they ran down the
steps. The usually quiet street was crowded in an instant.

The burnisher's wife stood on the steps of the vacant
house with her sister, watching the throng debouch into
the street. All at once the sister exclaimed, "There he
is!" and the other began to call, "Oscar, Oscar!" waving her hand to one of the workmen on the other side of
the street. It was her husband, the burnisher, and he
came across the street, crowding his lunch basket into the
pocket of his coat. He was a thin little man with a timid
air, his face white and fat and covered with a sparse un-
shaven stubble of a pale straw colour. An odour as of a
harness shop hung about him. Vandover gathered up his
broom and pail and soap preparing to go home.

"Well, Oscar, I've taken the house!" said his wife to
the burnisher as he came up the steps. "But I couldn't
get him to say that he'd let me have it for fifteen, water
included. The landlord himself, Mr. Geary, was here to-
day and I made the dicker with him. He's had a man here
all day cleaning up." She explained the bargain, the burnisher approving of everything, nodding his head continually. His wife showed him about the house, her sister
and the little boy following in silence. "He's a good landlord, I guess," continued the young woman; "anybody in
the row will tell you that, and he means to keep his houses
in good repair. Now you see, here's the kitchen. You

see how big it is. Here's our laundry tubs, our iron sink,
our boiler, and everything we want. It's all as clean as a
whistle; and get on to this big cubby under the sink where
I can stow away things." She opened its door to show her
husband, but all at once straightened up, exclaiming,
"Well, dear me *suz* — did you *ever* see anything like that?"
The cubby under the sink was abominably dirty. Vandover had altogether forgotten it.

The little burnisher himself bent down and peered in.

"Oh, that'll never do!" he cried. "Has that man gone
home yet? He mustn't; he's got to clean this out first!"
He had a weak, faint voice, small and timid like his figure.
He hurried out to the front door and called Vandover back
just as he was going down the steps. The two went back
into the kitchen and stood in front of the sink. "Look
under there!" piped the burnisher. "You can't leave
that, that way."

"You know," protested his wife, "that this all was to be
done to our satisfaction. Mr. Geary said so. That's
the only way I came to take the house."

"It's about six o'clock, though," observed her fat sister,
who smelt of cooked cabbage. "Perhaps he'd want to
go home to his dinner." But at this both the others cried
out in one voice, the burnisher exclaiming: "I can't help
that, this has got to be done first," while his wife protested
that she couldn't naturally stand dirt, adding, "This all
was to be done to our satisfaction, and we ain't satisfied
yet by a long shot." Delighted at this excitement, the
little boy forgot to eat into his bread and butter, rolling
his eyes wildly from one to the other, still silent.

Meanwhile, without replying, Vandover had gone down

upon the floor again, poking about amid the filth under
the sink. The four others, the burnisher, his wife, his
sister-in-law and his little boy, stood about in a half-circle
behind him, seeing to it that he did the work properly,
giving orders as to how he should proceed.

"Now, be sure you get everything out that's under
there," said the burnisher. "Ouf! how it smells! They
made a regular dump heap of it."

"What's that over in the corner there?" cried the wife,
bending down. "I can't see, it's so dark under there —
something gray; can't you see, in under there? You'll have
to crawl way in to get at it — go way in!" Vandover
obeyed. The sink pipes were so close above him that he
was obliged to crouch lower and lower; at length he lay
flat upon his stomach. Prone in the filth under the sink,
in the sour water, the grease, the refuse, he groped
about with his hand searching for the something gray
that the burnisher's wife had seen. He found it and
drew it out. It was an old hambone covered with a greenish fuzz.

"Oh, did you *ever!*" cried the burnisher, holding up
his hands. "Here, don't drop that on my clean floor;
put it in your pail. Now get out the rest of the dirt, and
hurry up, it's late." Vandover crawled back, half the
way under the sink again, this time bringing out a rusty
pan half full of some kind of congealed gravy that exhaled
a choking, acrid odour; next it was an old stocking, and
then an ink bottle, a broken rat-trap, a battered teapot
lacking a nozzle, a piece of rubber hose, an old comb
choked with a great handful of hair, a torn overshoe,
newspapers, and a great quantity of other débris that had

accumulated there during the occupancy of the previous
tenant.

"Now go over the floor with a rag," ordered the little
burnisher, when the last of these articles had been brought
out. "Wipe up all that nasty muck! Look there by
your knee to your left! Scrub that big spot there with
your brush — looks like grease. That's the style — scrub
it hard!" His wife joined her directions to his. Then it
was over here, and over there, now in that corner, now in
this, and now with his brush and soap, and now with his
dry rag, and hurry up all the time because it was growing
late. But the little boy, carried away by the interest of the
occasion, suddenly broke silence for the first time, crying
out shrilly, his mouth full of bread and butter, "Hey
there! Get up, you old lazee-bones!"

The others shouted with laughter. *There* was a smart
little boy for you. Ah, he'd be a man before his mother.
It was wonderful how that boy saw everything that went
on. He took an *interest*, that was it. You ought to see,
he watched everything, and sometimes he'd plump out
with things that were astonishing for a boy of his years.
Only four and a half, too, and they reminded each other
of the first day he put on knickerbockers; stood in front of
the house on the sidewalk all day long with his hands in
his pockets. The interest was directed from Vandover,
they turned their backs, grouping themselves about the
little boy. The burnisher's sister-in-law felt called upon
to tell about her little girl, a matter of family pride. *She*
was going on twelve, and would you suppose that little
thing was in next to the last grade in the grammar school?
Her teacher had said that she was a real wonder; never

had had such a bright pupil.   Ah, but one should see how
she studied over her books all the time.   Next year they
were to try to get her into the high school.   Of course
she was not ready for the high school yet, and it was against
the rule to let children in that way, she was too young, but
they had a pull, you understand.   Oh, yes, for sure they
had a pull.   *They'd* work her in all right.   The burnisher's
wife was not listening.   She wanted to draw the interest
back to her own little boy.   She bent down and straightened out his little jacket, saying, "Does he like his bread
'n butter?   Well, he could have all he wanted!"   But the
little boy paid no attention to her.   He had made a *bon-
mot*, ambition stirred in him, he had tasted the delights
of an appreciative audience.   Bread and butter had fallen
in his esteem.   He wished to repeat his former success,
and cried out shriller than ever:

"Hey, there!   Get up, you old lazee-bones!"

But his father corrected him — his mother ought not
to encourage him to be rude.   "That's not right, Oscar,"
he observed, shaking his head.   "You must be kind to the
poor man."

Vandover was sitting back on his heels to rest his back,
waiting till the others should finish.

"Well, all through?" inquired the burnisher in his thin
voice.   Vandover nodded.   But his wife was not satisfied until she had herself carefully peered into the cubby,
while her husband held a lighted match for her.   "Ah,
that's something like," she said finally.

It was nearly seven.   Vandover prepared to go home a
second time.   The little boy stood in front of him, looking
down at him as he made his brush and rags and broom

into a bundle; the boy slowly eating his bread and butter the while. In one corner of the room an excited whispered conference was going on between the burnisher, his wife, and his fat sister-in-law. From time to time one heard such expressions as "Overtime, you know — not afraid of work — ah! think I'd better, looks as though he needed it." In a moment the two women went out, calling in vain for the little boy to follow, and the burnisher crossed the room toward Vandover. Vandover was on his knees tying up his bundle with a bit of bale rope.

"I'm sorry," began the burnisher awkwardly. "We didn't mean to keep you from your supper — here," he went on, holding out a quarter to Vandover, "here, you take this, that's all right — you worked overtime for us, that's all right. Come along, Oscar; come along, m' son."

Vandover put the quarter in his vest pocket.

"Thank you, sir," he said.

The burnisher hurried away, calling back, "Come along, m' son; don't keep your mama waiting for supper." But the little boy remained very interested in watching Vandover, still on the floor, tying the last knots. As he finished, he glanced up. For an instant the two remained there motionless, looking into each other's eyes, Vandover on the floor, one hand twisted into the bale rope about his bundle, the little boy standing before him eating the last mouthful of his bread and butter.

THE END